11+ Non-Verbal Reasoning

For **GL** Assessment

These 10-Minute Tests from CGP are perfect for short bursts of 11+ practice — just what children need to keep their skills fresh in the run-up to the test.

Each test is packed with realistic GL-style practice, with fun puzzle pages and answers to every question. There's even a handy progress chart at the back of the book.

This is Book 2. For even more quick-fire tests at the same level, don't miss Book 1!

10-Minute Tests

Ages 10-11

Unlock your Online Edition

Just scan the QR code below or go to **cgpbooks.co.uk/extras** and enter this code!

1794 9129 5896 0949

By the way, this code only works for one person. If somebody else has used this book before you, they might have already claimed the code.

How to use this book

This book is made up of 10-minute tests and puzzle pages.
There are answers and detailed explanations at the back of the book.

10-Minute Tests

- There are 30 tests in this book, each containing 14 or 15 questions.
  Each test is a bite-sized version of a full-length 11+ test.

- Each test is designed to cover a good range of the question styles and topics that your child could come across in their 11+ test, at the same difficulty level.

- Your child should aim to score at least 12 in each 10-minute test.
  If they score less than this, use their results to work out the areas they need more practice on.

- If your child hasn't managed to finish the test in time, they need to work on increasing their speed, whereas if they have made a lot of mistakes, they need to work more carefully.

- Keep track of your child's scores using the progress chart on the inside back cover of the book.

Puzzle Pages

- There are 10 puzzle pages in this book, which are a great break from test-style questions.
  They encourage children to practise the same skills that they will need in the test, but in a fun way.

Published by CGP

Editors:
Molly Barker, Emma Clayton, Katherine Faudemer, Emily Forsberg, Duncan Lindsay, Sarah Pattison, Julie Wakeling

With thanks to Glenn Rogers for the proofreading.

ISBN: 978 1 83774 106 9.
Printed by Elanders Ltd, Newcastle upon Tyne
Clipart from Corel®

Based on the classic CGP style created by Richard Parsons.

Contents

Question Type Examples 2

Test 1 6
Test 2 9
Test 3 12

Puzzles 1 15

Test 4 16
Test 5 19
Test 6 22

Puzzles 2 25

Test 7 26
Test 8 29
Test 9 32

Puzzles 3 35

Test 10 36
Test 11 39
Test 12 42

Puzzles 4 45

Test 13 46
Test 14 49
Test 15 52

Puzzles 5 55

Test 16 56
Test 17 59
Test 18 62

Puzzles 6 65

Test 19 66
Test 20 69
Test 21 72

Puzzles 7 75

Test 22 76
Test 23 79
Test 24 82

Puzzles 8 85

Test 25 86
Test 26 89
Test 27 92

Puzzles 9 95

Test 28 96
Test 29 99
Test 30 102

Puzzles 10 105

Glossary 106

Answers 107

Question Type Examples

These pages contain a completed example question for each question type that appears in this book. Have a look through them to familiarise yourself with the question types before you do the tests.

Odd One Out

The question below has five figures.
Find the figure which is most unlike the others.

Example:

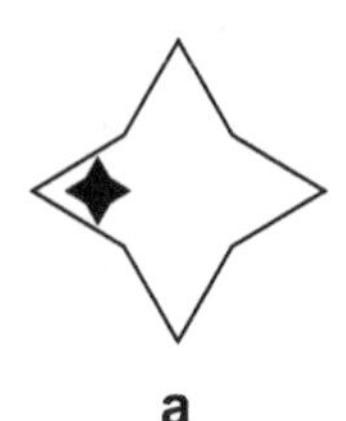
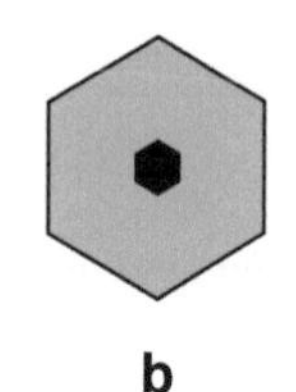
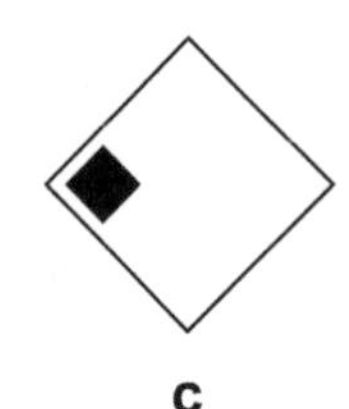
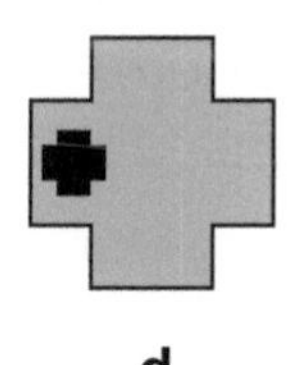
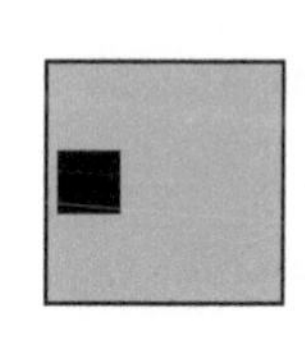

a b c d e

Answer: b

In all other figures, the black inner shape is on the left-hand side.

Find the Figure Like the First Two

In the question below there are two figures that are like each other in some way. Find which of the five figures on the right is most like the two figures on the left.

Example:

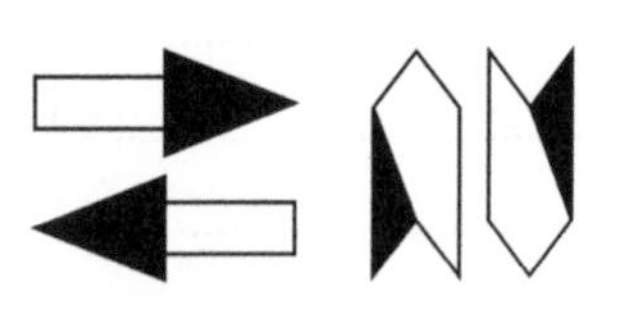
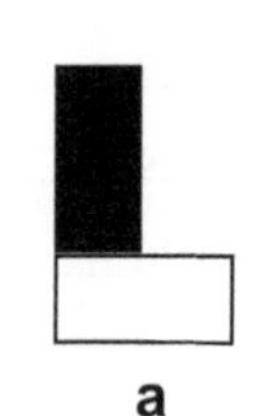
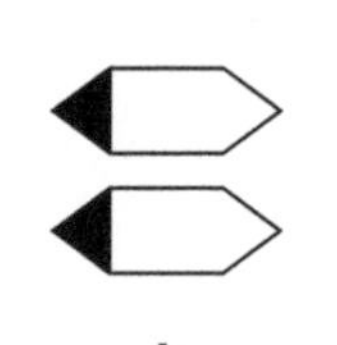

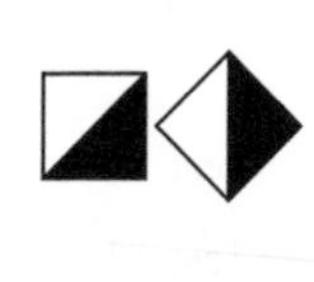

a b c d e

Answer: d

In all figures, one shape must be a 180 degree rotation of the other shape.

Find the Figure Like the First Three

In the question below there are three figures that are like each other in some way. Find which of the five figures on the right is most like the three figures on the left.

Example:

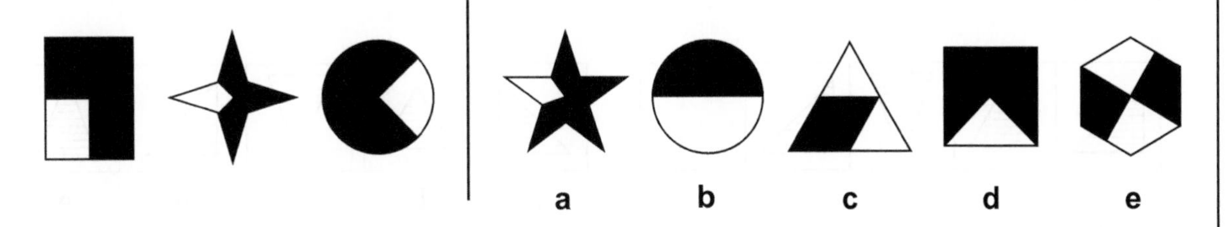

Answer: d

Three-quarters of the shape must be shaded black.

Complete the Grid

On the left of the question below is a big square with one small empty square. Find which of the five squares on the right should replace the empty square.

Example:

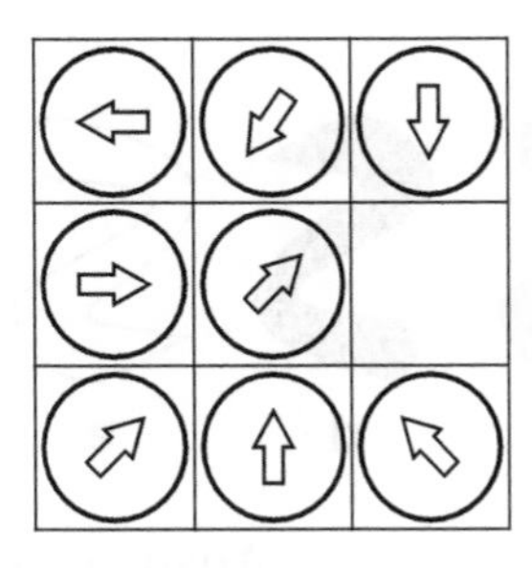

a

b

c

d

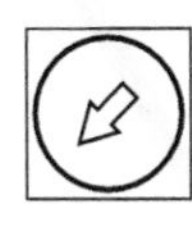

e

Answer: c

Moving from left to right, the arrow rotates 45 degrees anticlockwise in each grid square.

Complete the Series

The question below has five squares on the left that are arranged in order. One of the squares is missing. One of the squares on the right should go in its place. Find which one of the five squares on the right should go in place of the empty square.

Example:

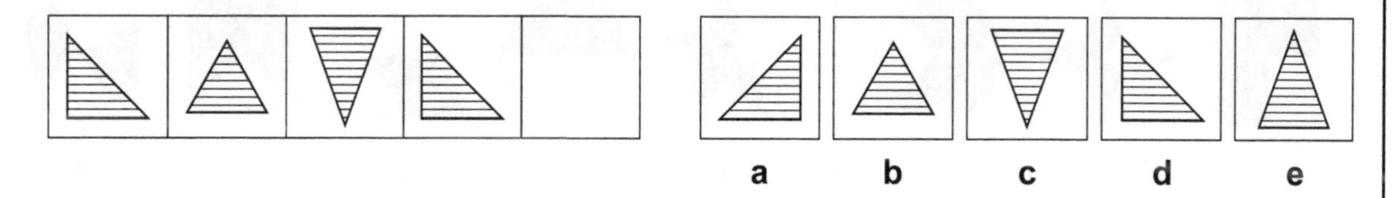

Answer: b

The series cycles through three different triangles — a right-angled triangle, an equilateral triangle and then an isosceles triangle.

Complete the Pair

The question below has two shapes on the left with an arrow between them. The first shape is changed in some way to become the second. There is then a third shape followed by an arrow and a choice of five shapes. Choose the shape on the right that relates to the third shape like the second does to the first.

Example:

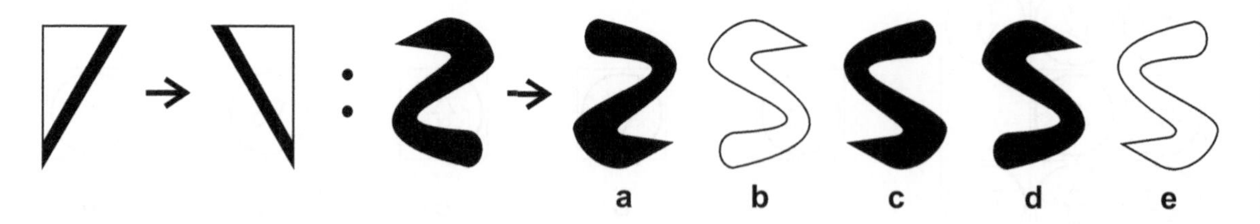

Answer: d

The figure reflects across.

Vertical Code

The question below has some shapes on the left with code letters that describe them. You need to work out what the code letters mean — do this one letter at a time. There is then a shape on its own next to a choice of five codes. Work out which code describes this shape.

Example:

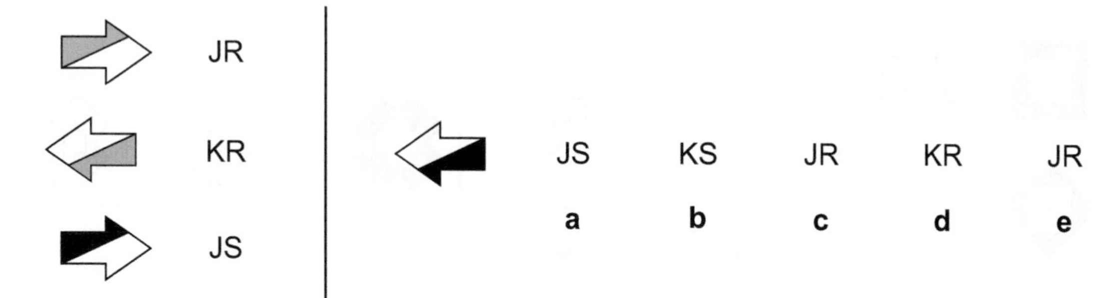

Answer: b

K means the arrow points left. S means the arrow has a black shape.

Horizontal Code

In the boxes on the left are shapes with code letters. The top letters have a different meaning to the bottom ones. Work out how the letters go with the shapes and then find the code for the new shape from the five codes on the right.

Example:

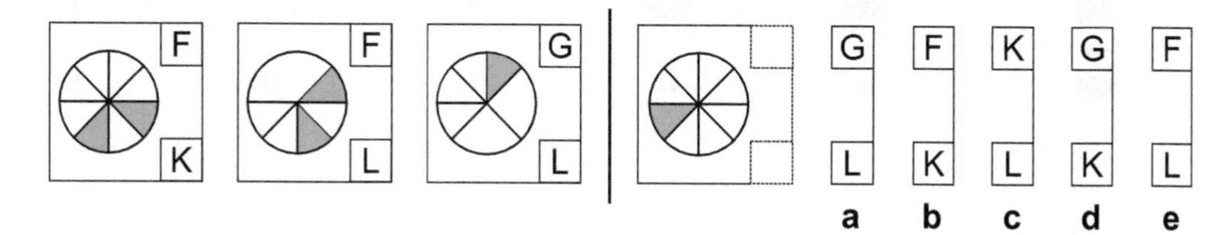

Answer: d

G means one grey section. K means eight sections in total.

Test 1

You have **10 minutes** to do this test. Circle the letter underneath each correct answer.

On the left of each question below is a big square with one small empty square. Find which of the five squares on the right should replace the empty square.

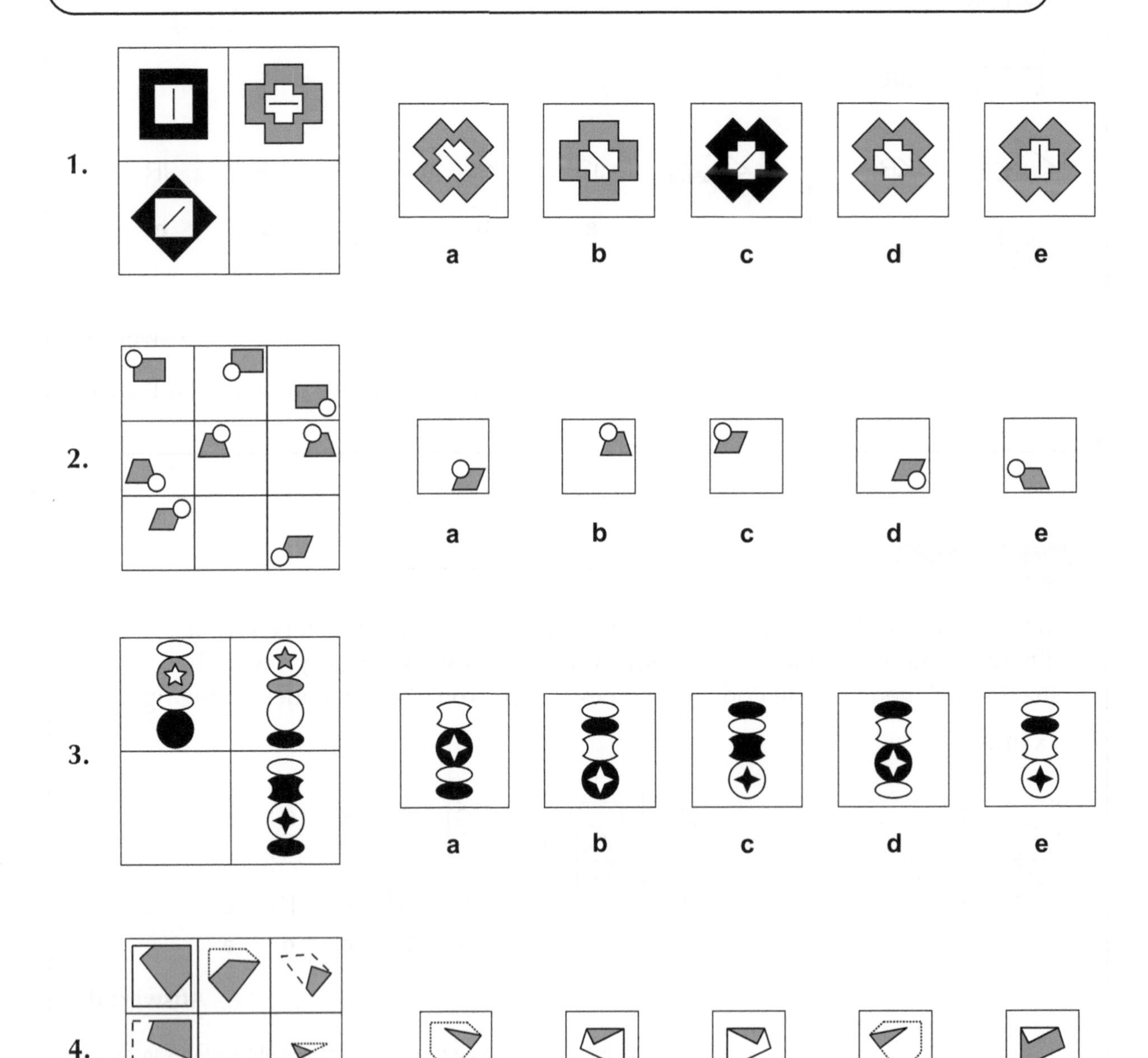

For each of the questions below there are three figures that are like each other in some way. Find which of the five figures on the right is most like the three figures on the left.

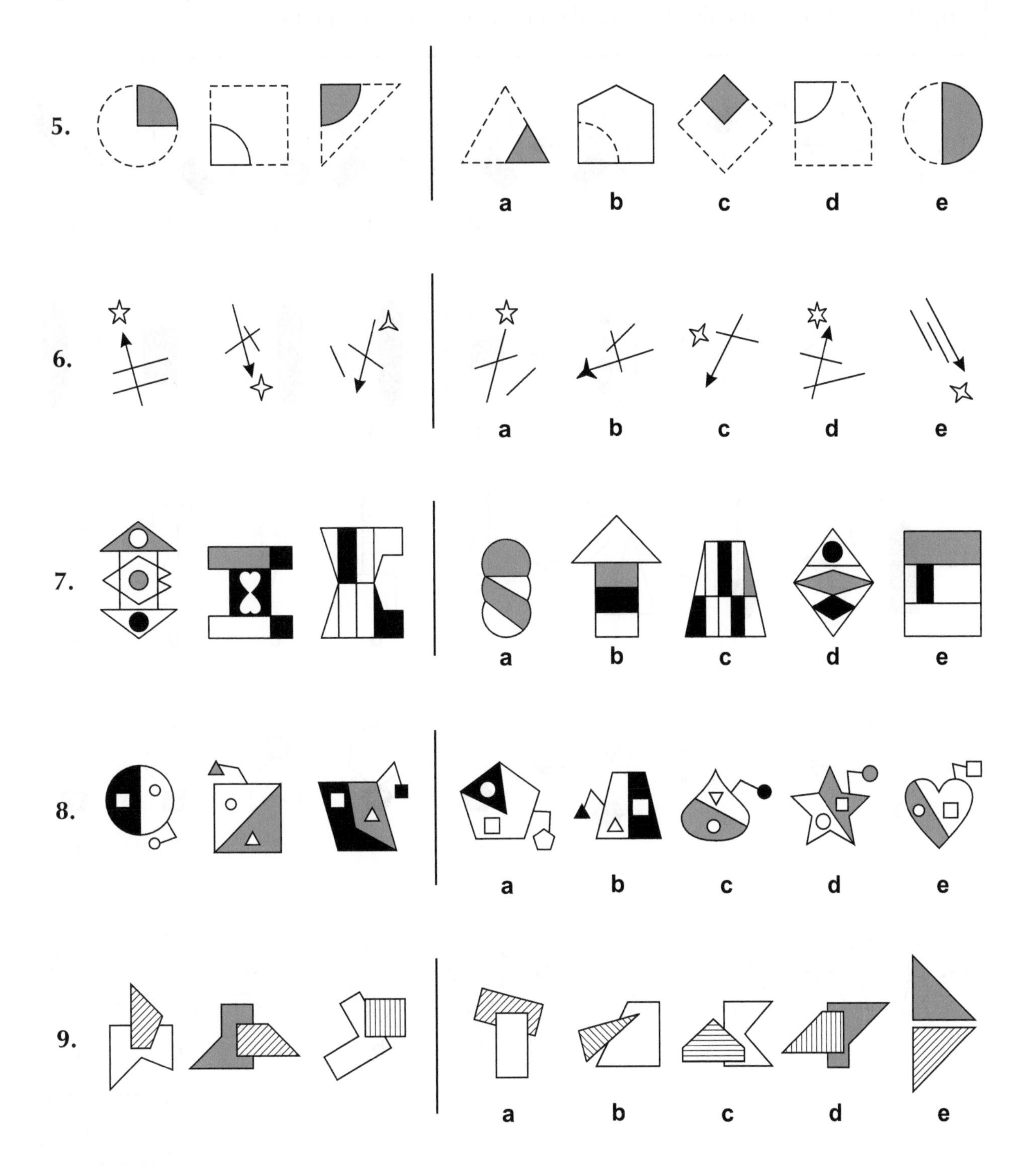

Each question has two shapes on the left with an arrow between them.
The first shape is changed in some way to become the second. There is then a third shape followed by an arrow and a choice of five shapes. Choose the shape on the right that relates to the third shape like the second does to the first.

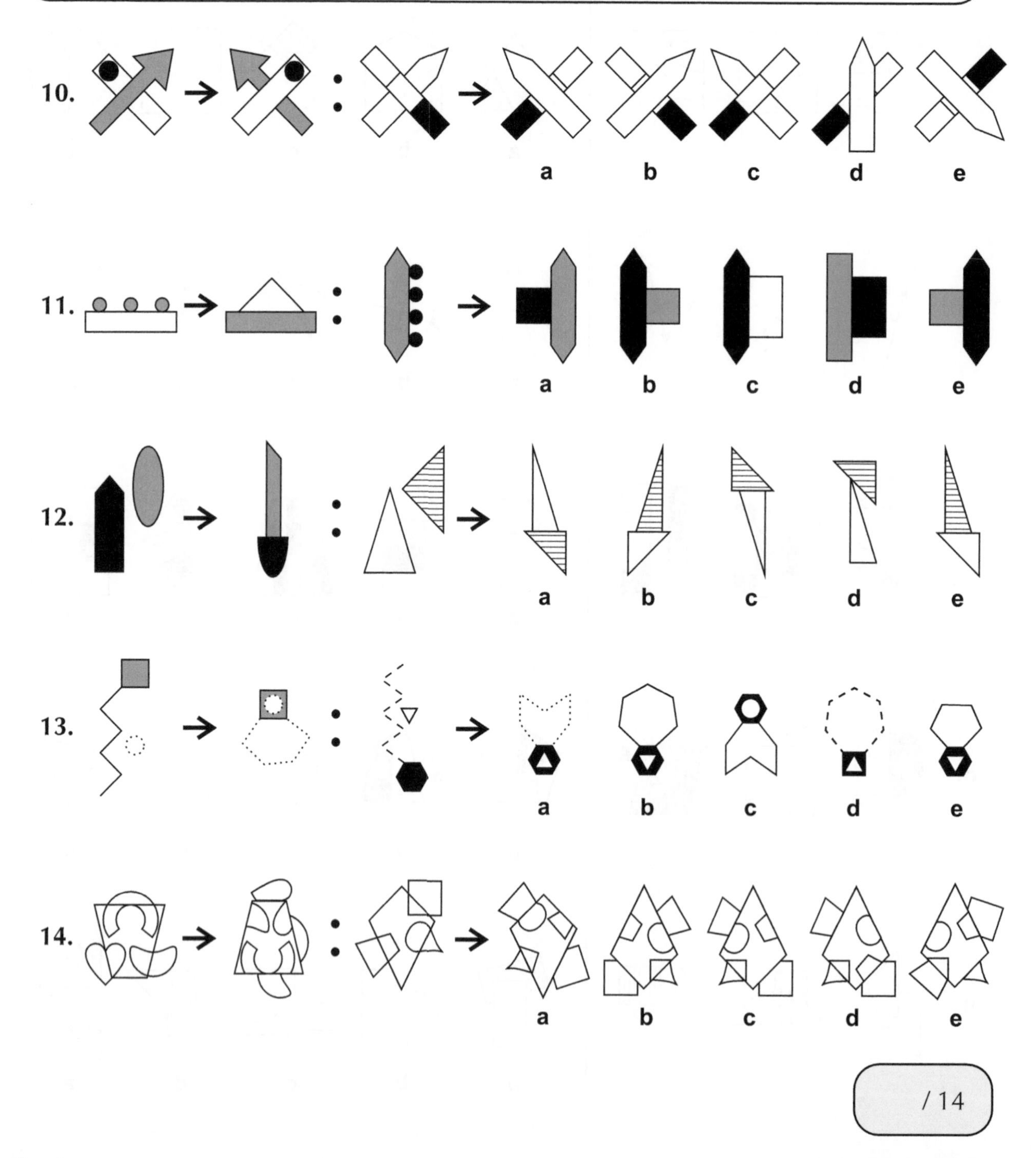

/ 14

Test 2

You have **10 minutes** to do this test. Circle the letter underneath each correct answer.

For each question below there are two figures that are like each other in some way. Find which of the five figures on the right is most like the two figures on the left.

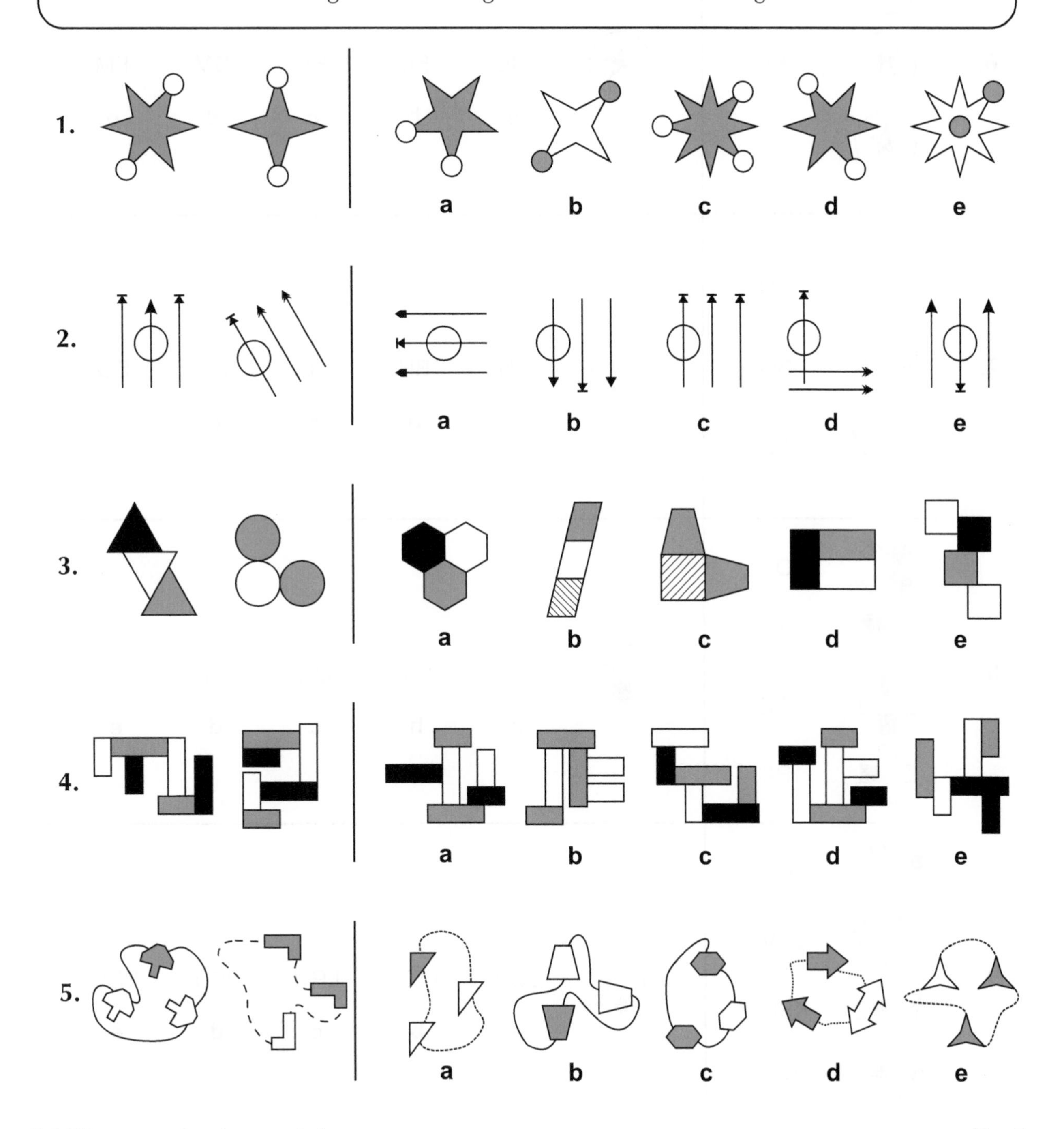

Each question has some shapes on the left with code letters that describe them. You need to work out what the code letters mean. There is then a shape on its own next to a choice of five codes. Work out which code describes this shape.

6.

DL
EL
DM

DL	EM	EL	DM	FM
a	**b**	**c**	**d**	**e**

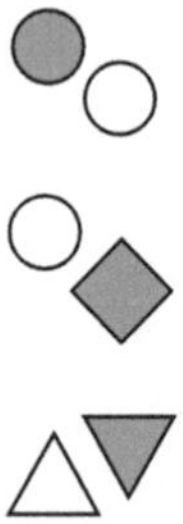

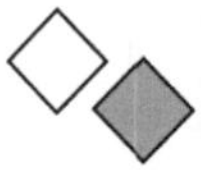

7.

AH
BG
AG

AH	BH	AG	BF	BG
a	**b**	**c**	**d**	**e**

8.

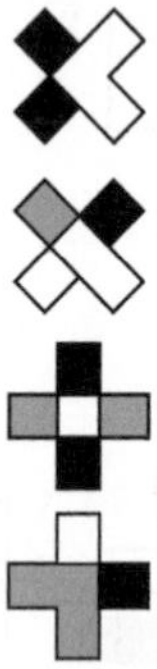

QX
QY
PZ
PX

PZ	QY	QX	PY	PX
a	**b**	**c**	**d**	**e**

9.

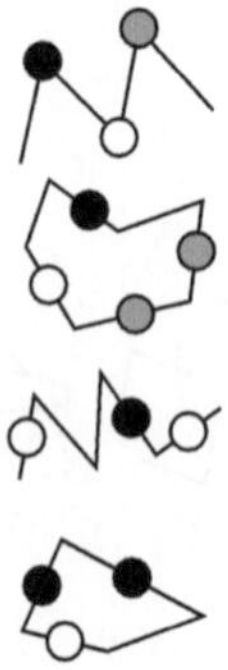

JRU
LSV
KSU
JSU

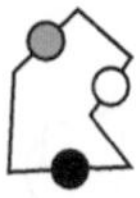

LSU	LSV	LRU	JSU	KSV
a	**b**	**c**	**d**	**e**

Each of the questions below has five figures.
Find which figure in each row is most unlike the others.

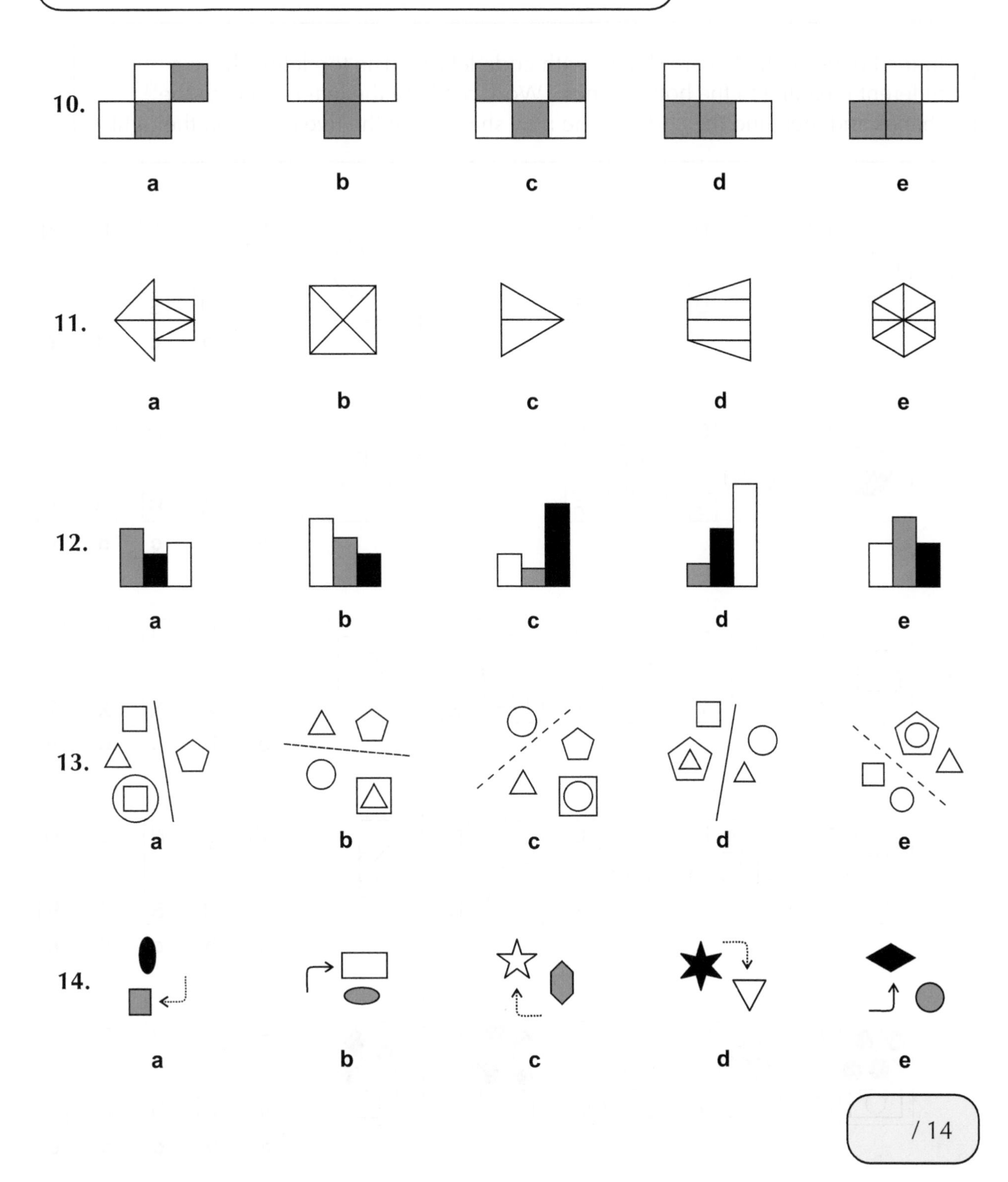

/ 14

Test 3

You have **10 minutes** to do this test. Circle the letter underneath each correct answer.

In the boxes on the left are shapes with code letters. The top letters have a different meaning to the bottom ones. Work out how the letters go with the shapes and then find the code for the new shape from the five codes on the right.

1.
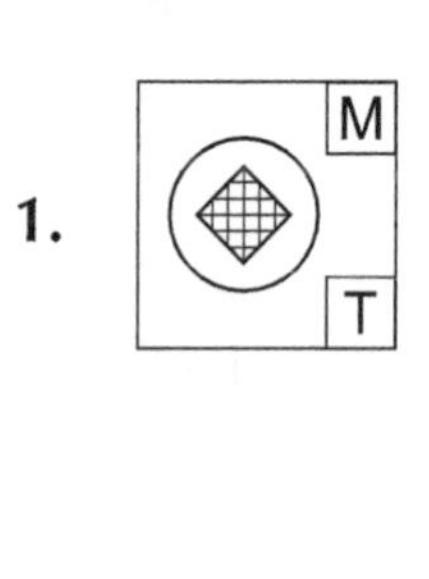
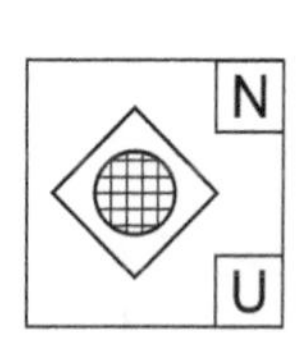
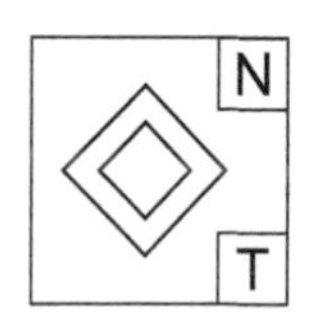
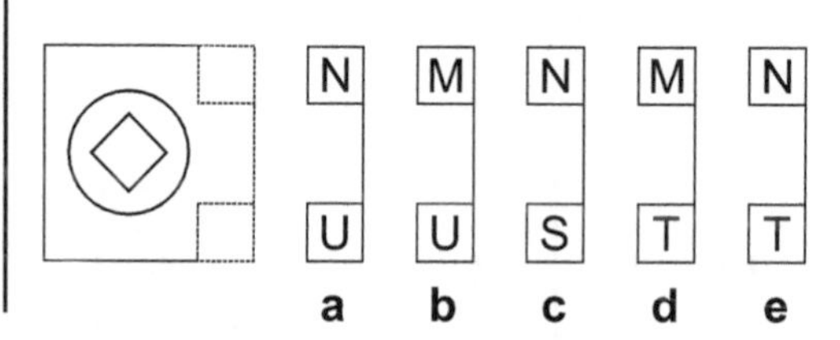

a	b	c	d	e
NU	MU	NS	MT	NT

2.
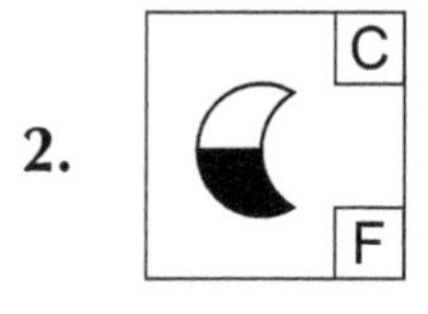
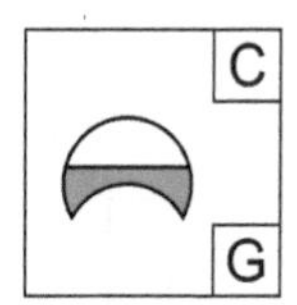
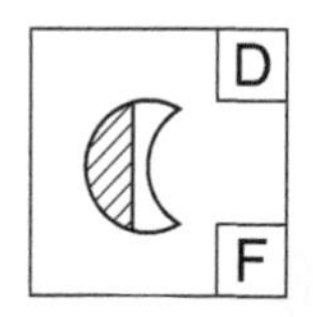
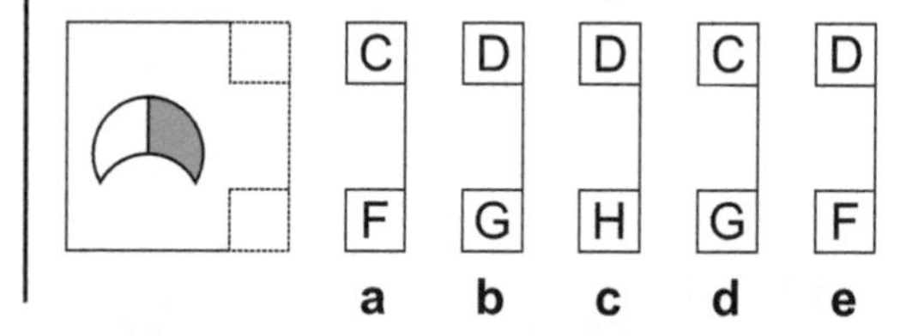

a	b	c	d	e
CF	DG	DH	CG	DF

3.
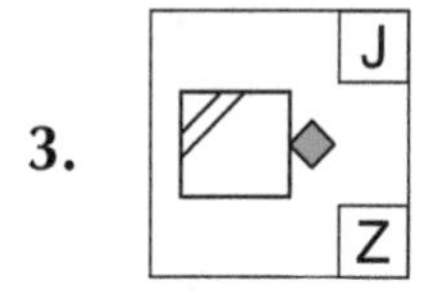
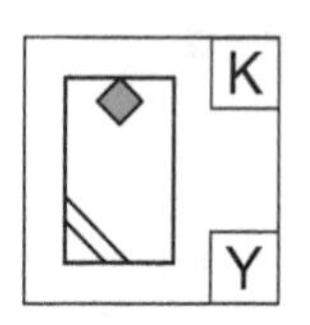
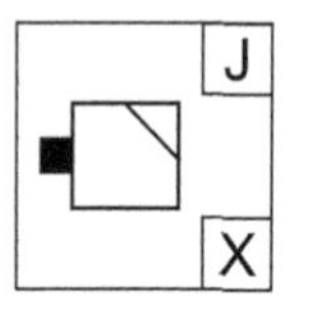
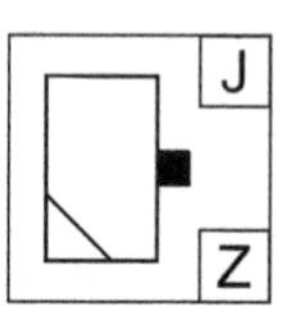
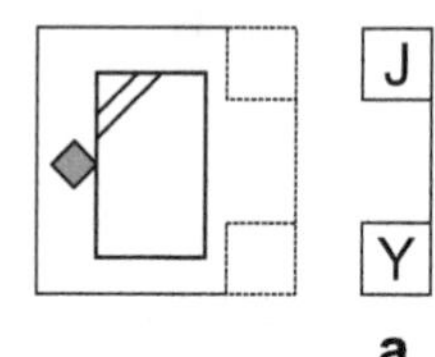
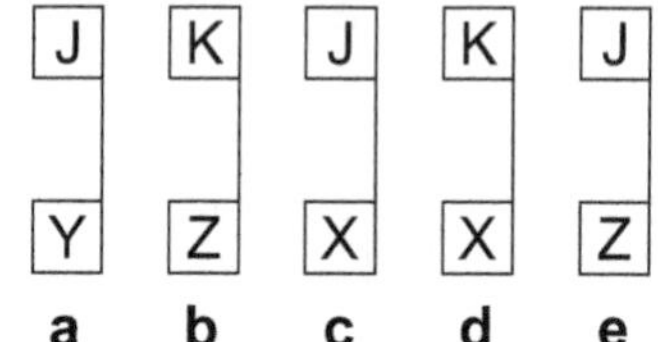

a	b	c	d	e
JY	KZ	JX	KX	JZ

4.

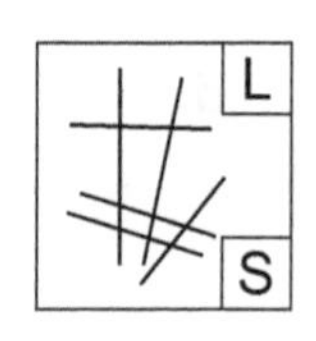
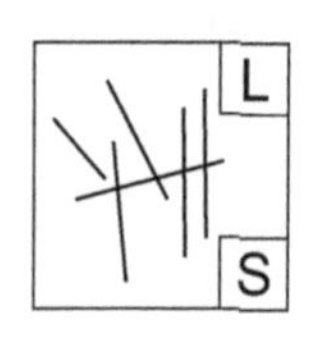
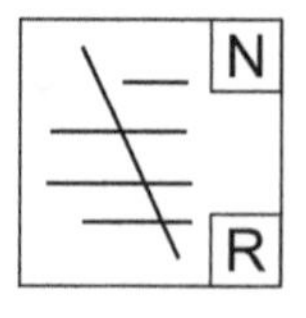
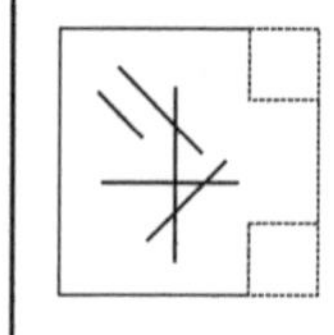

a	b	c	d	e
MS	LR	NS	LS	NR

5.
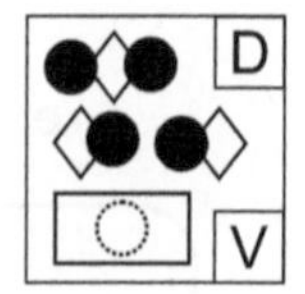
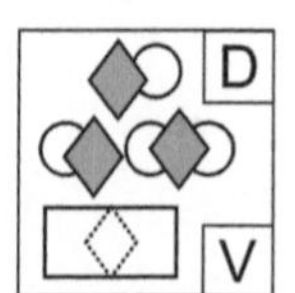
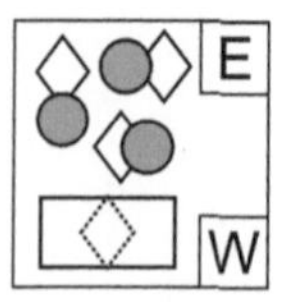
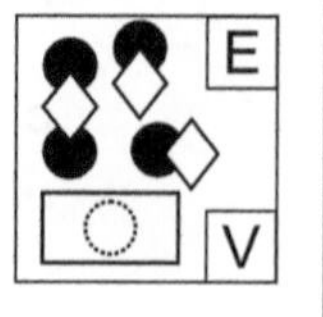

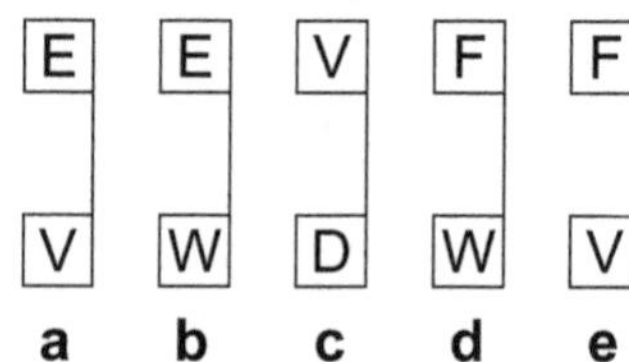

a	b	c	d	e
EV	EW	VD	FW	FV

For each of the questions below there are three figures that are like each other in some way. Find which of the five figures on the right is most like the three figures on the left.

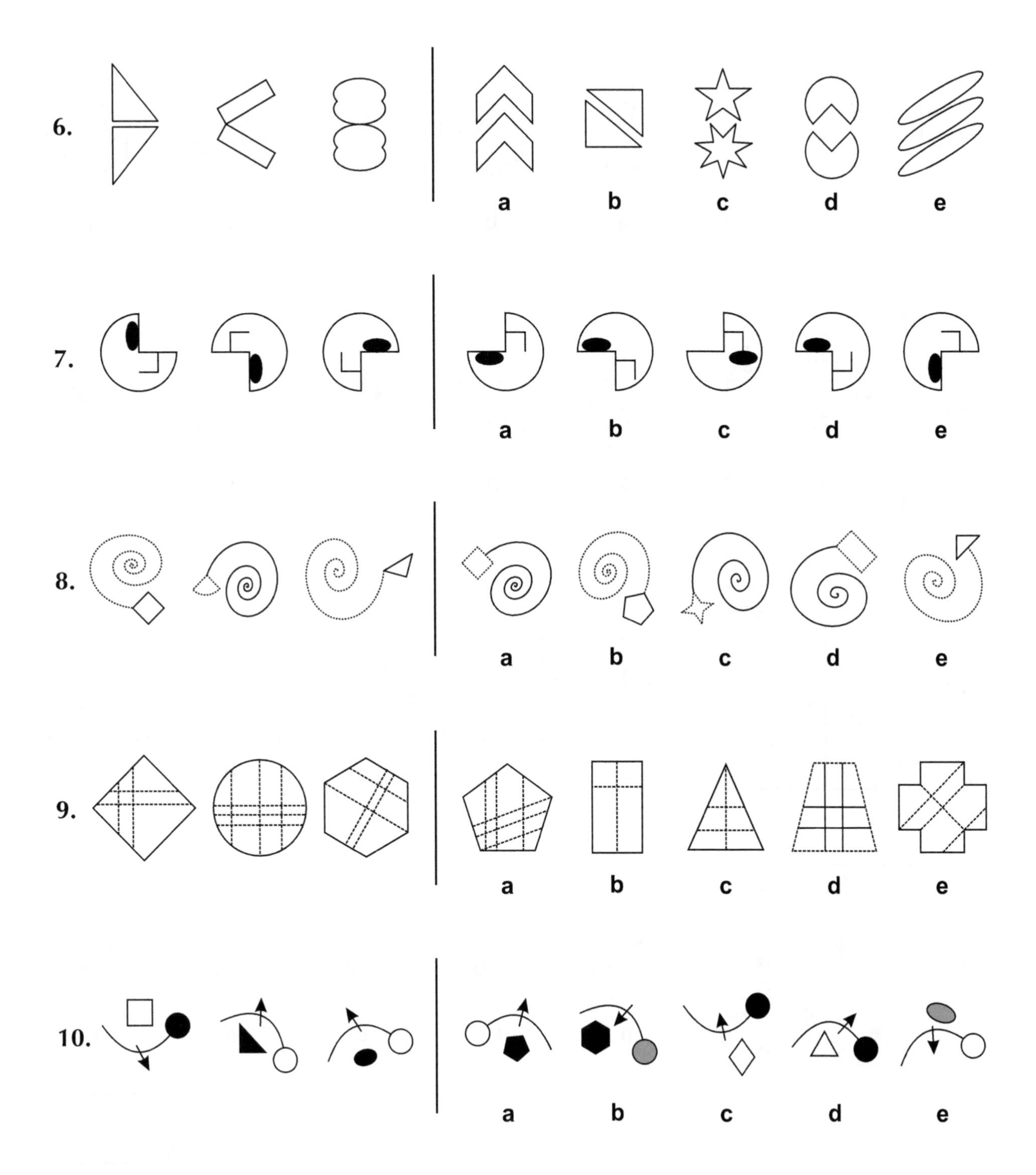

On the left of each question below is a big square with one small empty square.
Find which of the five squares on the right should replace the empty square.

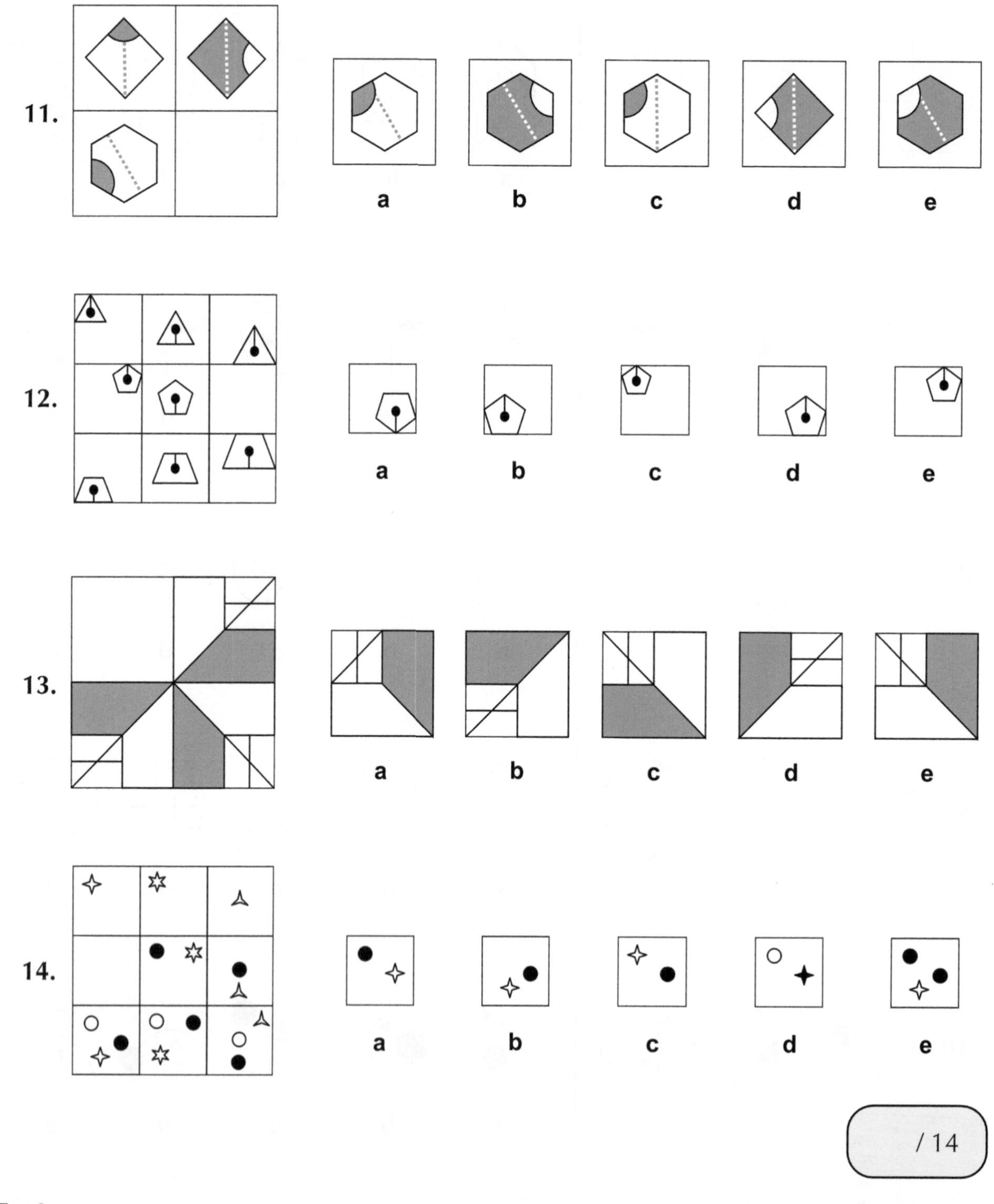

/ 14

Now try these puzzles! They'll help you to hone your skills at **spotting similarities**.

Cherry Picking

Riya and Jack are playing a game. The person who plays a card that is most like the card in the centre wins the game. Jack goes first and plays the card on the right. Which of the cards below should Riya play to win the game?

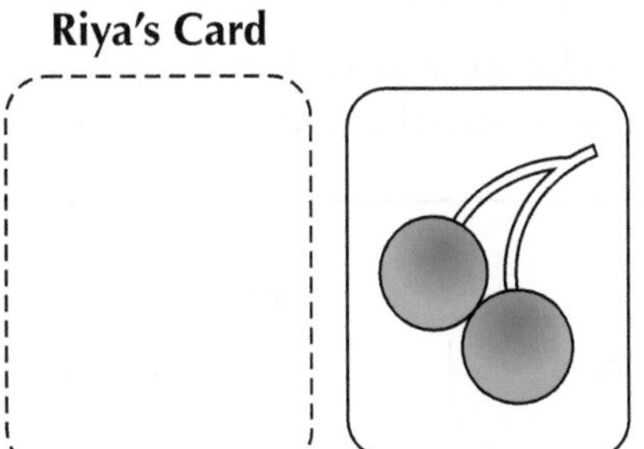

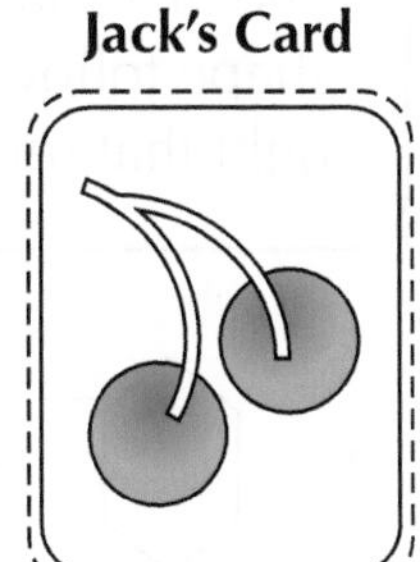

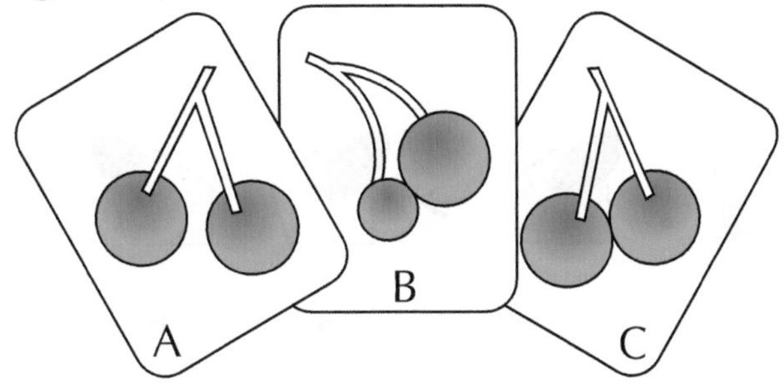

Spinning Circles

Each of the three figures on the left can be made by combining two of the figures on the right. Work out which pairs of figures go together to make the figures on the left. (Hint: you'll have to rotate them!)

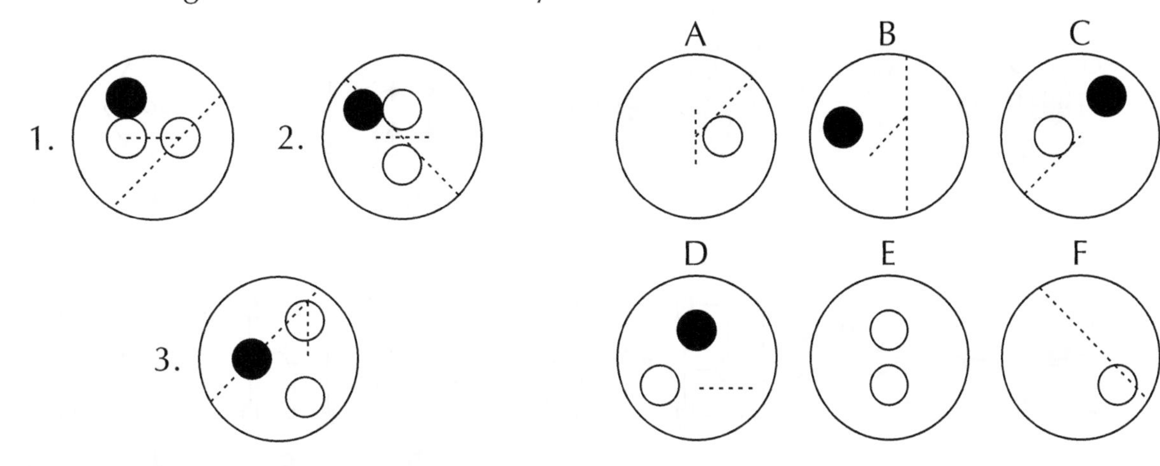

Test 4

You have **10 minutes** to do this test. Circle the letter underneath each correct answer.

Each question has two shapes on the left with an arrow between them.
The first shape is changed in some way to become the second. There is then a third shape followed by an arrow and a choice of five shapes. Choose the shape on the right that relates to the third shape like the second does to the first.

1.
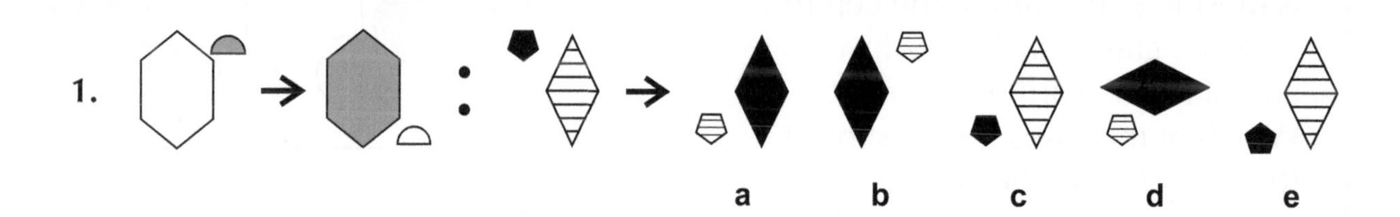

2.
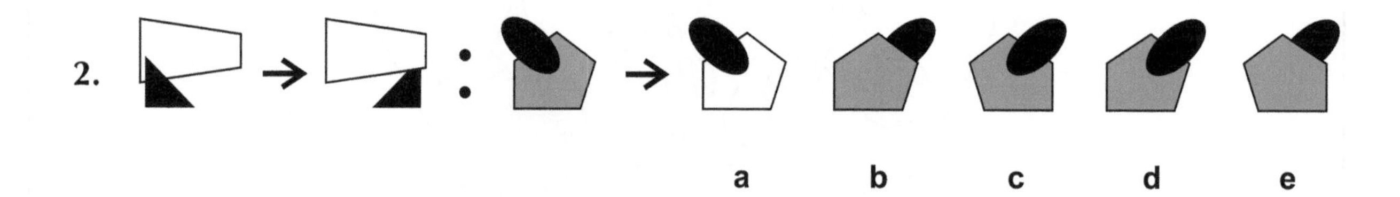

3.
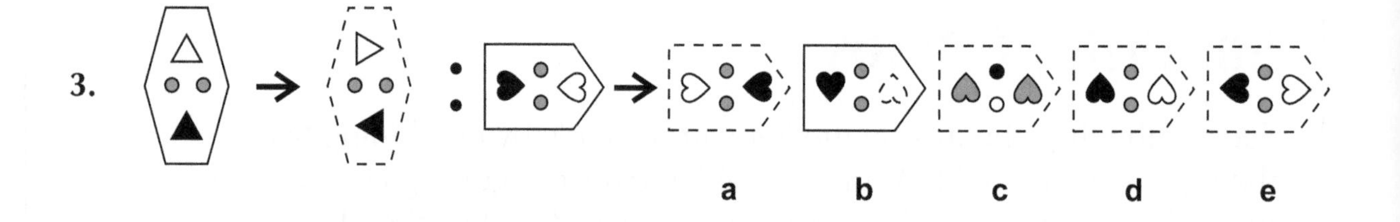

4.
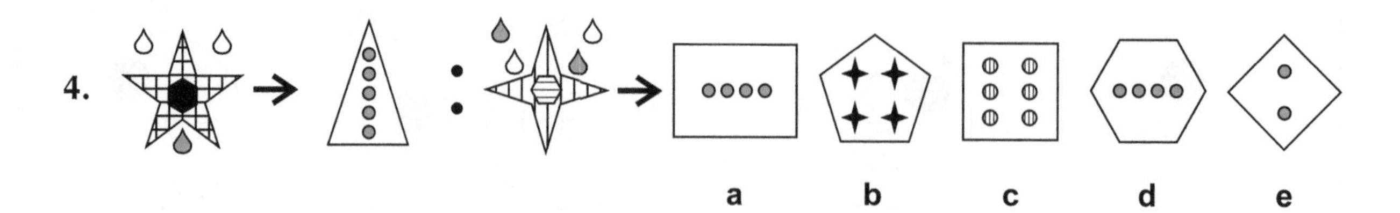

5.
a b c d e

Each question has some shapes on the left with code letters that describe them. You need to work out what the code letters mean. There is then a shape on its own next to a choice of five codes. Work out which code describes this shape.

6.

AJQ

BJP

BKQ

AKQ	BJQ	AJP	BKP	AKP
a	**b**	**c**	**d**	**e**

7.

FY

EX

DZ

EW

FZ	DY	FX	DW	EZ
a	**b**	**c**	**d**	**e**

8.

MQ

LQ

NR

MQ	LR	LQ	NQ	MR
a	**b**	**c**	**d**	**e**

9.

AGT

BGS

AFS

BHS

AHT	BFS	BHT	AHS	BGT
a	**b**	**c**	**d**	**e**

For each question below there are two figures that are like each other in some way. Find which of the five figures on the right is most like the two figures on the left.

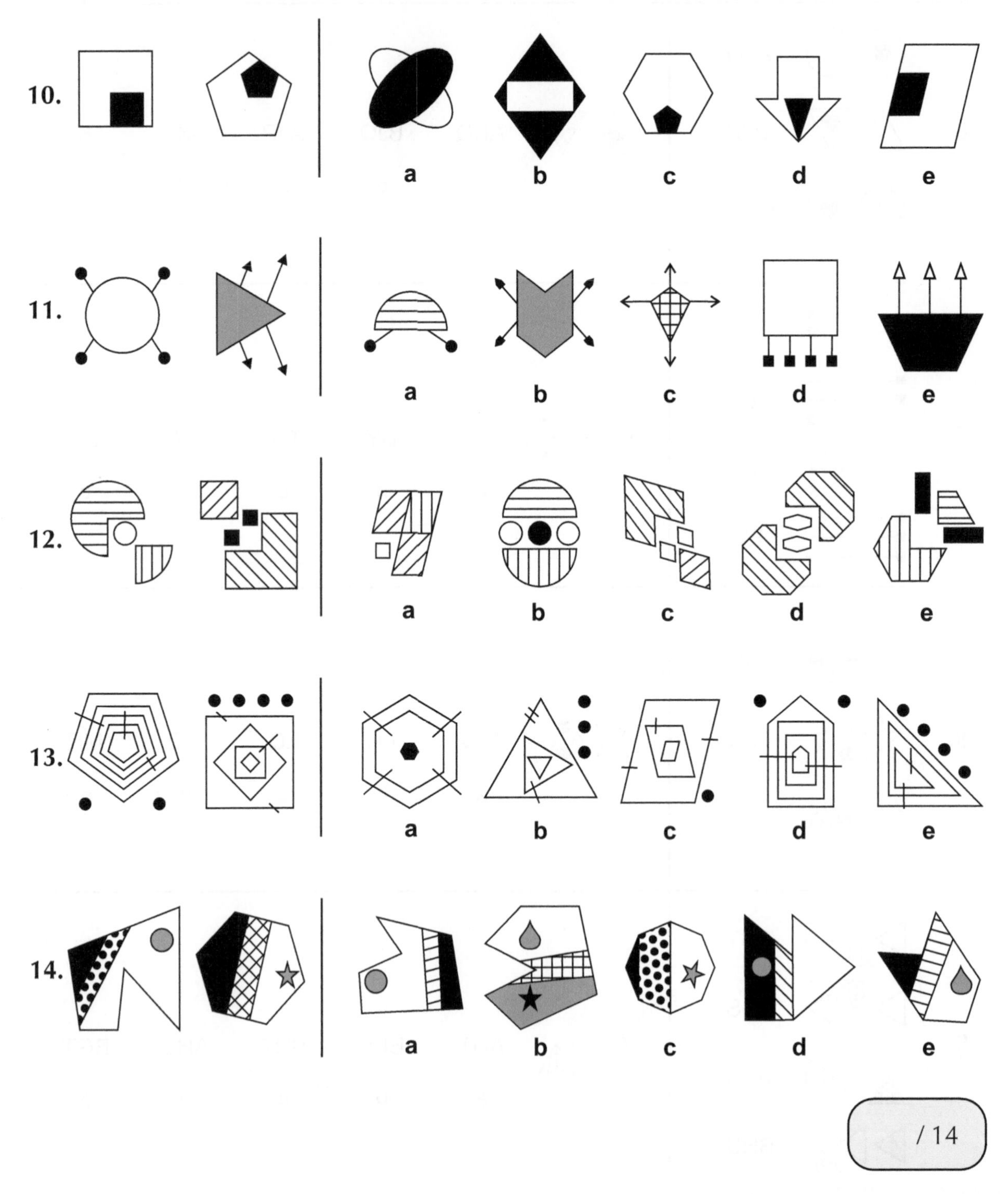

/ 14

Test 5

You have **10 minutes** to do this test. Circle the letter underneath each correct answer.

Each of the questions below has five figures.
Find which figure in each row is most unlike the others.

1.

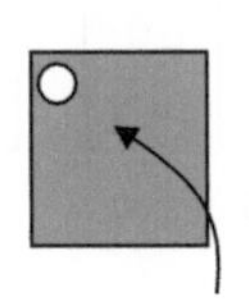 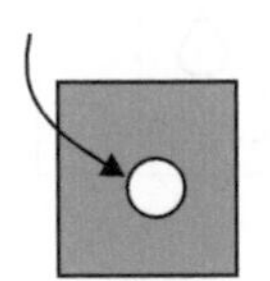 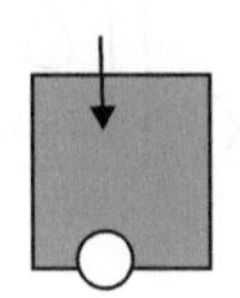 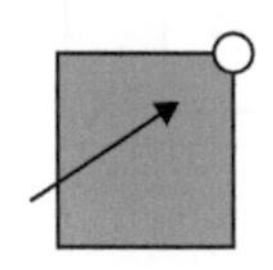 

a b c d e

2.

  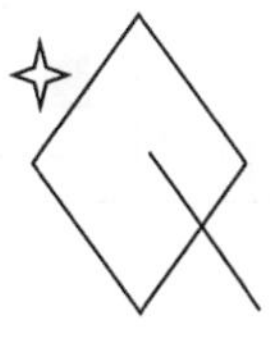  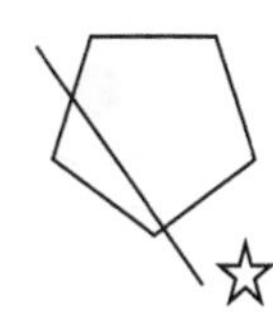

a b c d e

3.

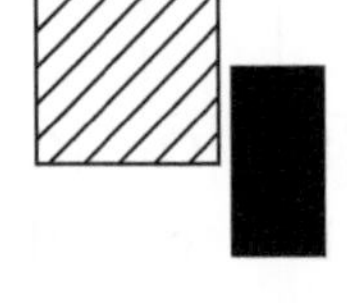 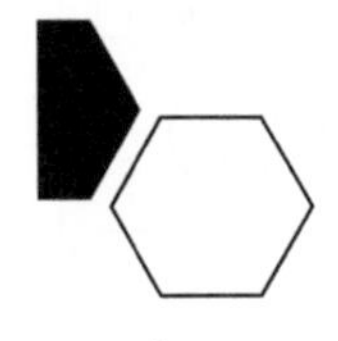 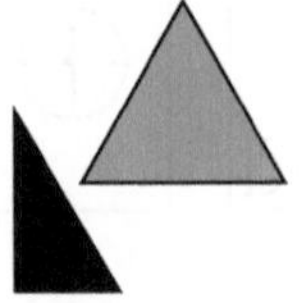 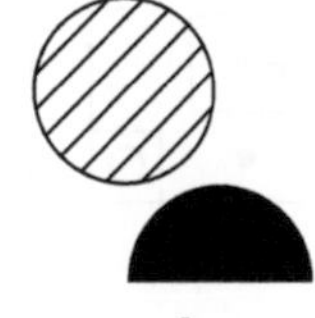 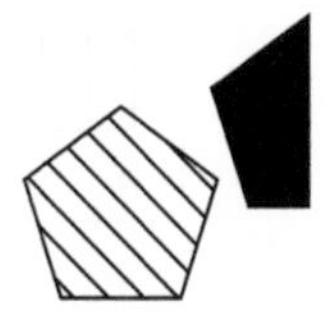

a b c d e

4.

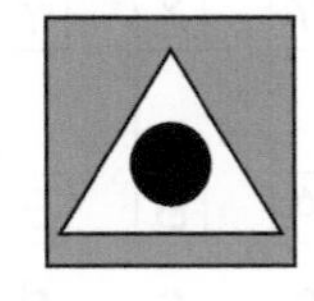 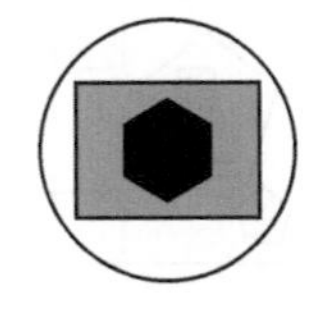   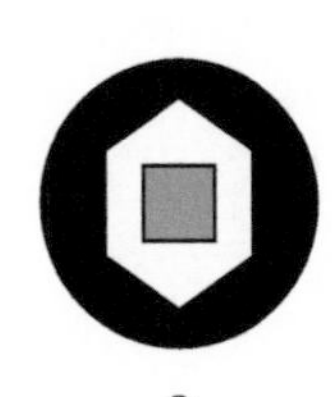

a b c d e

5.

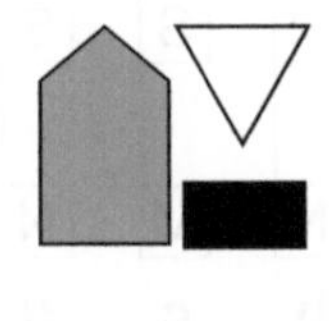 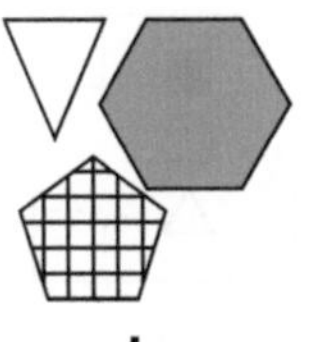 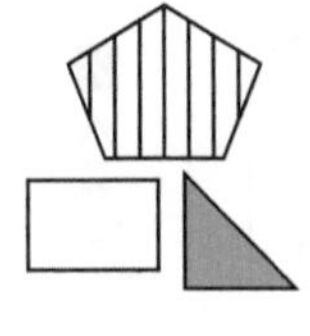 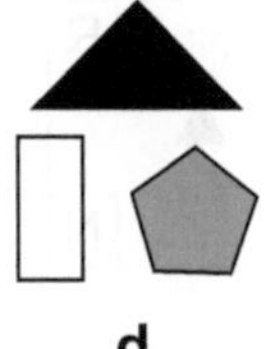 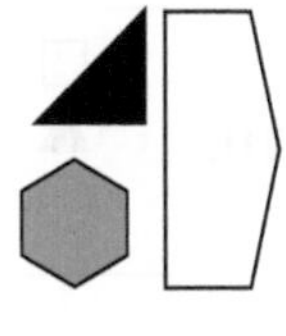

a b c d e

In the boxes on the left are shapes with code letters. The top letters have a different meaning to the bottom ones. Work out how the letters go with the shapes and then find the code for the new shape from the five codes on the right.

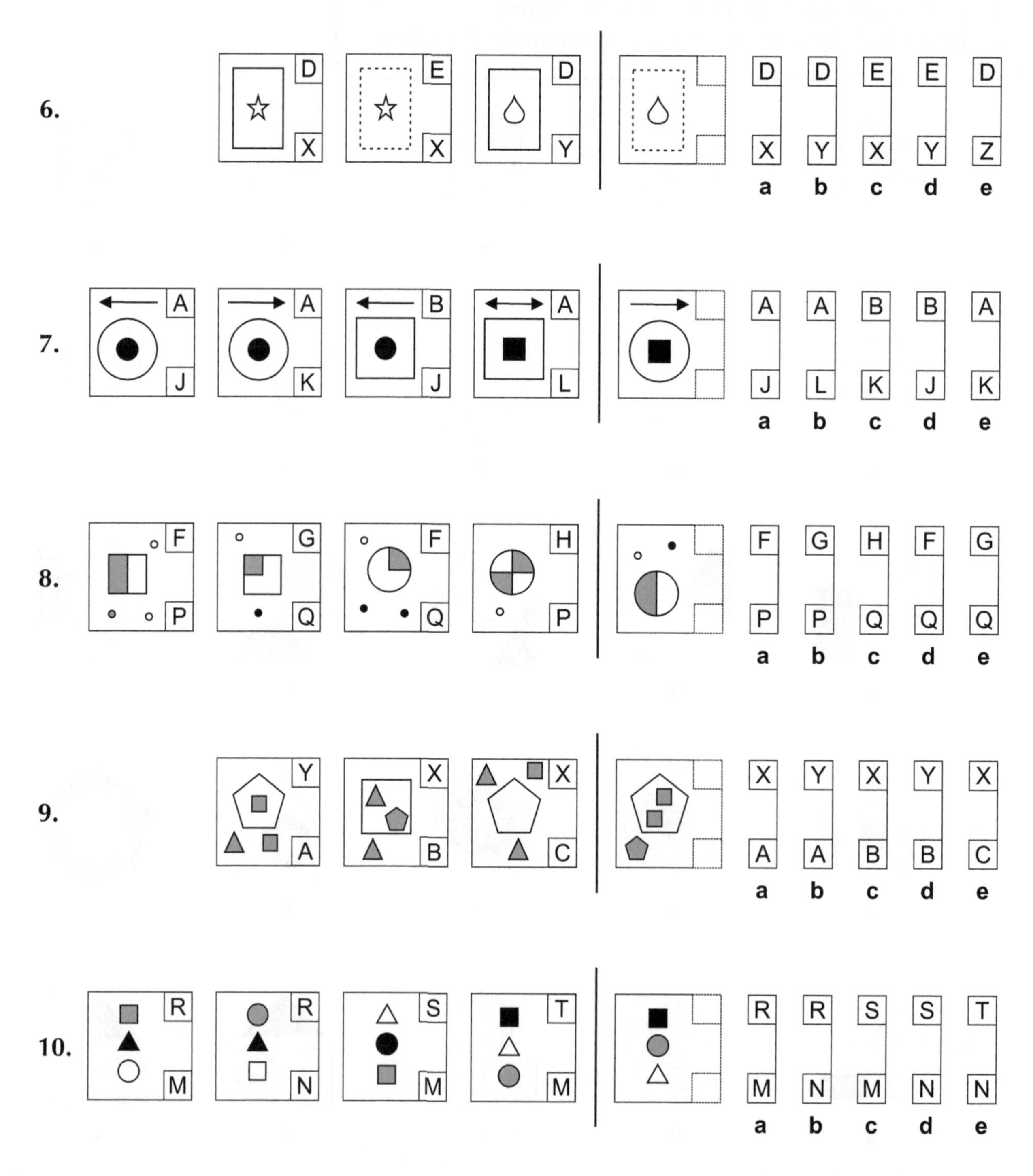

Each of these questions has five squares on the left that are arranged in order.
One of the squares is missing. One of the squares on the right should go in its place.
Find which one of the five squares on the right should go in place of the empty square.

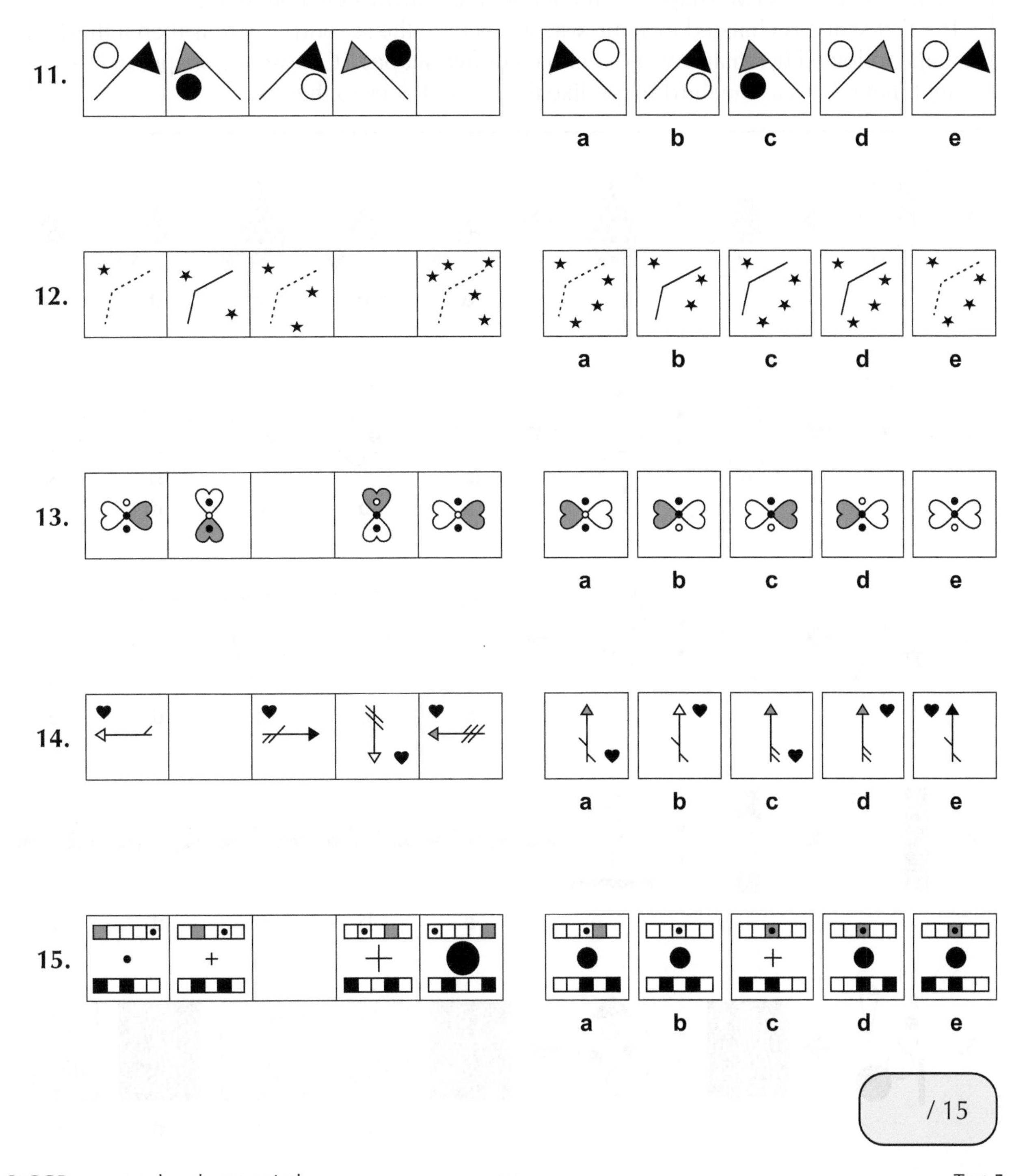

/ 15

Test 6

You have **10 minutes** to do this test. Circle the letter underneath each correct answer.

Each question has two shapes on the left with an arrow between them.
The first shape is changed in some way to become the second. There is then a third shape followed by an arrow and a choice of five shapes. Choose the shape on the right that relates to the third shape like the second does to the first.

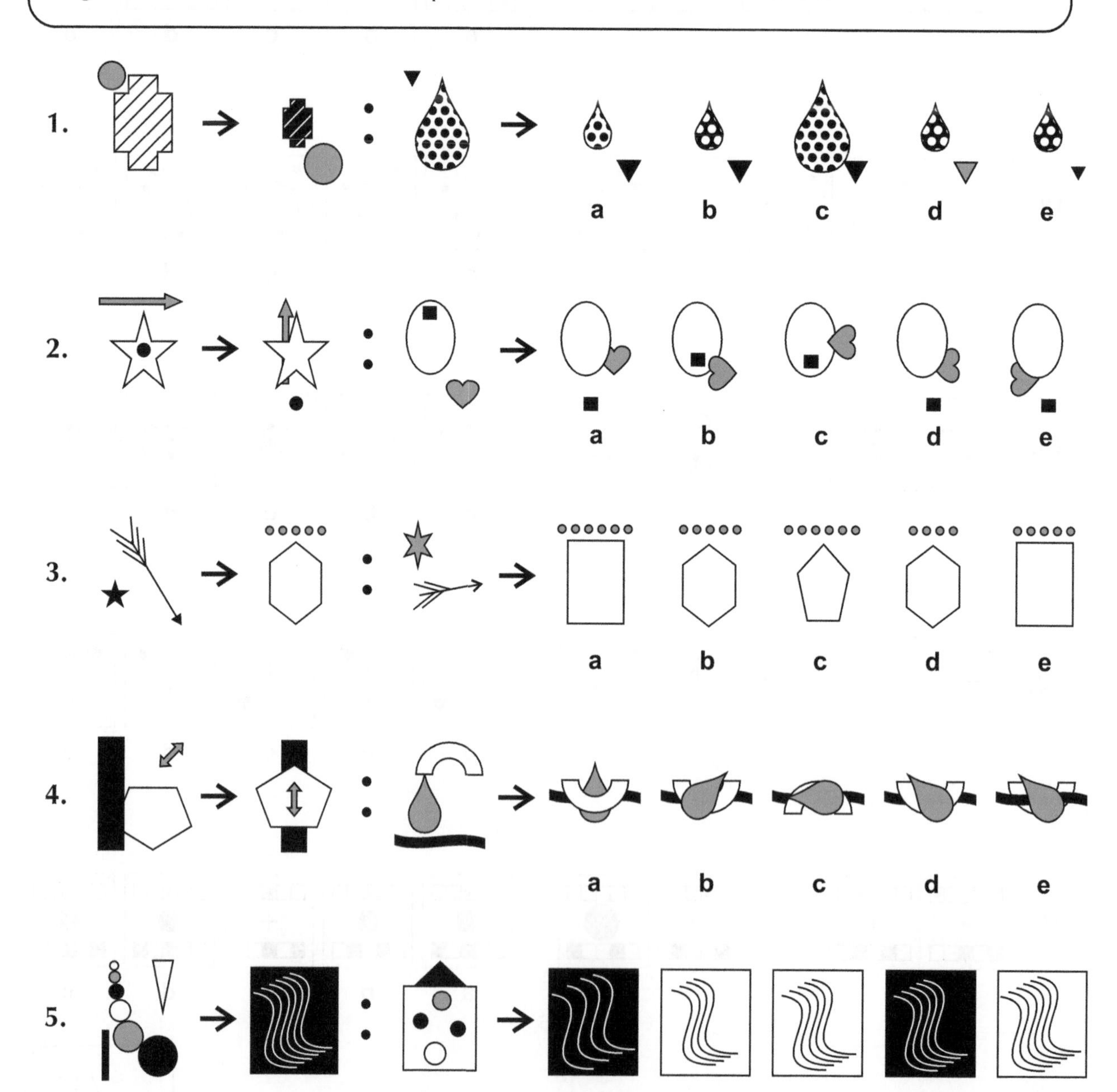

For each question below there are two figures that are like each other in some way. Find which of the five figures on the right is most like the two figures on the left.

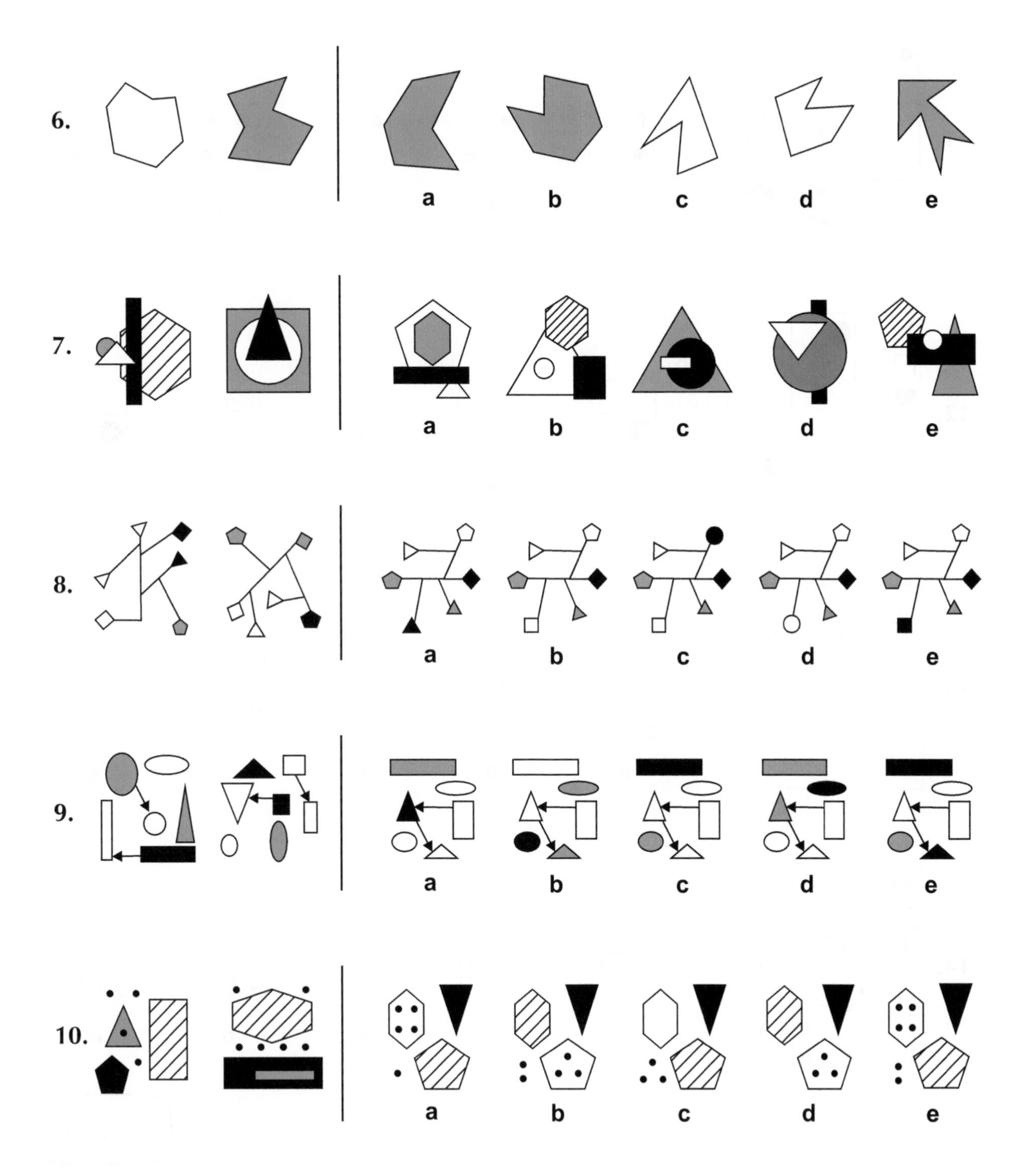

On the left of each question below is a big square with one small empty square. Find which of the five squares on the right should replace the empty square.

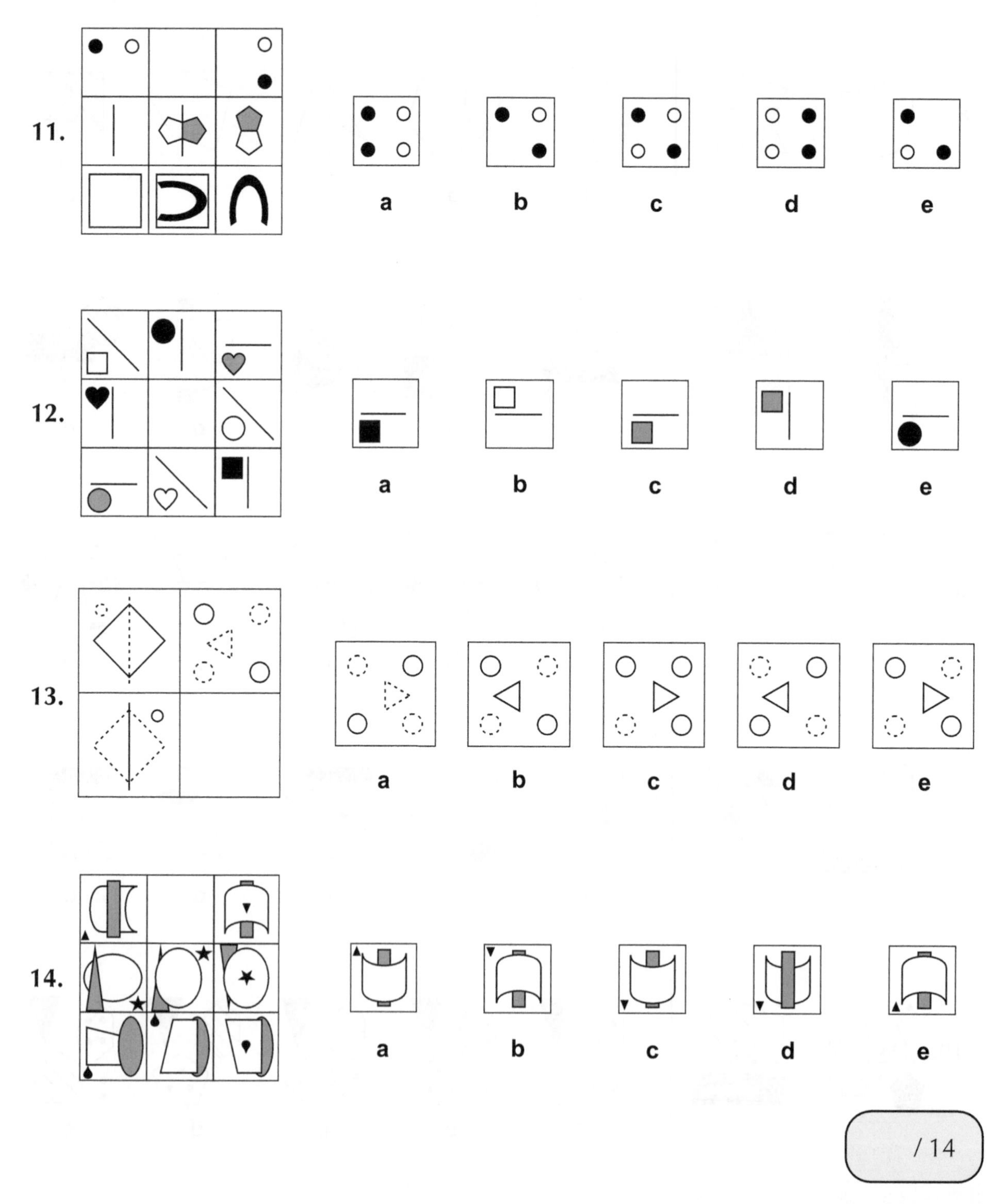

/ 14

It's puzzle time — these ones will help you get to grips with **rotation** and **patterns**.

Rotating Hexagons

Which of the tiles below can be placed in the middle of the puzzle to complete the pattern? (Hint: you'll have to rotate it!)

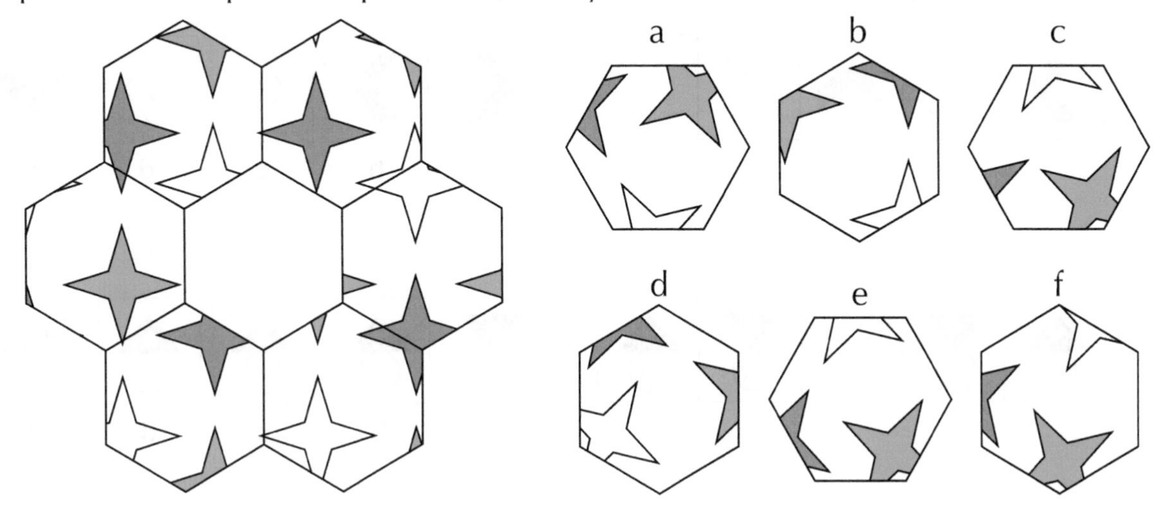

Locked Up!

In Pandora's house, the pattern on each lock relates to the key that opens it. Two of Pandora's locks and their keys are shown below. Design a key that Pandora could use to open the lock on the right.

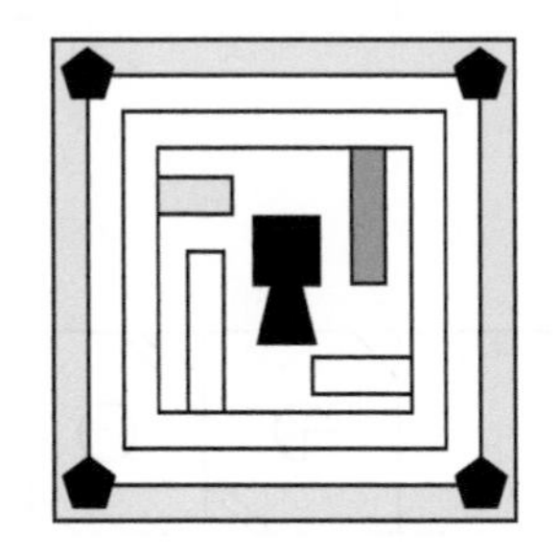

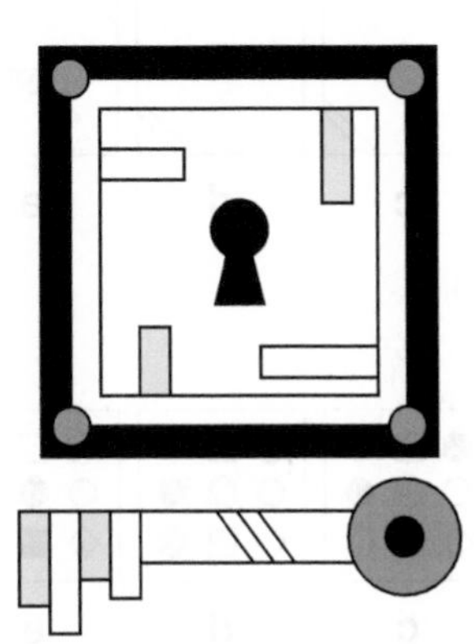

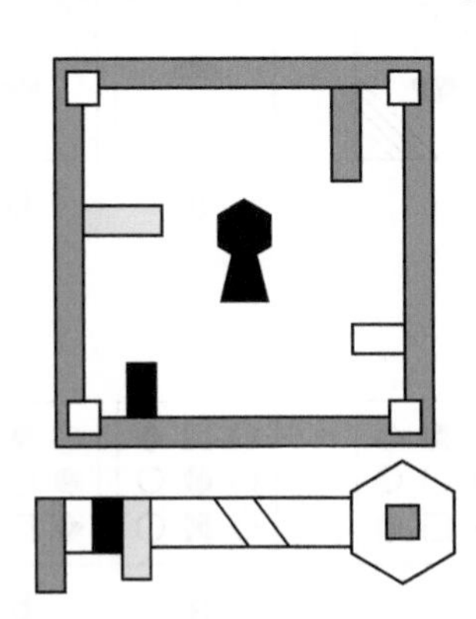

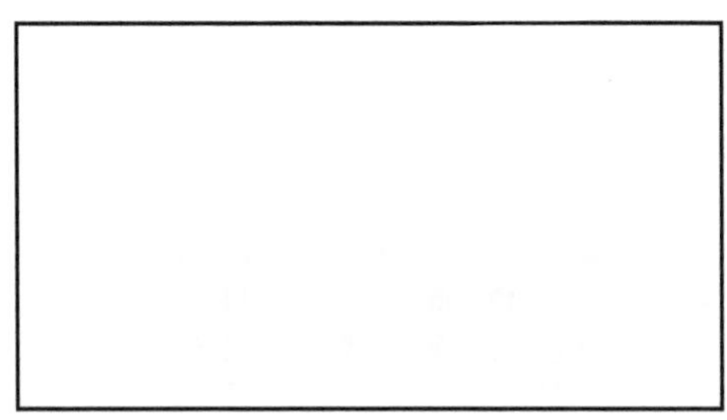

Test 7

You have **10 minutes** to do this test. Circle the letter underneath each correct answer.

Each of these questions has five squares on the left that are arranged in order.
One of the squares is missing. One of the squares on the right should go in its place.
Find which one of the five squares on the right should go in place of the empty square.

1. 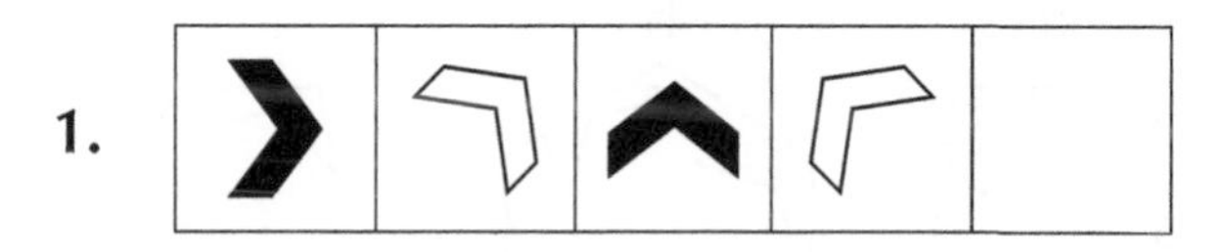 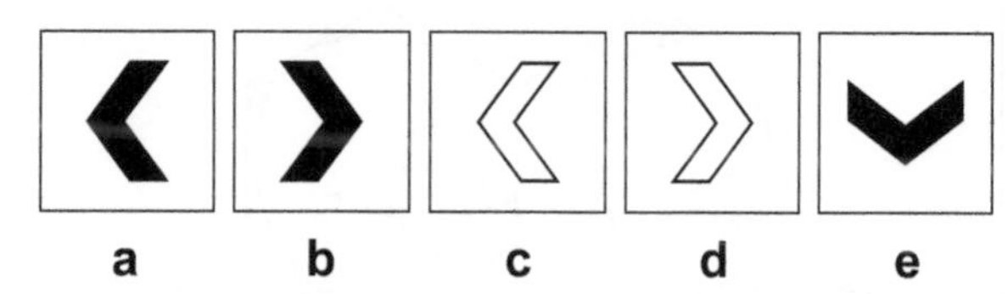

a b c d e

2. 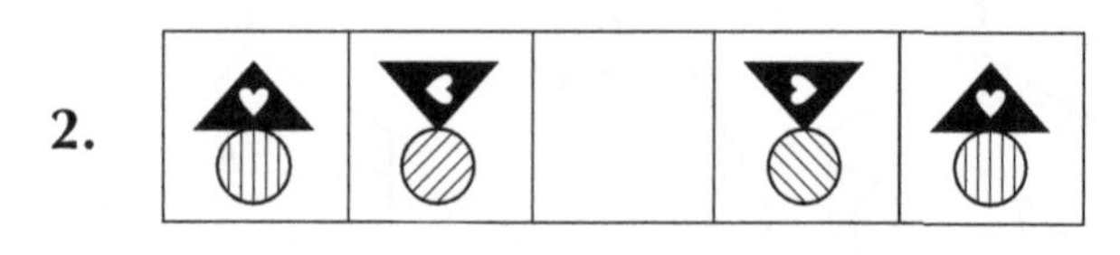 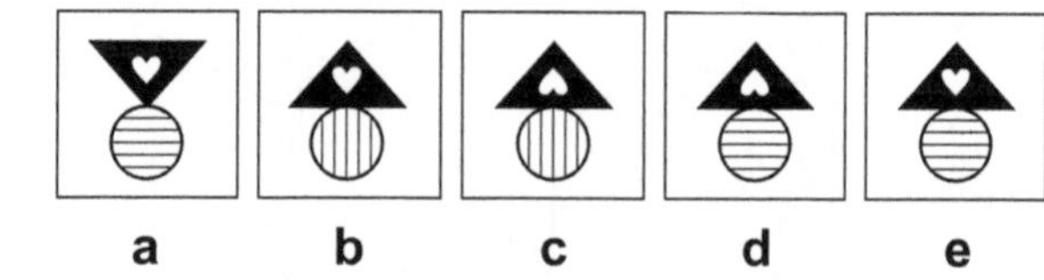

a b c d e

3. 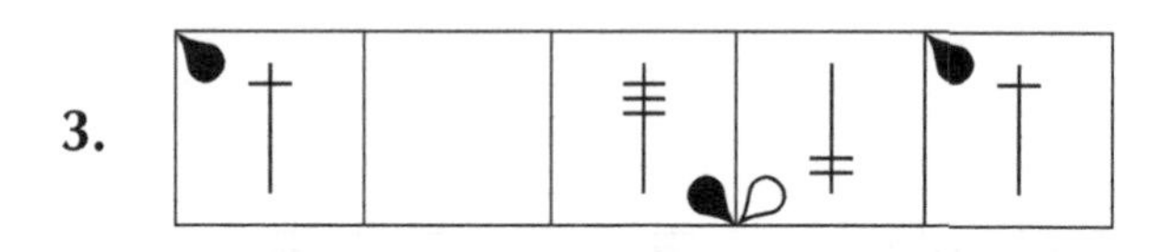 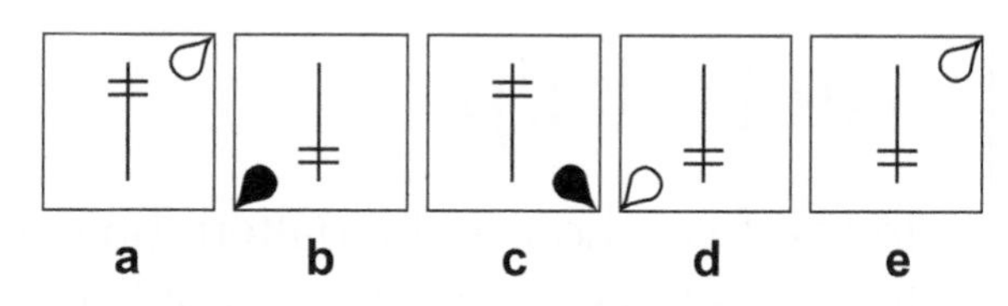

a b c d e

4. 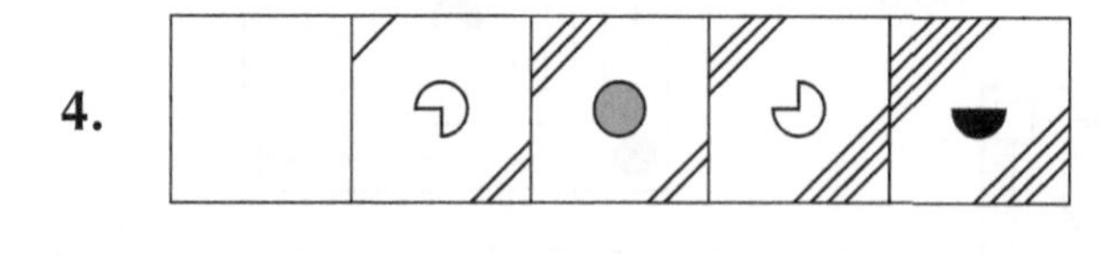 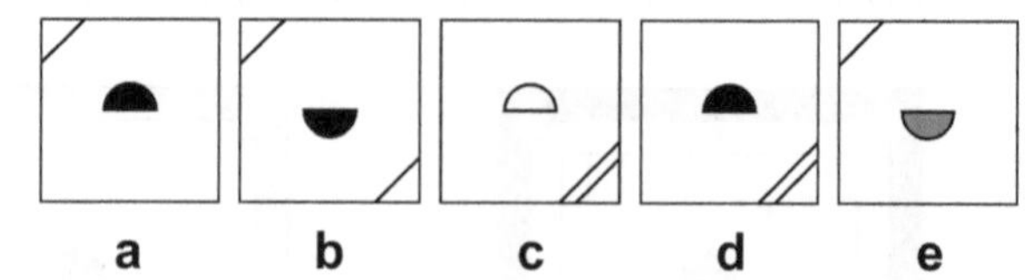

a b c d e

5. 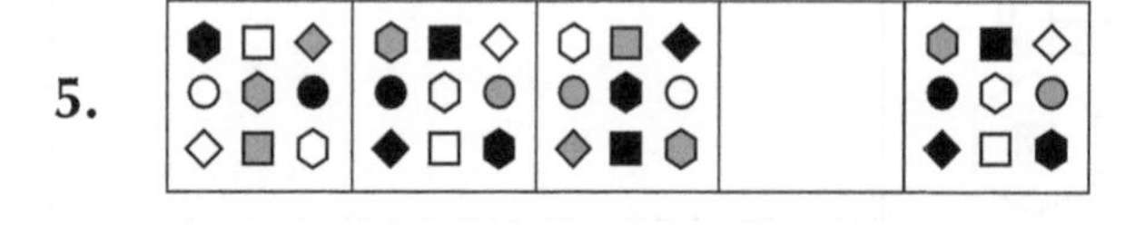 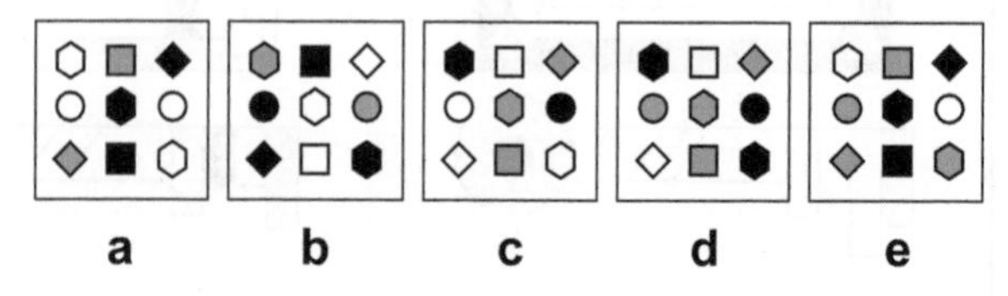

a b c d e

Each question has some shapes on the left with code letters that describe them. You need to work out what the code letters mean. There is then a shape on its own next to a choice of five codes. Work out which code describes this shape.

6.

	XA
	XB
	YC

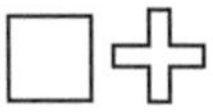

XA	XB	YA	YB	YC
a	**b**	**c**	**d**	**e**

7.

	EM
	FM
	FN
	GN

EN	EM	FN	FM	GM
a	**b**	**c**	**d**	**e**

8.

	DPV
	DQW
	EQV

DQW	DPV	EQW	EPW	EQV
a	**b**	**c**	**d**	**e**

9.

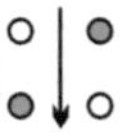

	AJR
	BKS
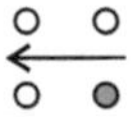	CKR
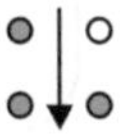	ALR

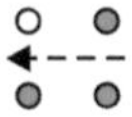

CKR	ALS	BJS	BLR	CLS
a	**b**	**c**	**d**	**e**

Each of the questions below has five figures.
Find which figure in each row is most unlike the others.

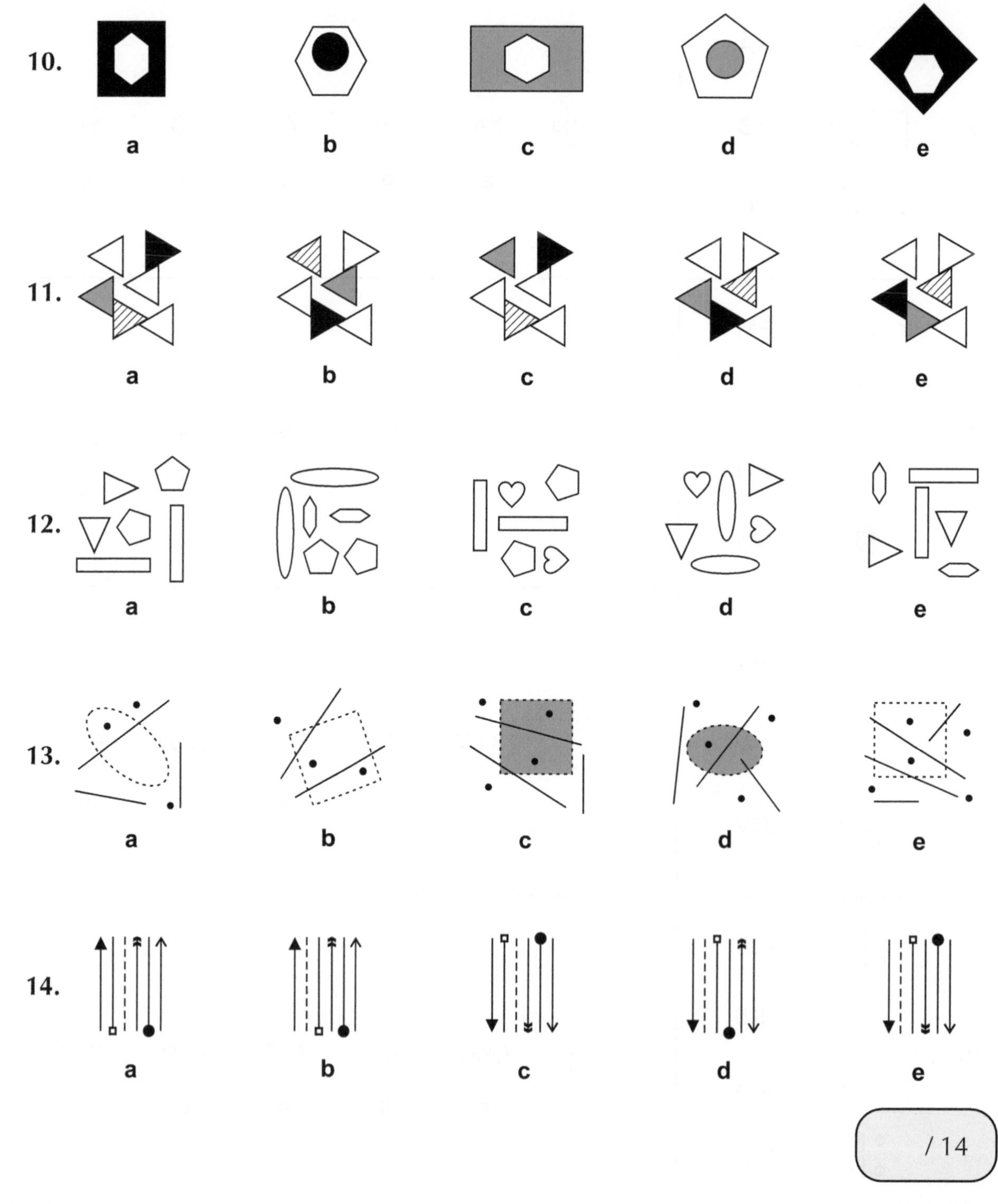

Test 8

You have **10 minutes** to do this test. Circle the letter underneath each correct answer.

On the left of each question below is a big square with one small empty square. Find which of the five squares on the right should replace the empty square.

1. 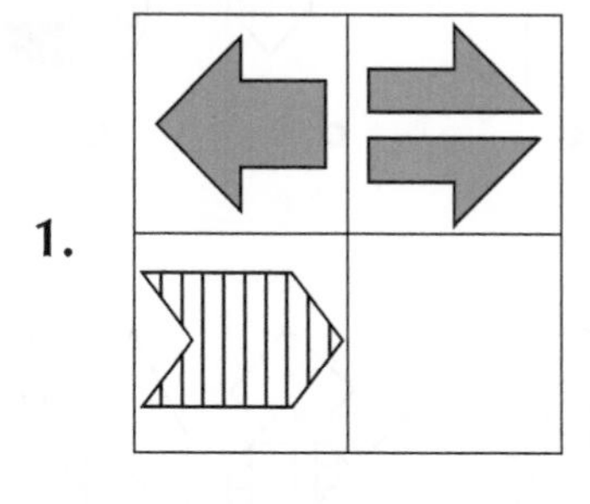

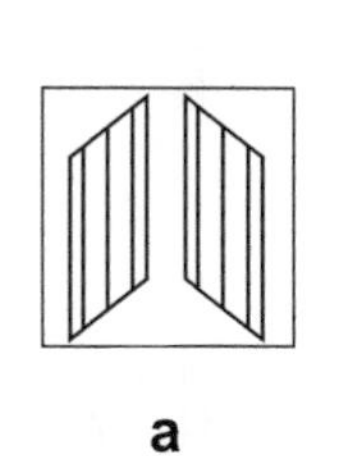 a 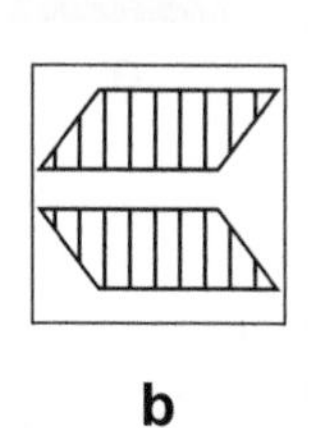 b 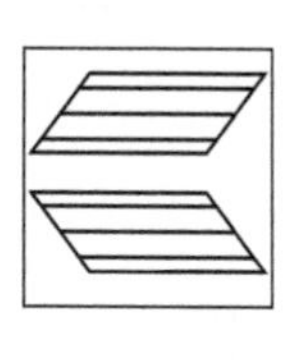 c 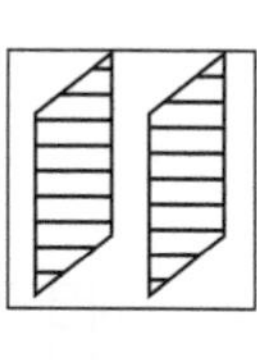 d 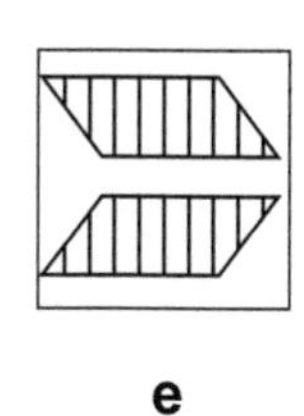 e

2. 

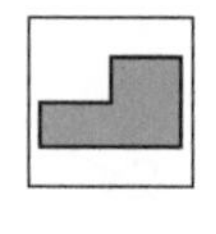 a 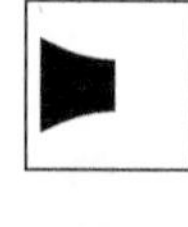 b  c 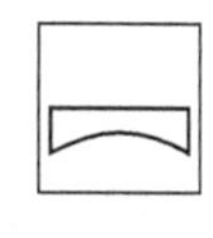 d 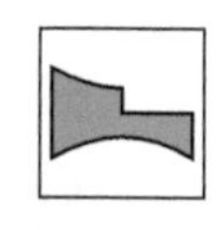 e

3. 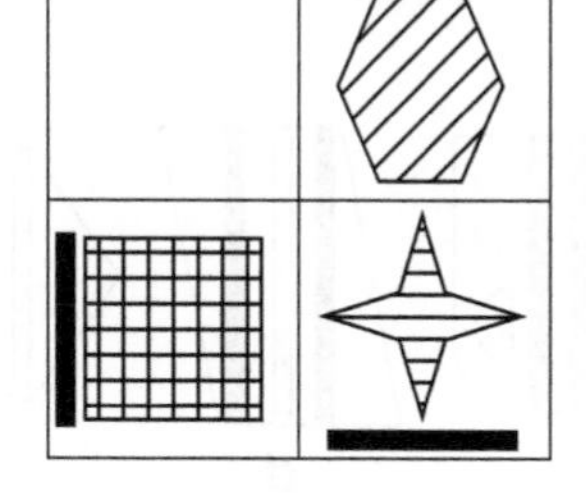

 a 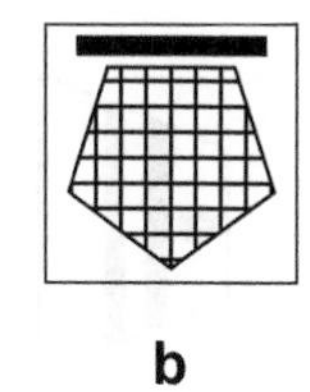 b 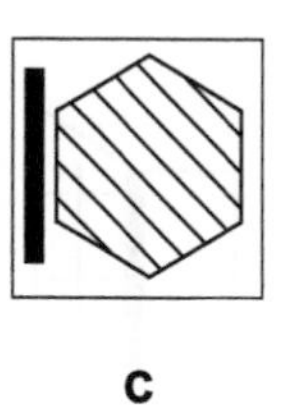 c  d 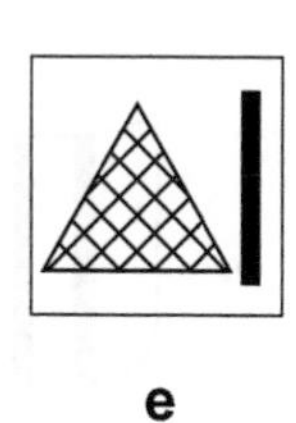 e

4. 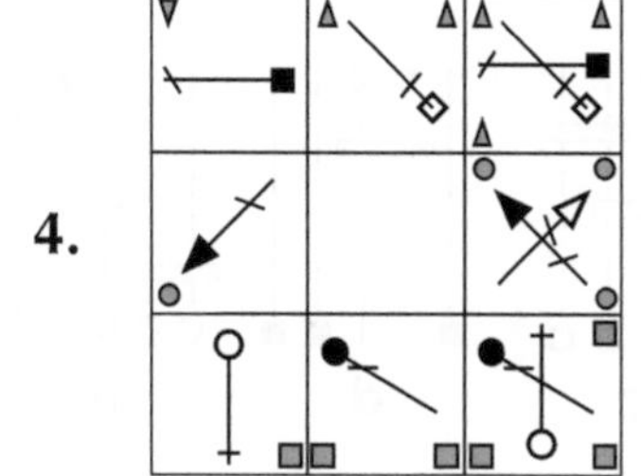

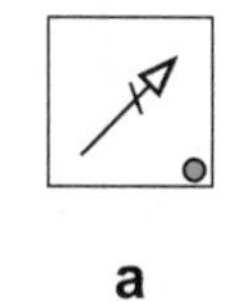 a 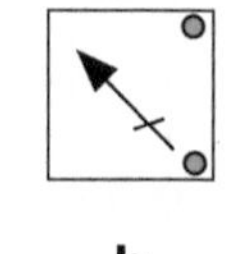 b 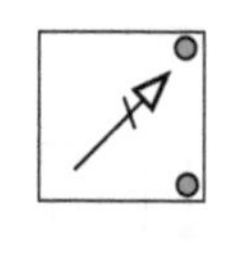 c 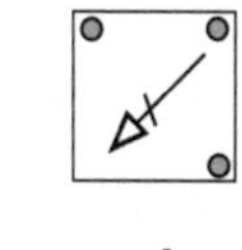 d 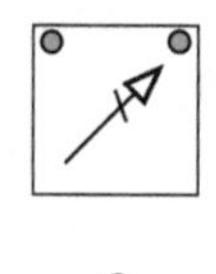 e

For each of the questions below there are three figures that are like each other in some way. Find which of the five figures on the right is most like the three figures on the left.

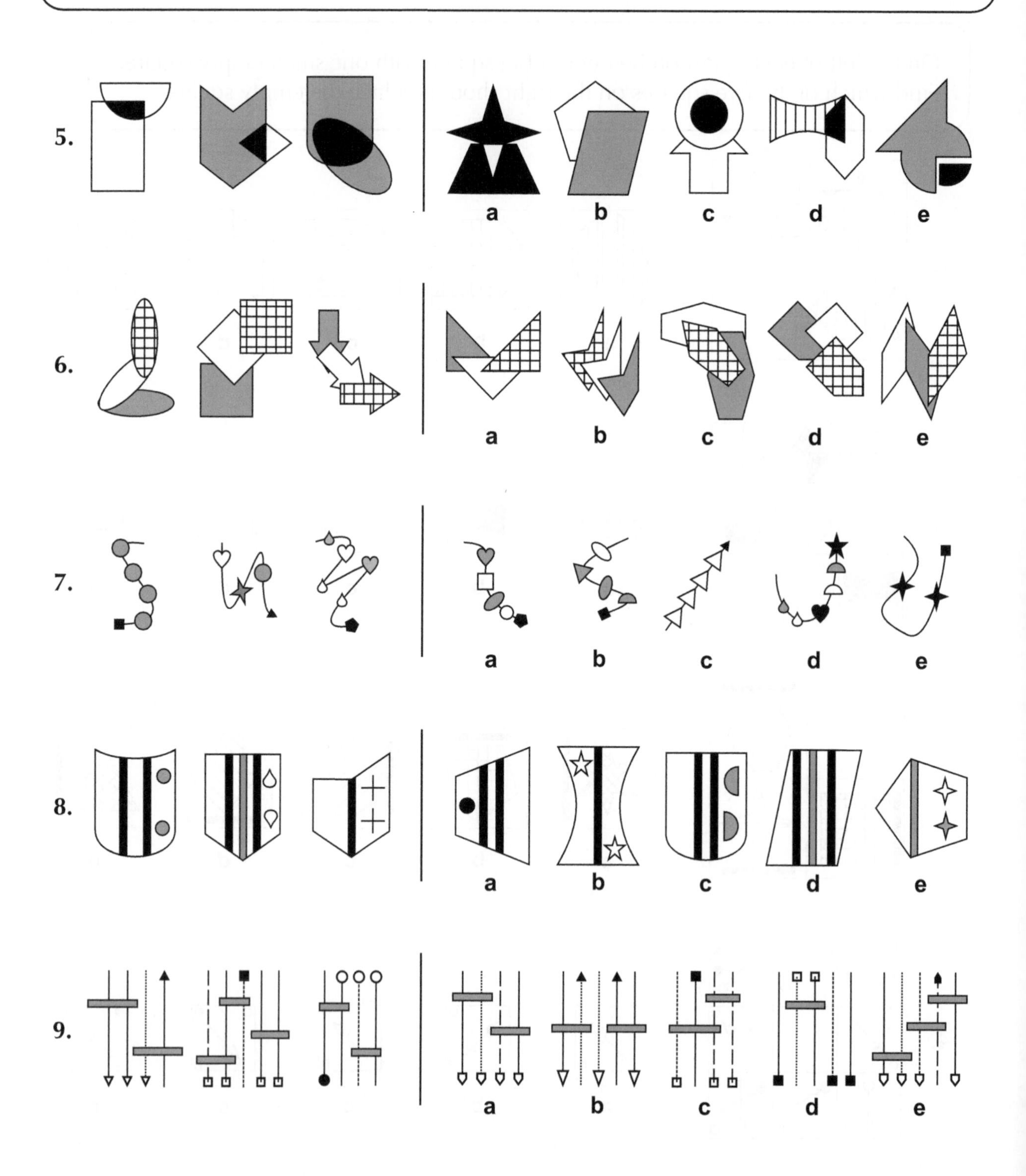

In the boxes on the left are shapes with code letters. The top letters have a different meaning to the bottom ones. Work out how the letters go with the shapes and then find the code for the new shape from the five codes on the right.

10. U S, V R, V Q

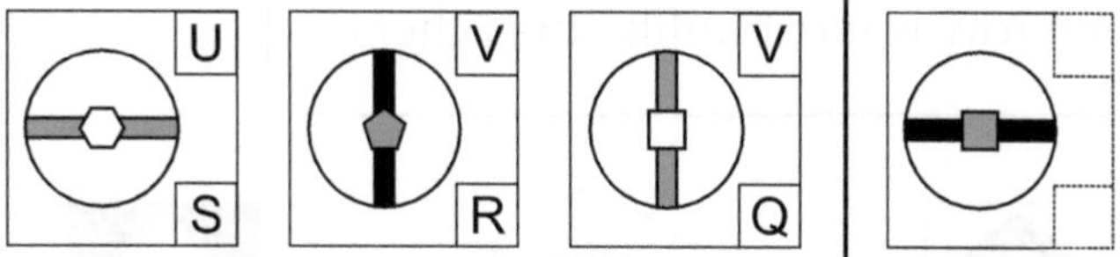

a	b	c	d	e
U S	V S	U Q	U R	V Q

11. F X, G V, E W, E X

a	b	c	d	e
E V	F W	G X	F V	G W

12. D K, C M, D L

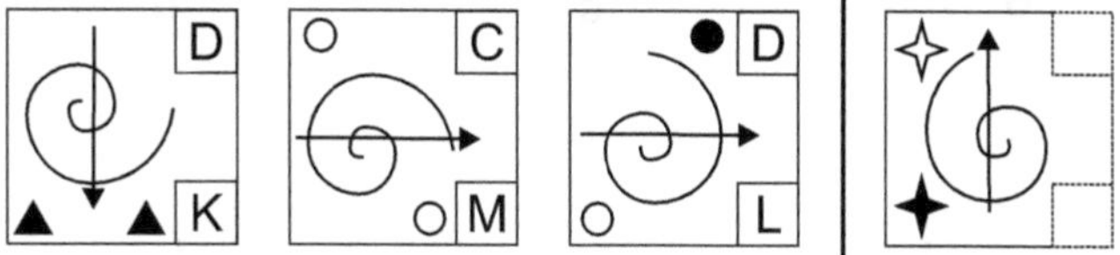

a	b	c	d	e
D M	C L	C K	D L	C M

13. T X, U Z, V Y, U X

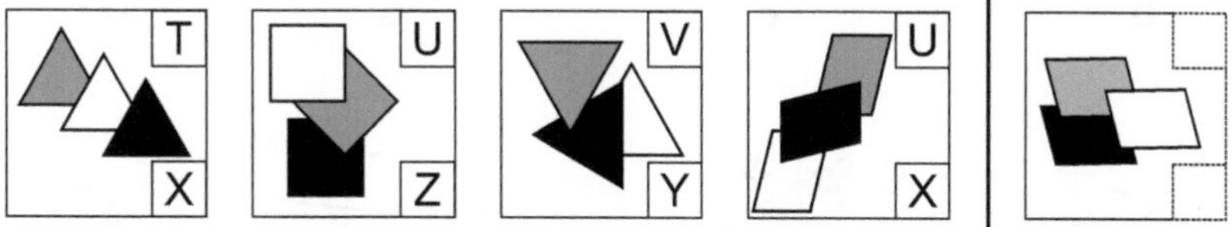

a	b	c	d	e
T Z	U Y	V X	V Z	U X

14. A L, B M, A M, C N

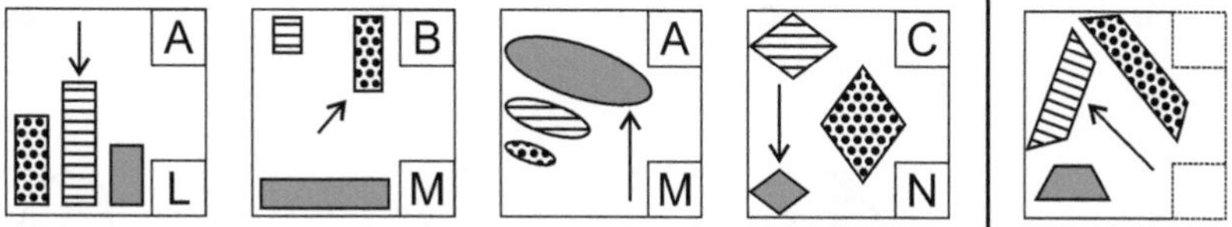

a	b	c	d	e
A L	B L	C N	C M	B N

/ 14

Test 9

You have **10 minutes** to do this test. Circle the letter underneath each correct answer.

Each of the questions below has five figures.
Find which figure in each row is most unlike the others.

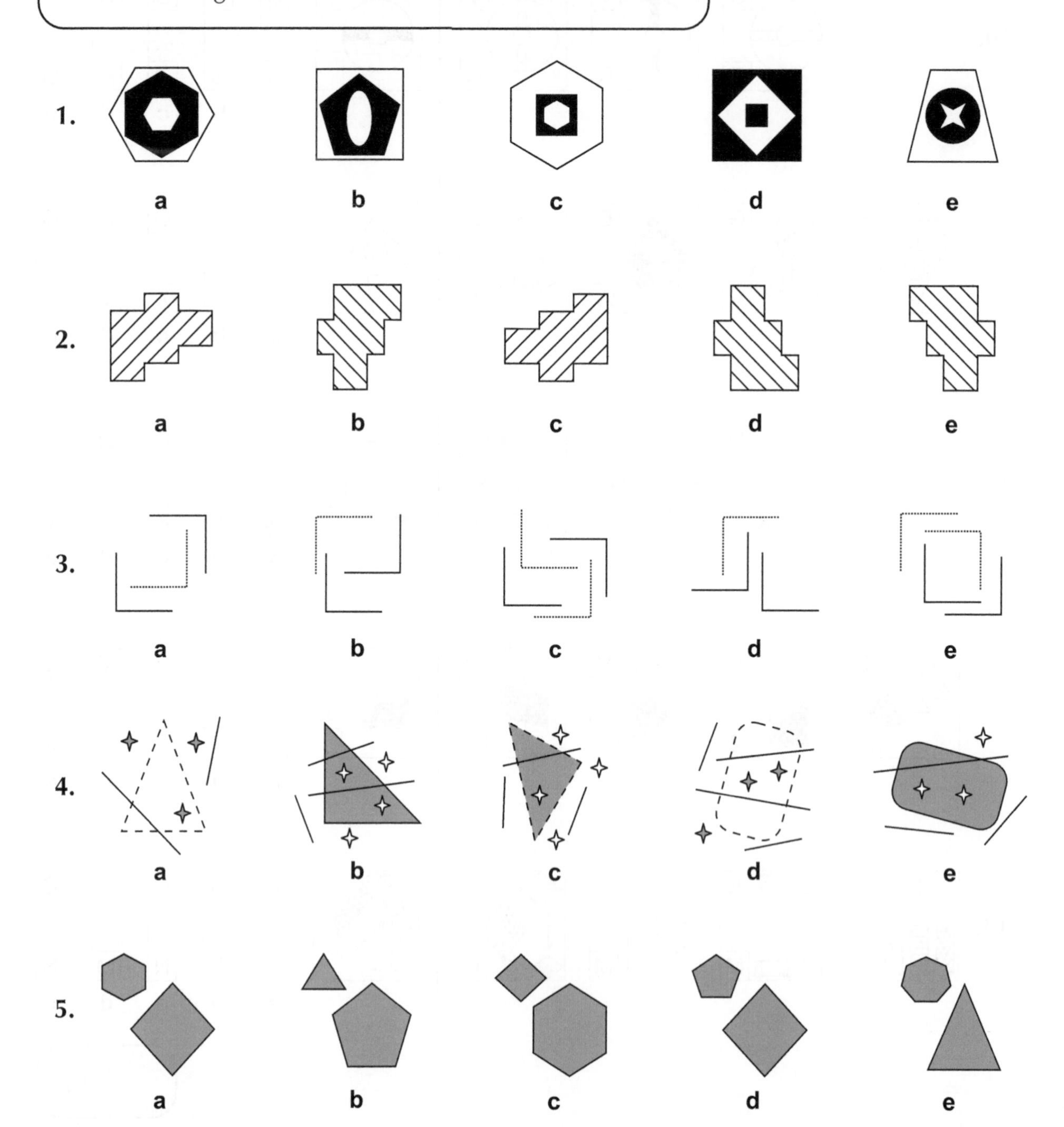

Each question has some shapes on the left with code letters that describe them. You need to work out what the code letters mean. There is then a shape on its own next to a choice of five codes. Work out which code describes this shape.

6.

BF

BG

CF

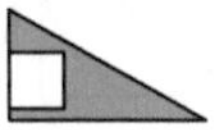

BF	CF	BG	CB	CG
a	**b**	**c**	**d**	**e**

7.

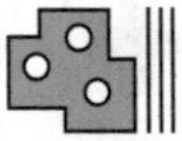

MU

NU

NT

NT

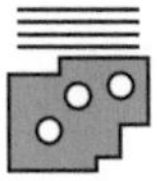

NT	MT	LT	NU	MU
a	**b**	**c**	**d**	**e**

8.

JT

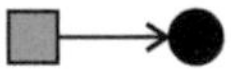

KU

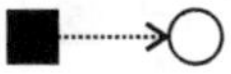

JS

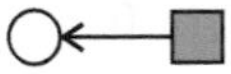

JU

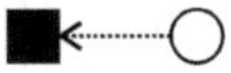

JU	KT	KU	JS	KS
a	**b**	**c**	**d**	**e**

9.

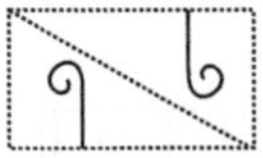

HPW

GQW

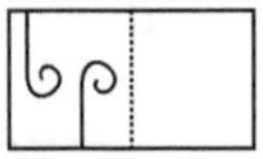

GPW

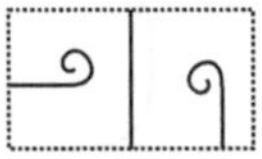

HQX

HQX	GPX	HPW	GQX	HQW
a	**b**	**c**	**d**	**e**

Each of these questions has five squares on the left that are arranged in order.
One of the squares is missing. One of the squares on the right should go in its place.
Find which one of the five squares on the right should go in place of the empty square.

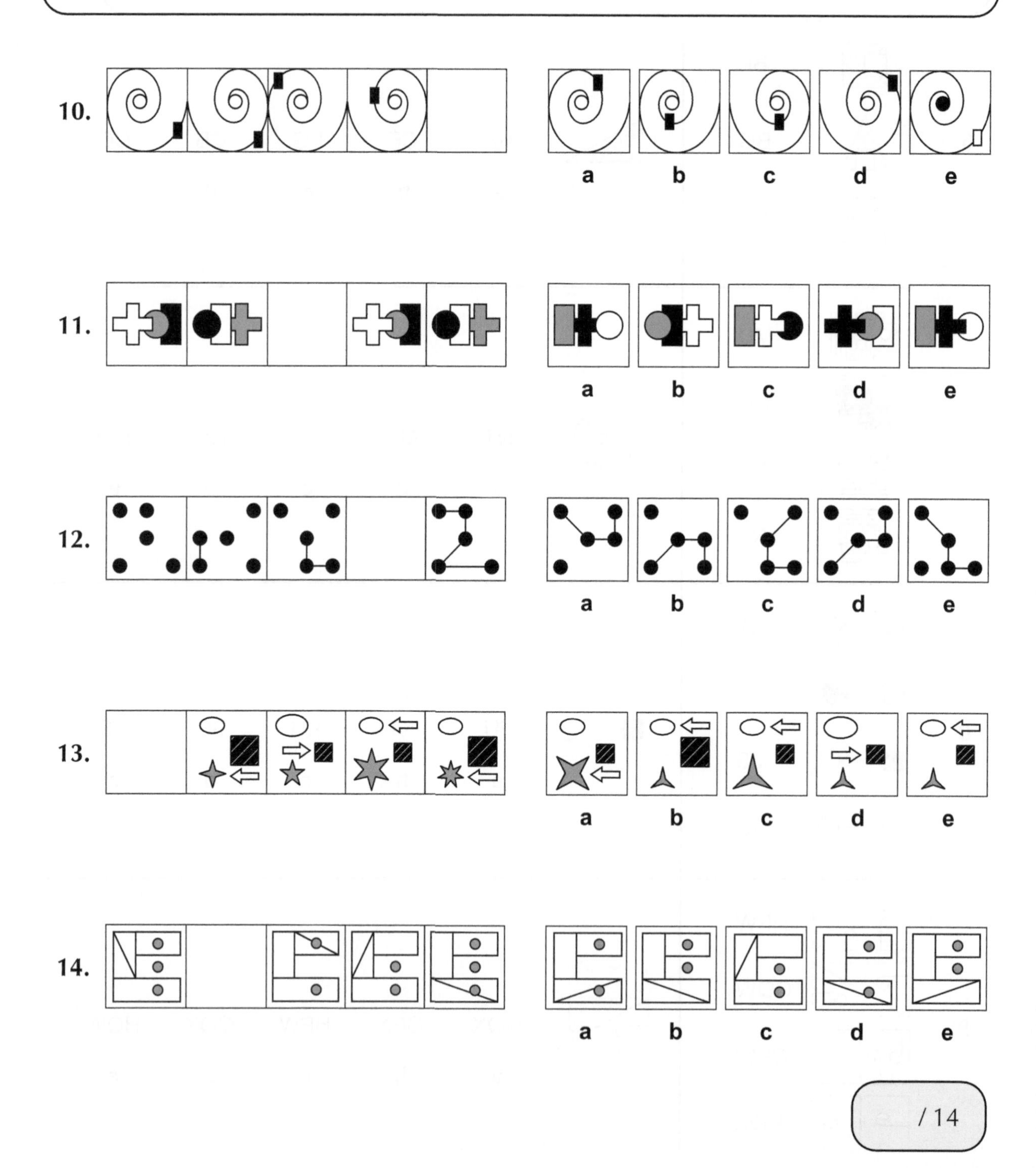

/ 14

Puzzles 3

Time for puzzles! These will help you practice finding **similarities** and **differences**.

Strange Stars

There is a pattern of stars, called a *constellation*, in each square of the grid on the right.

There are two groups of four constellations that are similar in some way.

One constellation doesn't fit into either group.

Which constellation is the odd one out?

____

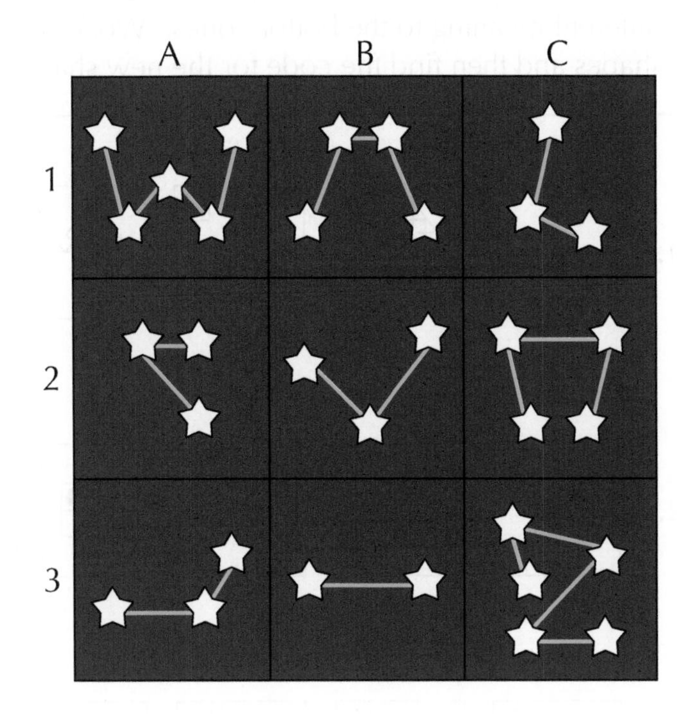

Queen Bee

The queen is the bee that looks the most different from the others.
Which bee is the queen bee?

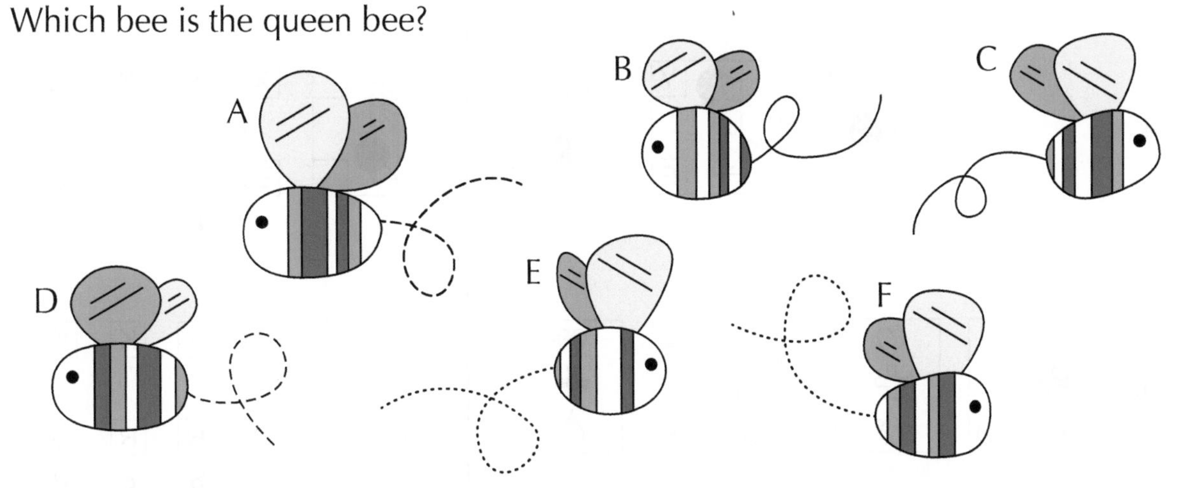

Test 10

You have **10 minutes** to do this test. Circle the letter underneath each correct answer.

In the boxes on the left are shapes with code letters. The top letters have a different meaning to the bottom ones. Work out how the letters go with the shapes and then find the code for the new shape from the five codes on the right.

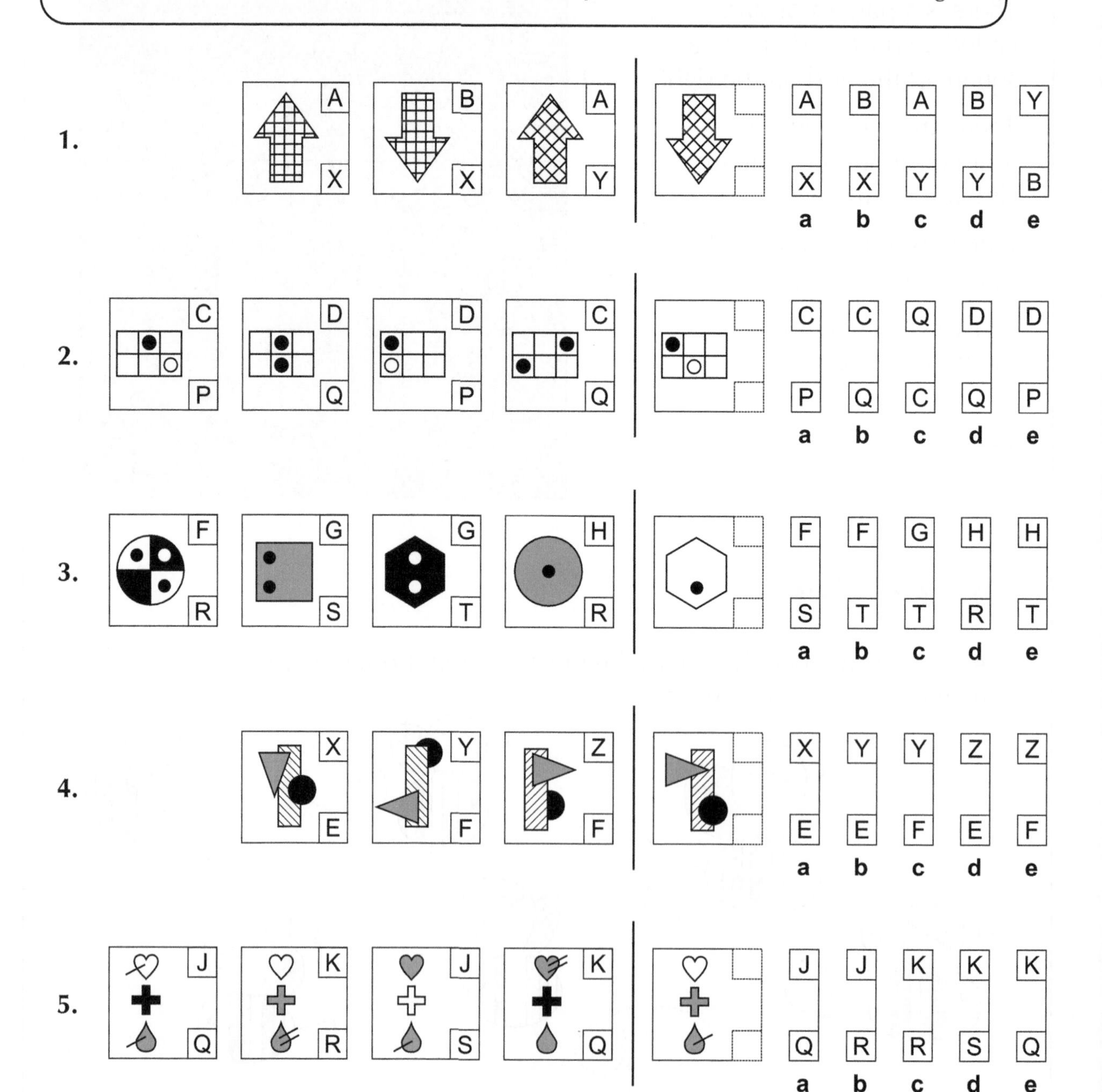

For each of the questions below there are three figures that are like each other in some way. Find which of the five figures on the right is most like the three figures on the left.

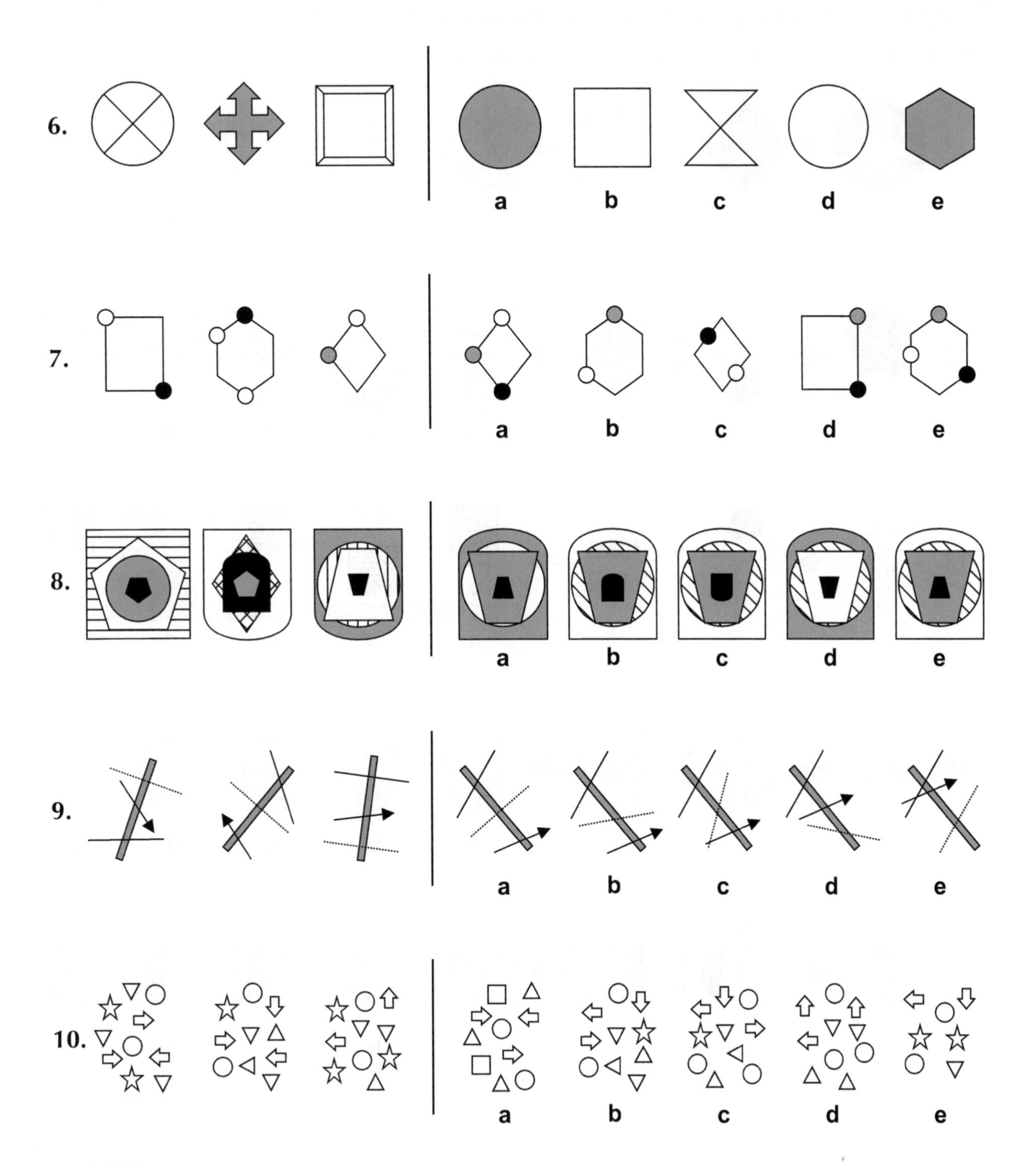

Each question has two shapes on the left with an arrow between them.
The first shape is changed in some way to become the second. There is then a third shape followed by an arrow and a choice of five shapes. Choose the shape on the right that relates to the third shape like the second does to the first.

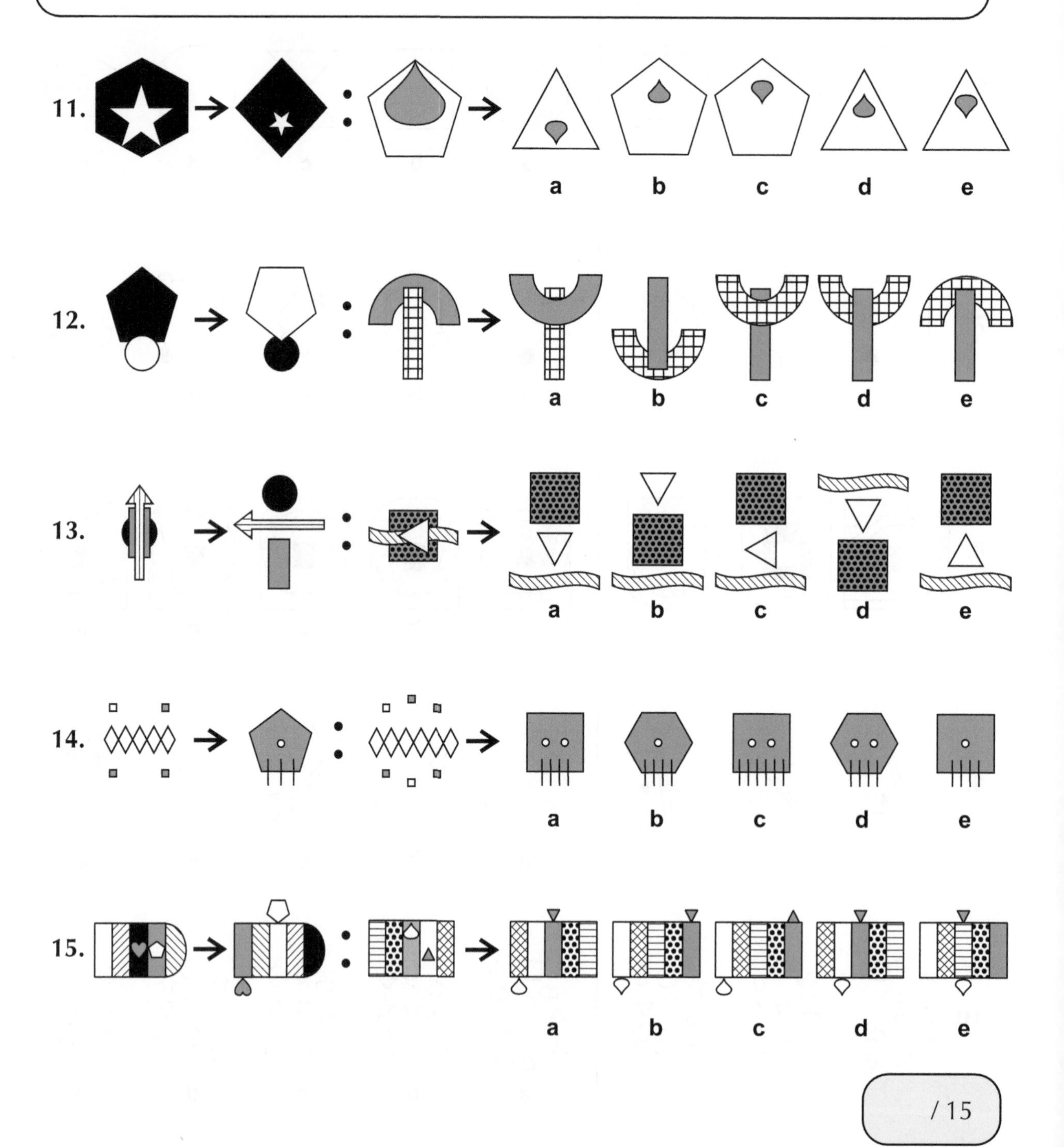

/ 15

Test 11

You have **10 minutes** to do this test. Circle the letter underneath each correct answer.

Each of these questions has five squares on the left that are arranged in order.
One of the squares is missing. One of the squares on the right should go in its place.
Find which one of the five squares on the right should go in place of the empty square.

1.

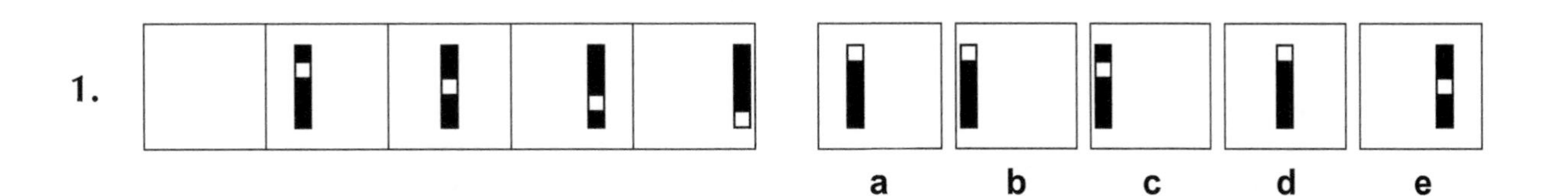

2.

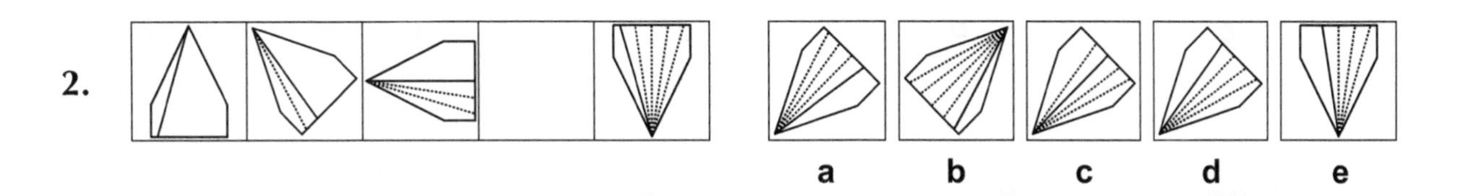

3.

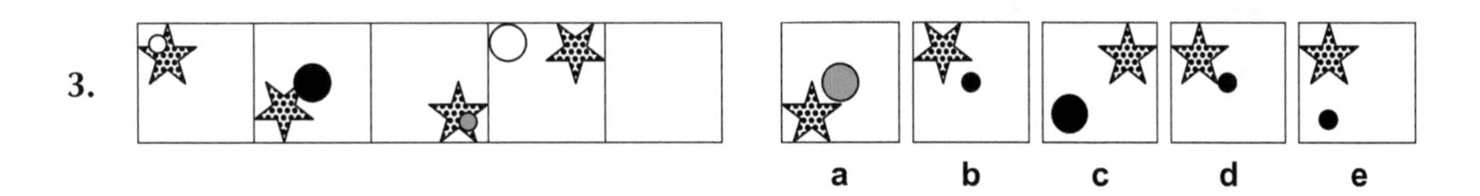

4.

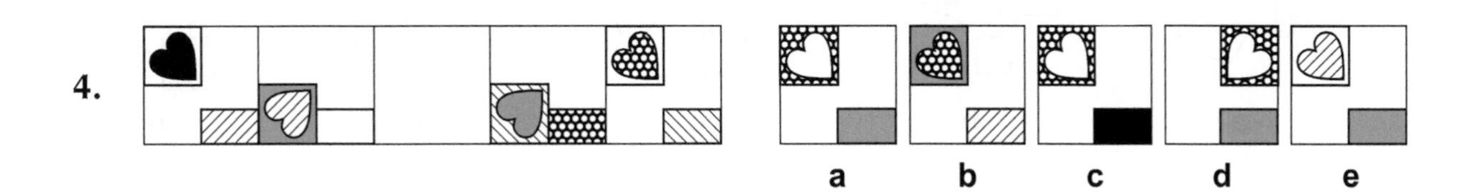

5.

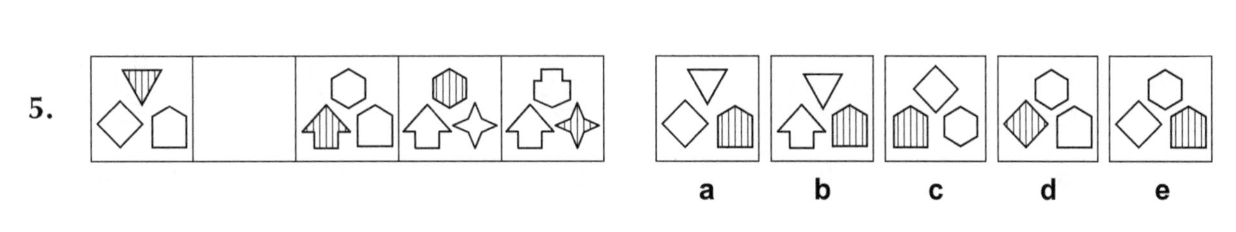

Each of the questions below has five figures.
Find which figure in each row is most unlike the others.

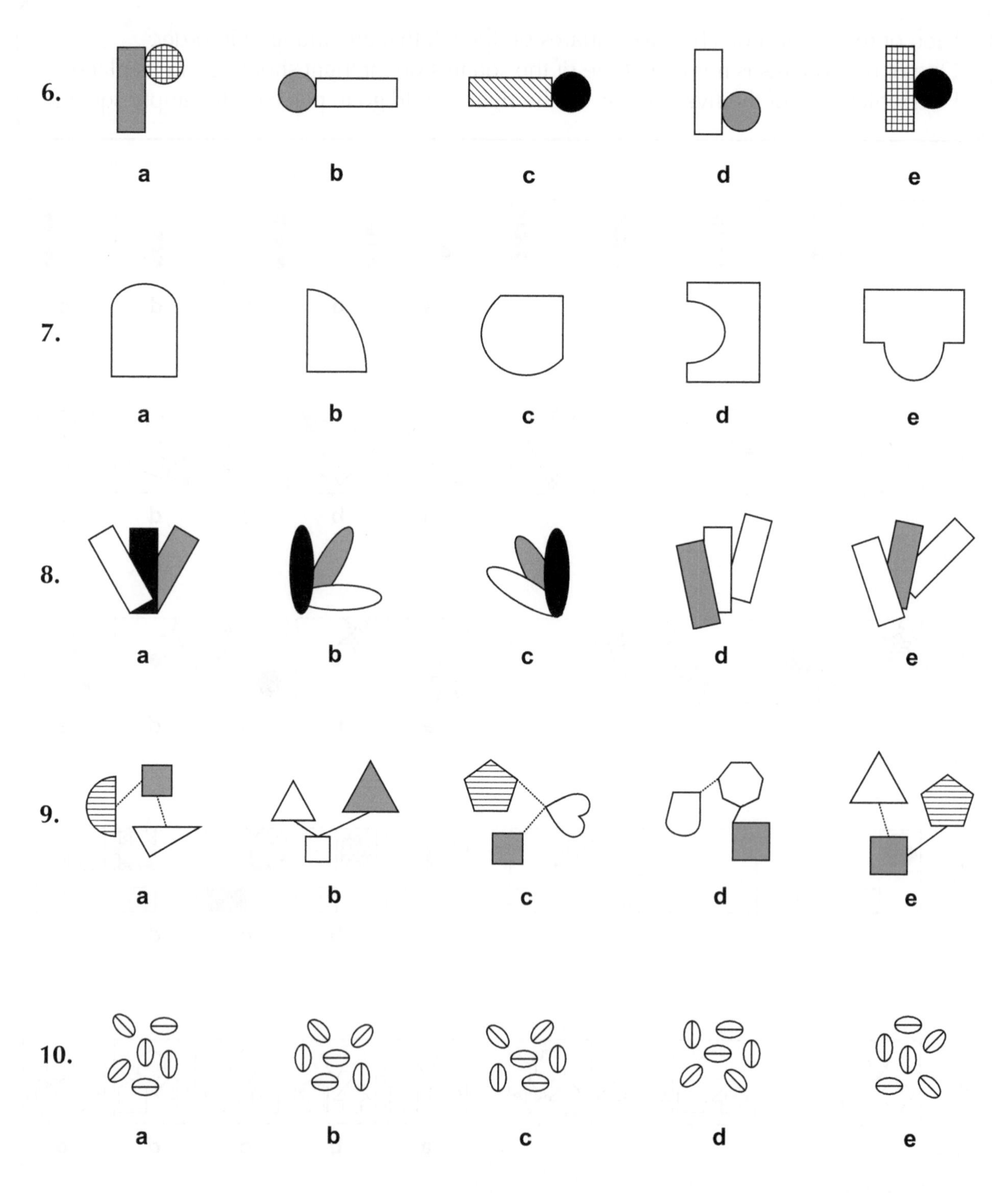

On the left of each question below is a big square with one small empty square. Find which of the five squares on the right should replace the empty square.

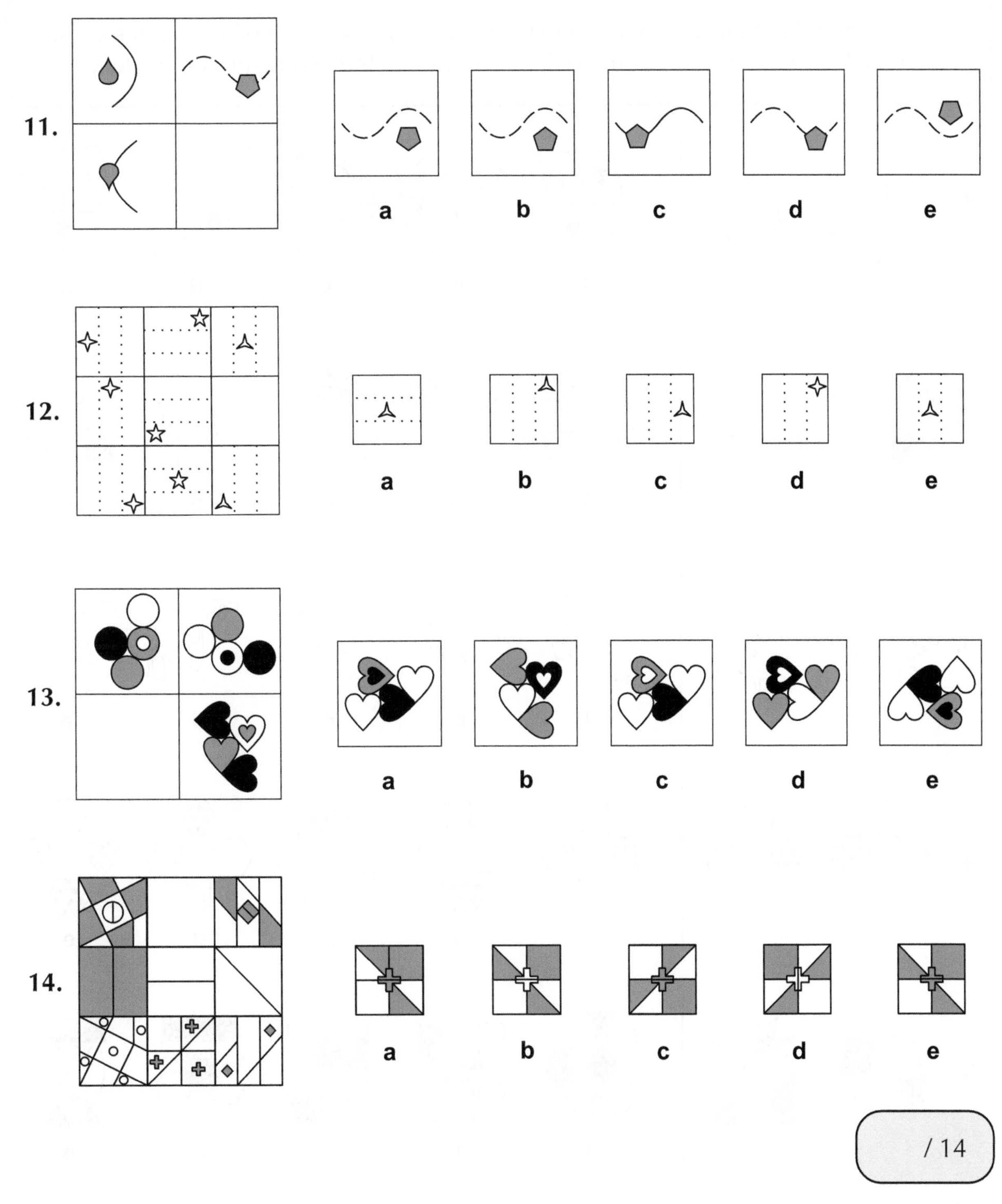

/ 14

Test 12

You have **10 minutes** to do this test. Circle the letter underneath each correct answer.

For each question below there are two figures that are like each other in some way. Find which of the five figures on the right is most like the two figures on the left.

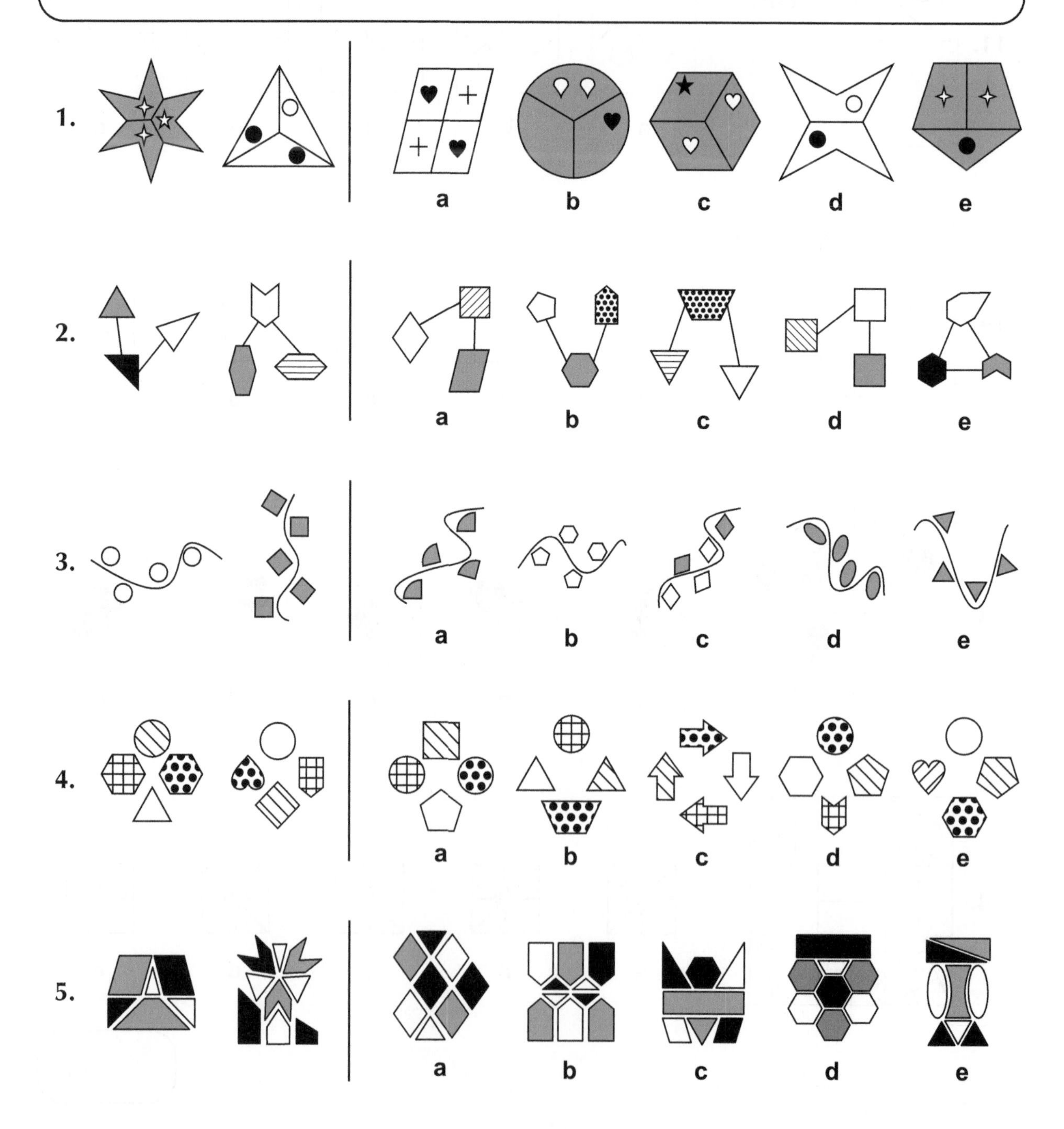

In the boxes on the left are shapes with code letters. The top letters have a different meaning to the bottom ones. Work out how the letters go with the shapes and then find the code for the new shape from the five codes on the right.

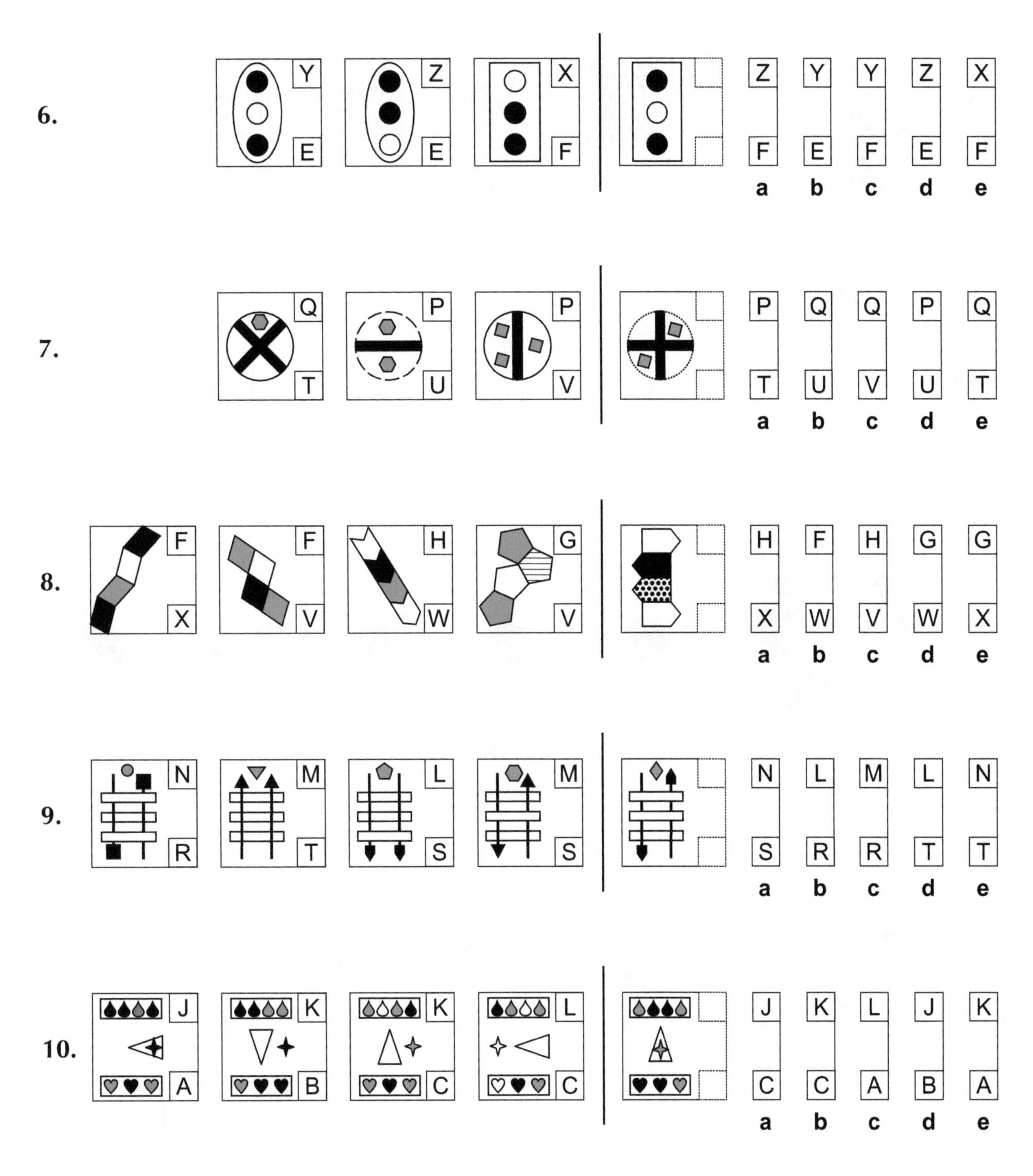

On the left of each question below is a big square with one small empty square.
Find which of the five squares on the right should replace the empty square.

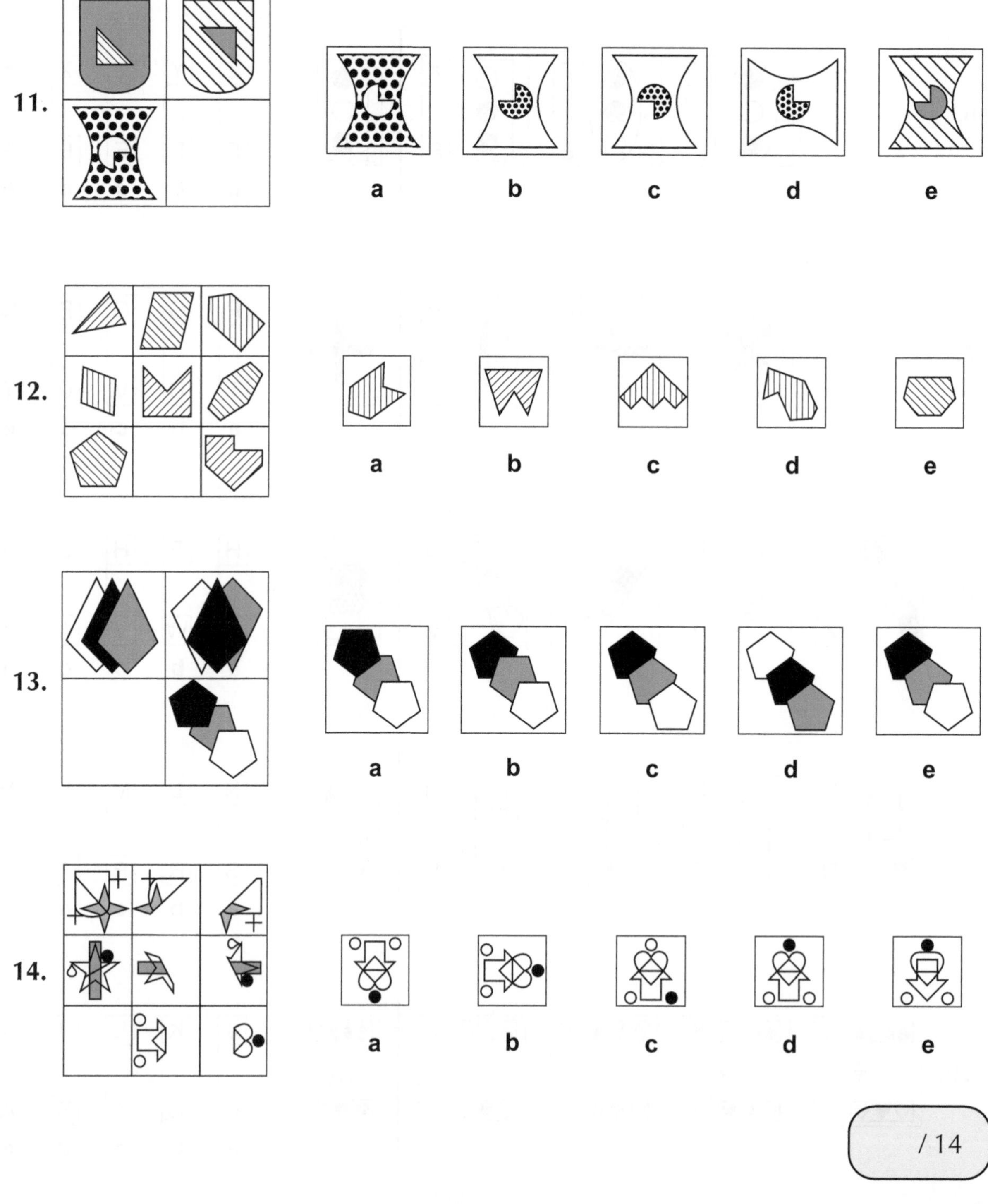

Pause for some puzzles! They'll help you perfect **comparing** and **reflecting** shapes.

Hidden Path

Find a path through the figures below by moving up, down, left or right.
You can only move between figures that have exactly **one** difference.

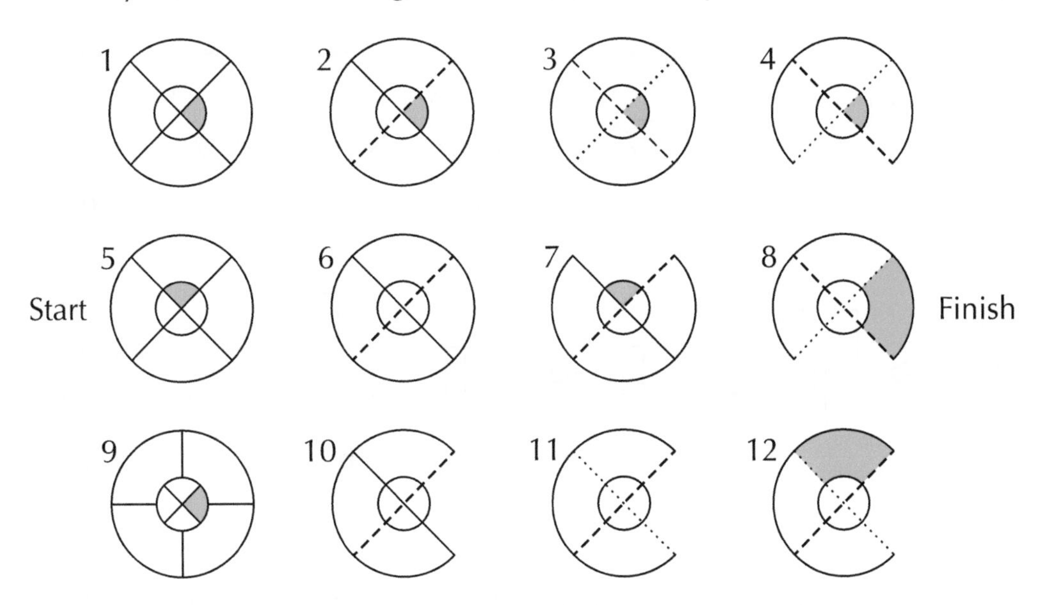

Misleading Mirrors

Look at the figure on the right.
Which of the mirrors below shows a reflection of this figure?

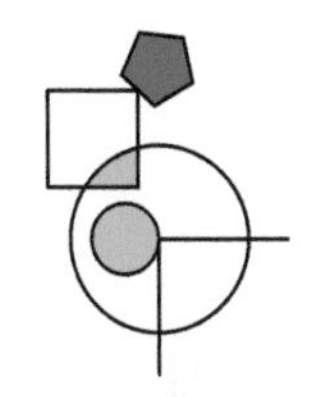

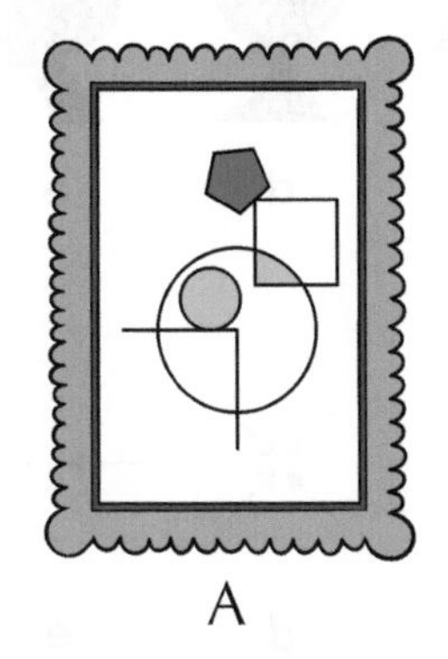
A

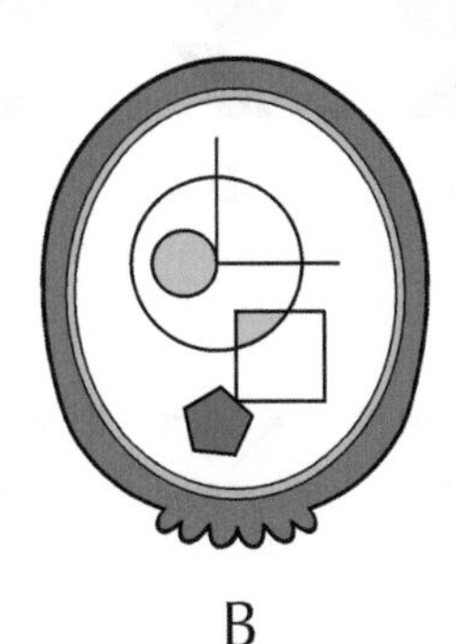
B

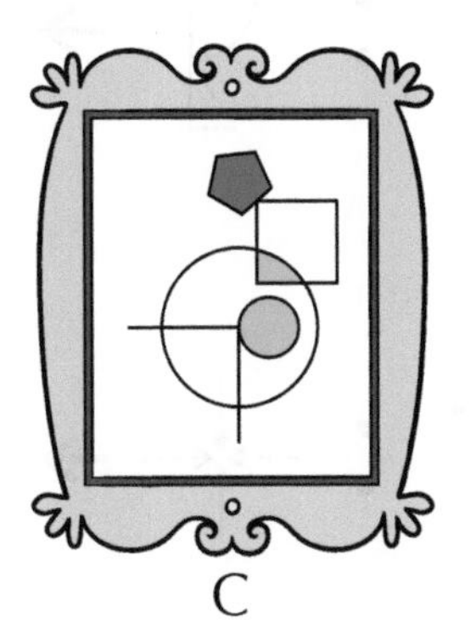
C

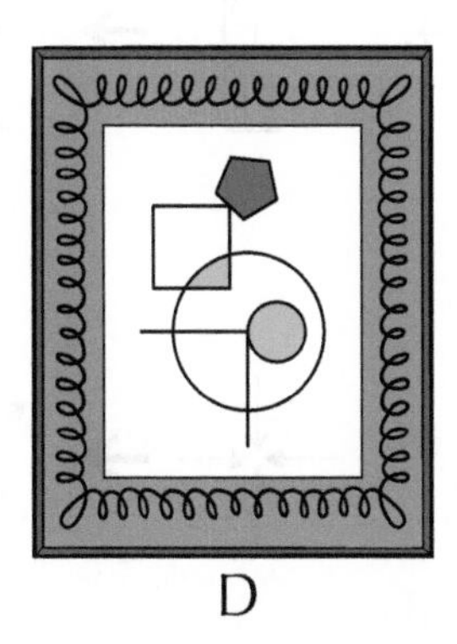
D

Test 13

You have **10 minutes** to do this test. Circle the letter underneath each correct answer.

Each question has two shapes on the left with an arrow between them.
The first shape is changed in some way to become the second. There is then a third shape followed by an arrow and a choice of five shapes. Choose the shape on the right that relates to the third shape like the second does to the first.

1.

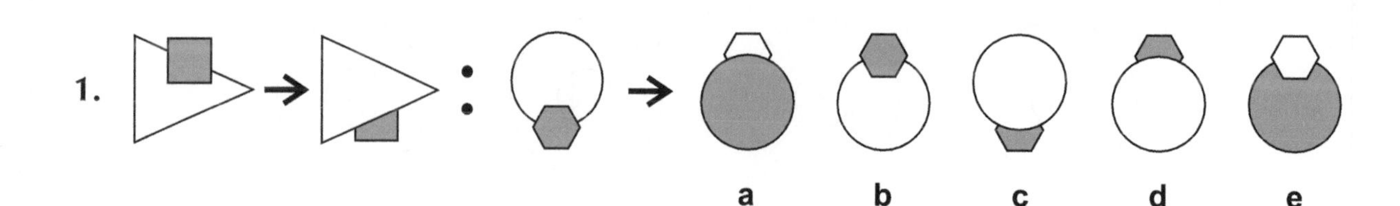

a b c d e

2.

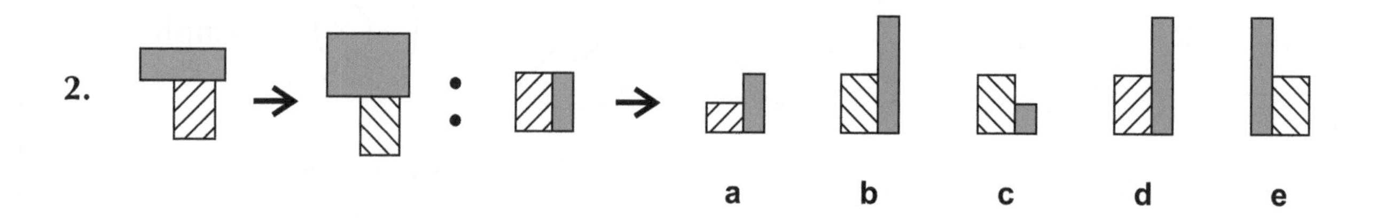

a b c d e

3.

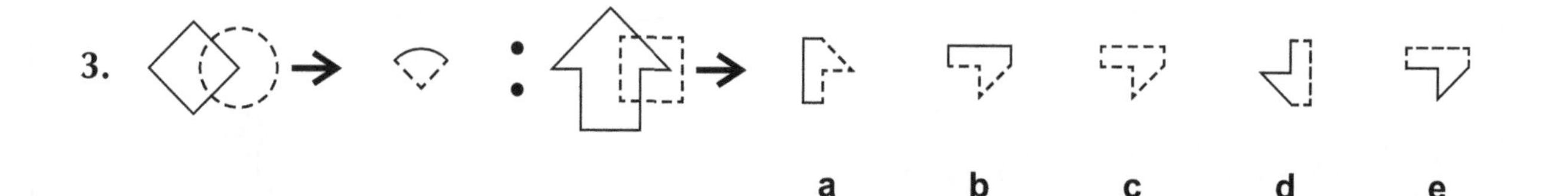

a b c d e

4.

a b c d e

5.

a b c d e

Each question has some shapes on the left with code letters that describe them. You need to work out what the code letters mean. There is then a shape on its own next to a choice of five codes. Work out which code describes this shape.

6.

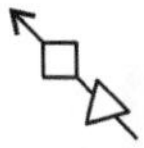

			a	b	c	d	e
AX			AX	BX	BA	AY	BY
BY							
AY							

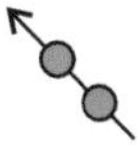

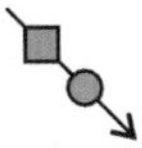

7.

	a	b	c	d	e
SG	SG	TE	SE	TG	SF
TE					
TF					
SE					

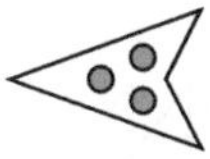

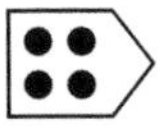

8.

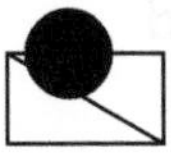

	a	b	c	d	e
MSY	NTZ	NSZ	NSY	MTY	MSZ
NTY					
MTZ					
NSZ					

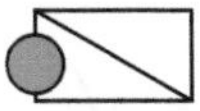

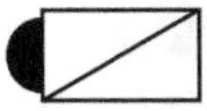

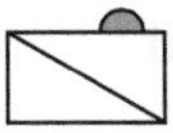

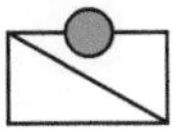

9.

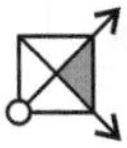

	a	b	c	d	e
PBJ	PBJ	QCK	PCL	QBK	PCJ
QBK					
QCL					

For each of the questions below there are three figures that are like each other in some way. Find which of the five figures on the right is most like the three figures on the left.

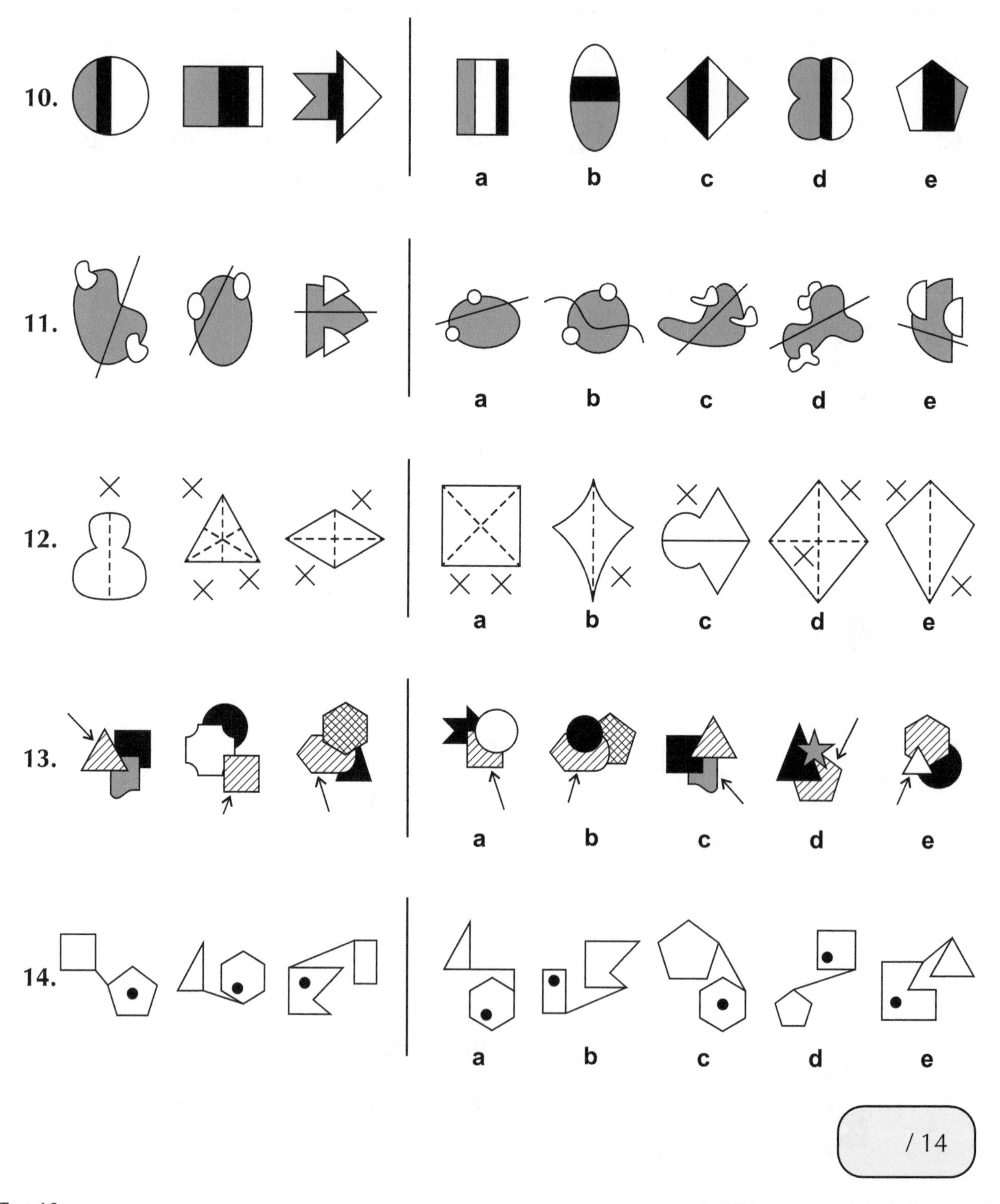

/ 14

Test 14

You have **10 minutes** to do this test. Circle the letter underneath each correct answer.

Each of these questions has five squares on the left that are arranged in order.
One of the squares is missing. One of the squares on the right should go in its place.
Find which one of the five squares on the right should go in place of the empty square.

1. 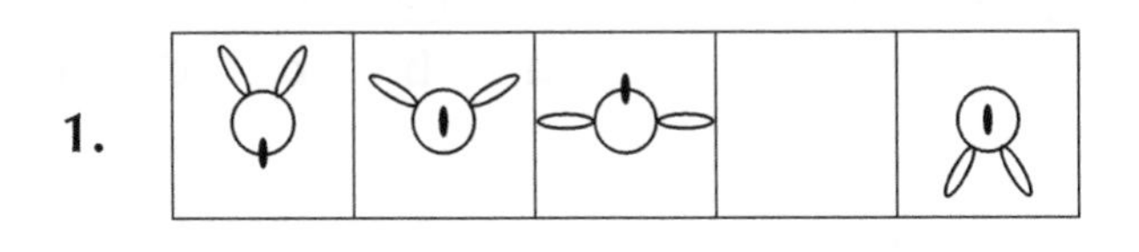 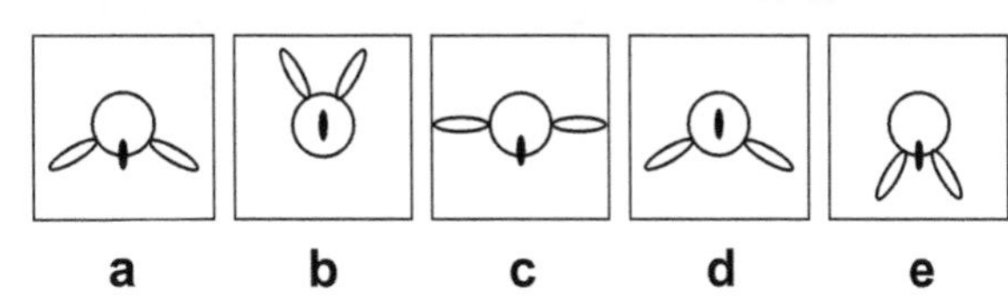

a b c d e

2. 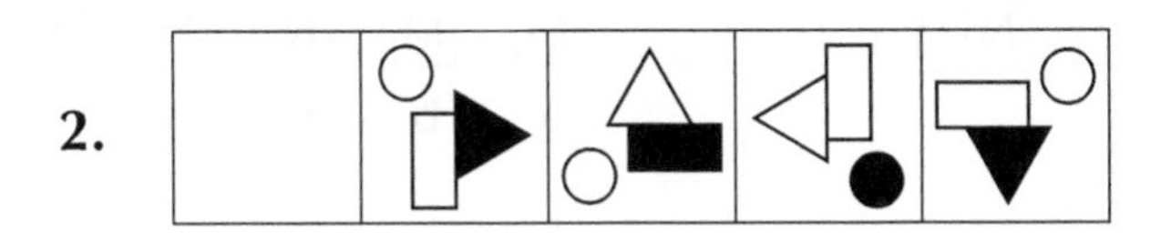 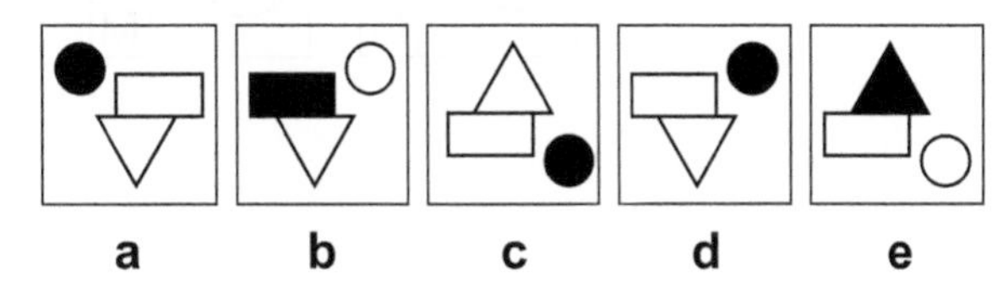

a b c d e

3. 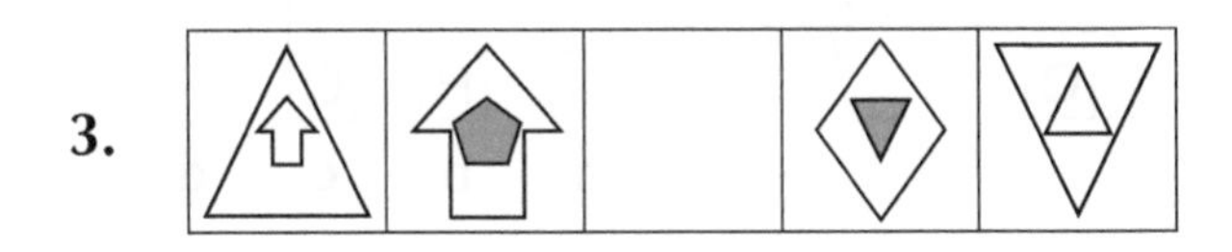 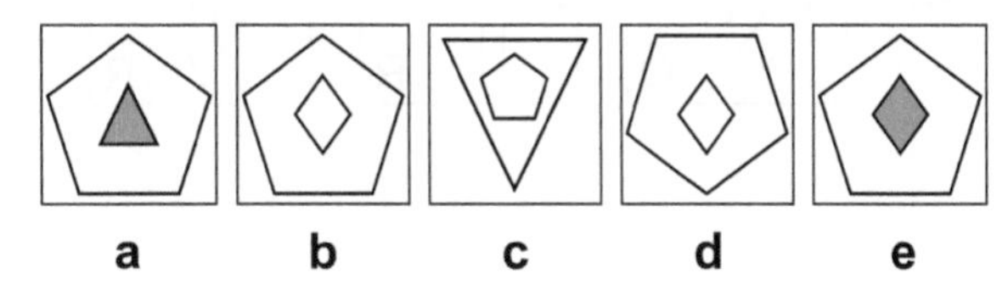

a b c d e

4. 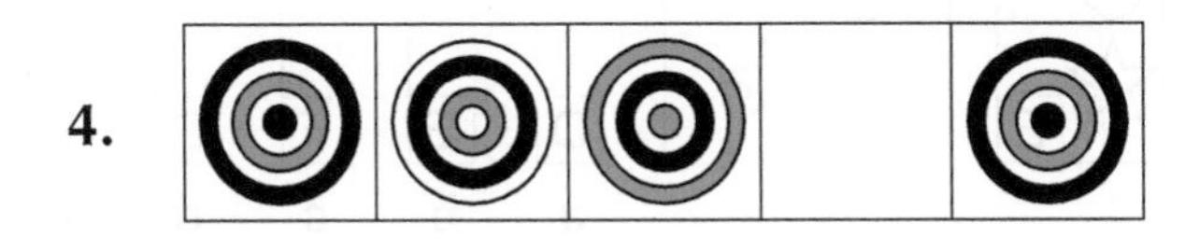 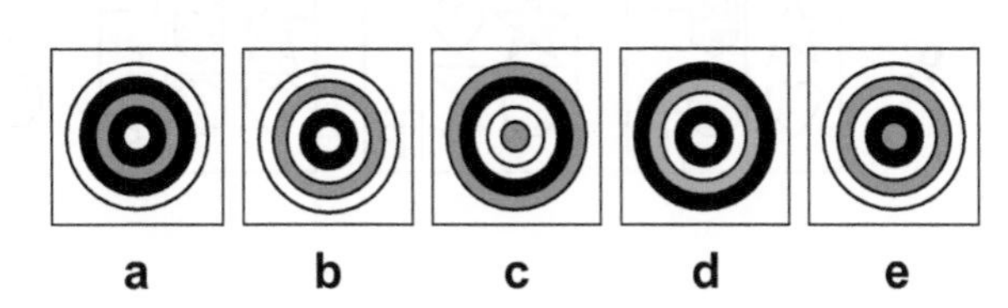

a b c d e

5. 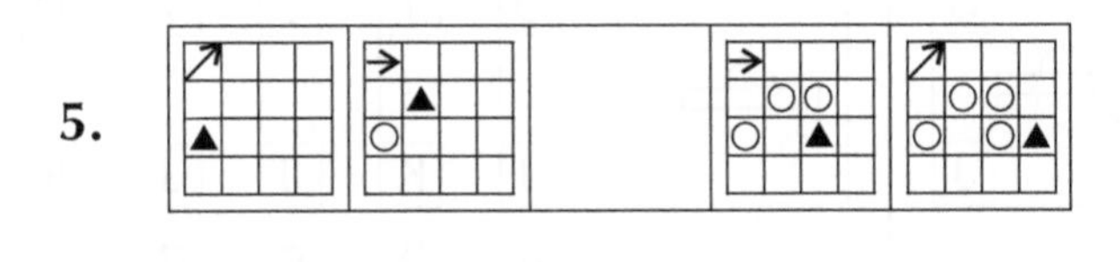 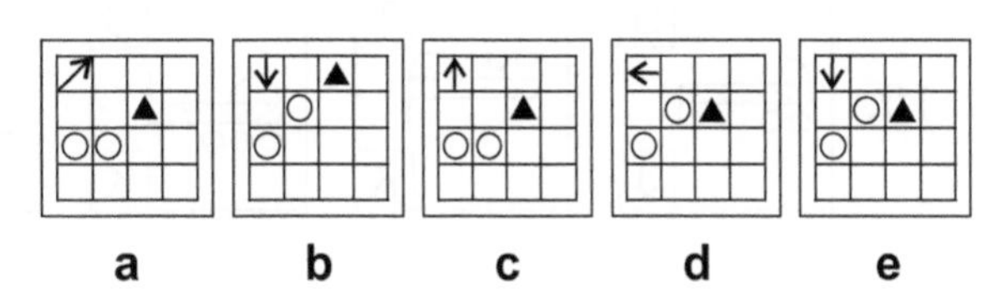

a b c d e

In the boxes on the left are shapes with code letters. The top letters have a different meaning to the bottom ones. Work out how the letters go with the shapes and then find the code for the new shape from the five codes on the right.

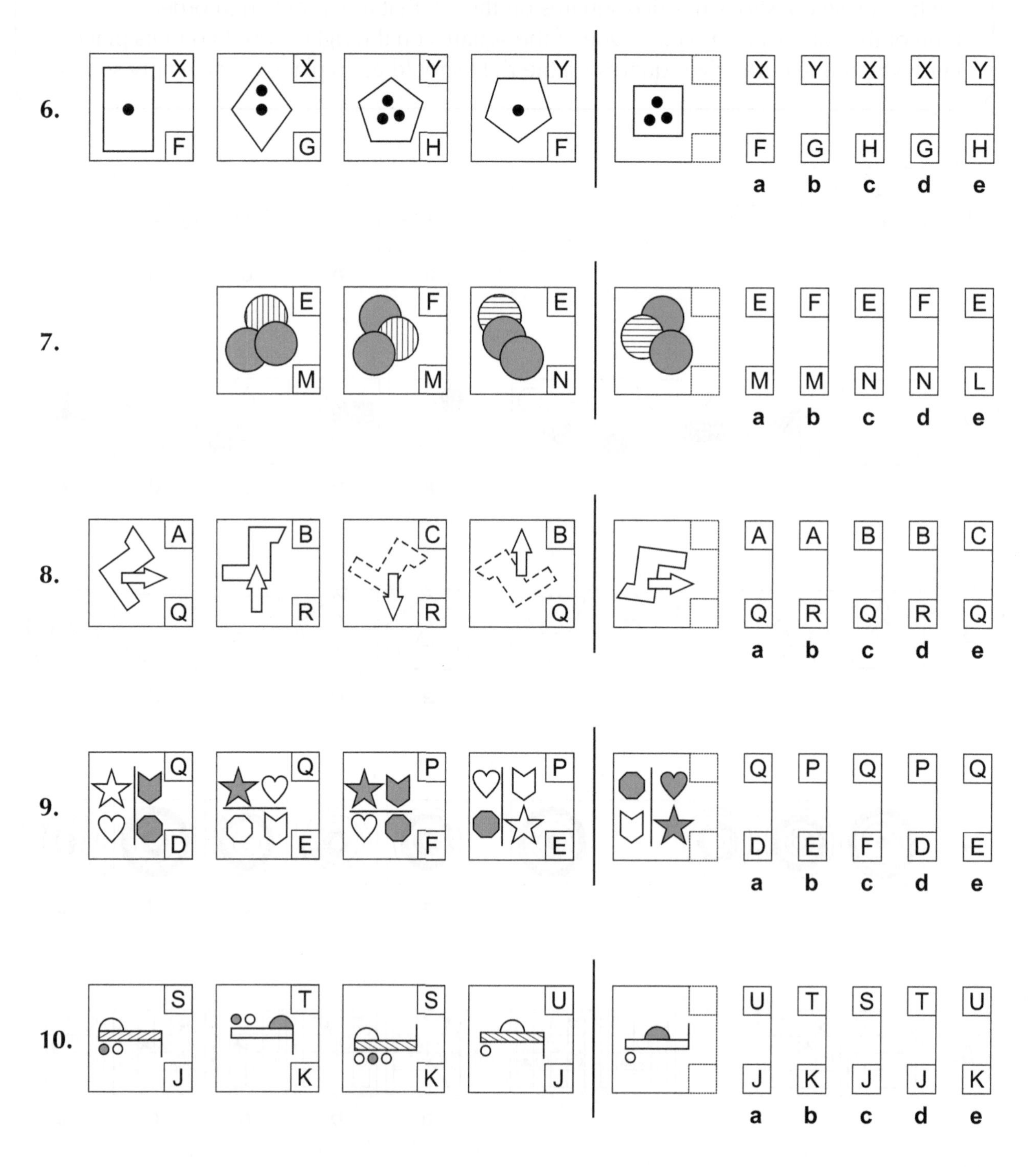

Each of the questions below has five figures.
Find which figure in each row is most unlike the others.

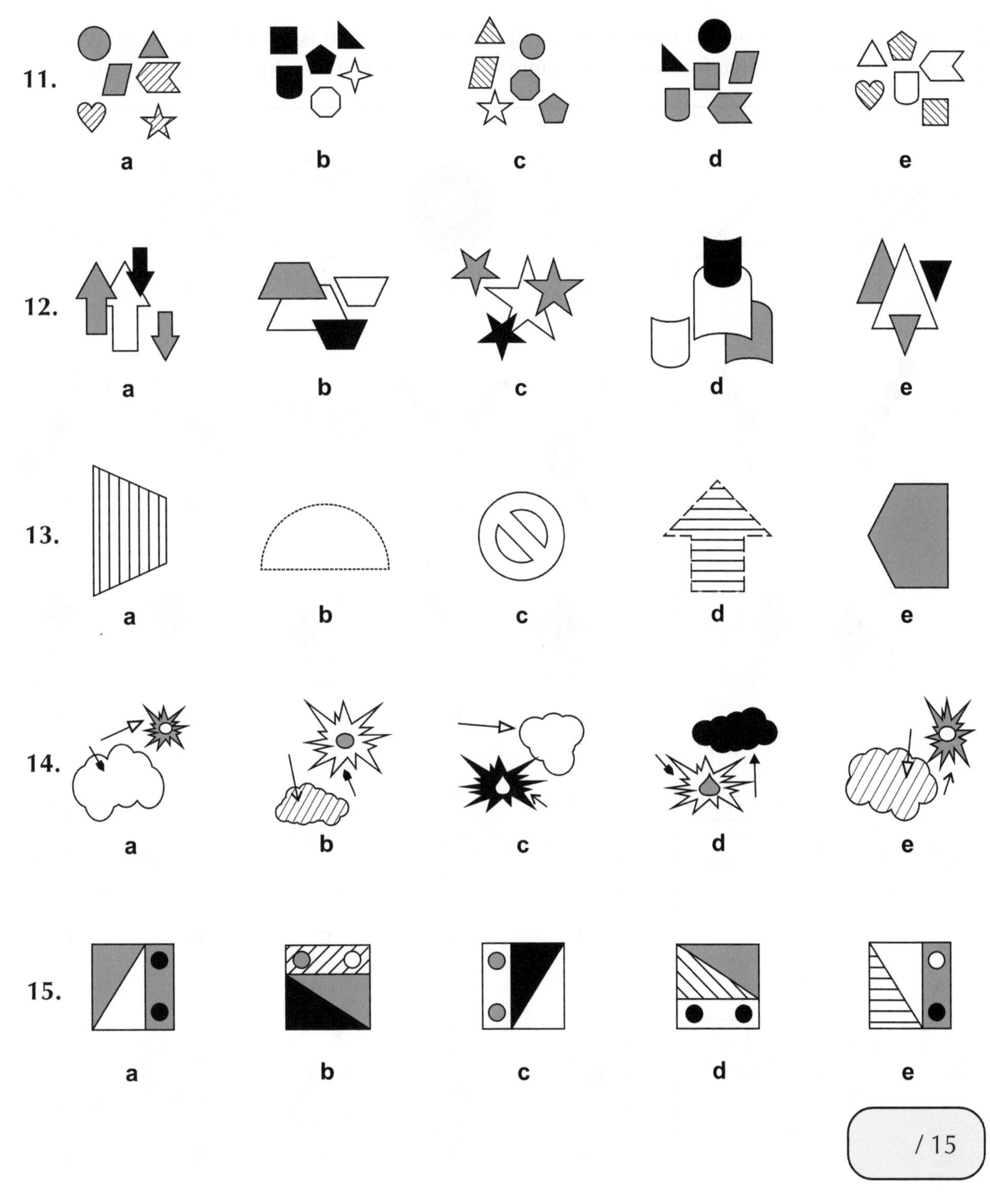

/ 15

Test 15

You have **10 minutes** to do this test. Circle the letter underneath each correct answer.

For each question below there are two figures that are like each other in some way. Find which of the five figures on the right is most like the two figures on the left.

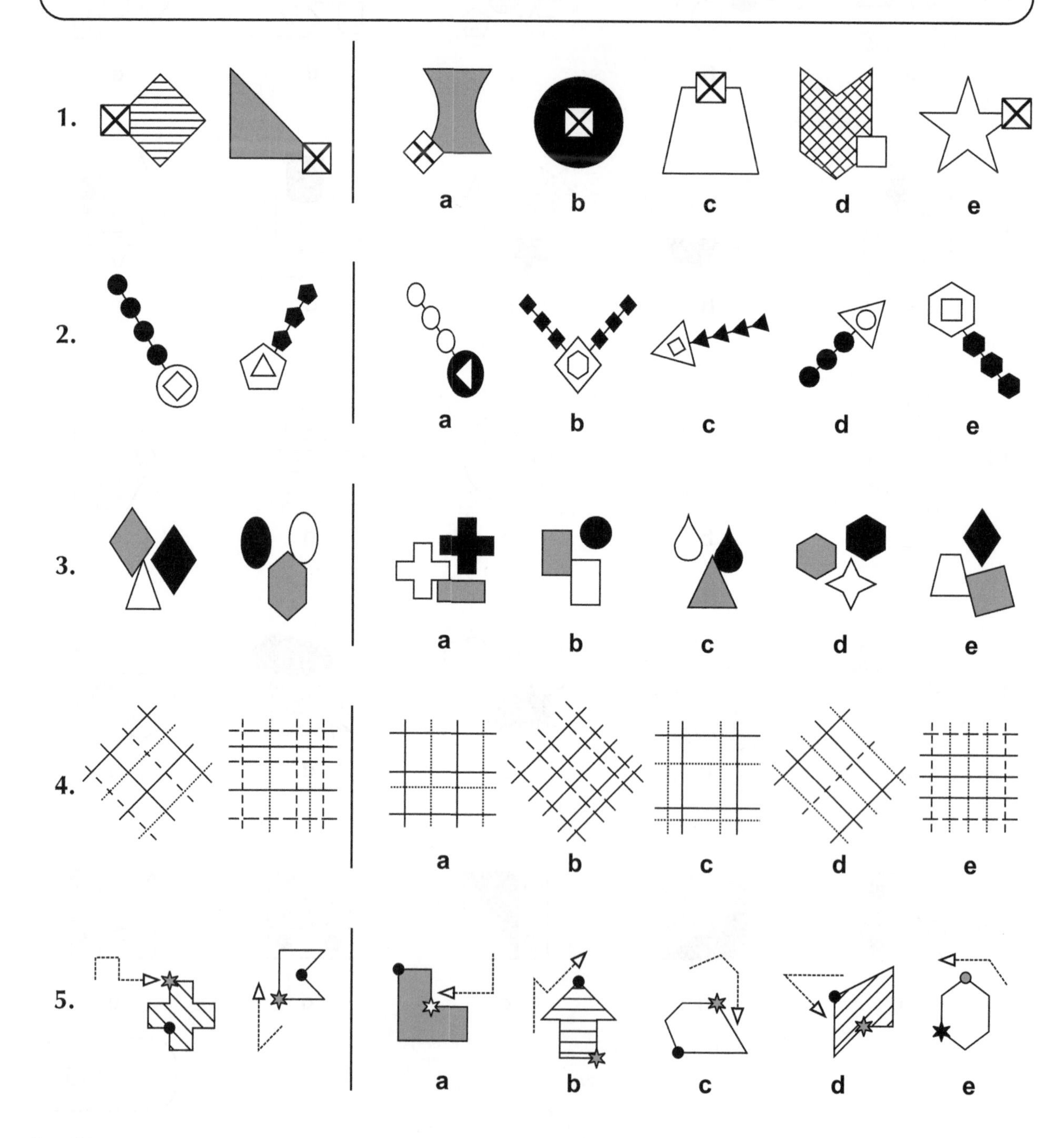

Each question has some shapes on the left with code letters that describe them. You need to work out what the code letters mean. There is then a shape on its own next to a choice of five codes. Work out which code describes this shape.

6.

UY	
VZ	
WY	

UY	VZ	VY	WZ	WY
a	**b**	**c**	**d**	**e**

7.

FMR	
FNS	
EMS	

FNS	FMS	ENR	FNR	EMS
a	**b**	**c**	**d**	**e**

8.

CHP	
CGP	
DHQ	
DGP	

DHQ	DGP	CGP	DGQ	CGQ
a	**b**	**c**	**d**	**e**

9.

KS	
JT	
JS	
LT	

JS	JT	KT	LS	KT
a	**b**	**c**	**d**	**e**

Each question has two shapes on the left with an arrow between them.
The first shape is changed in some way to become the second. There is then a third shape followed by an arrow and a choice of five shapes. Choose the shape on the right that relates to the third shape like the second does to the first.

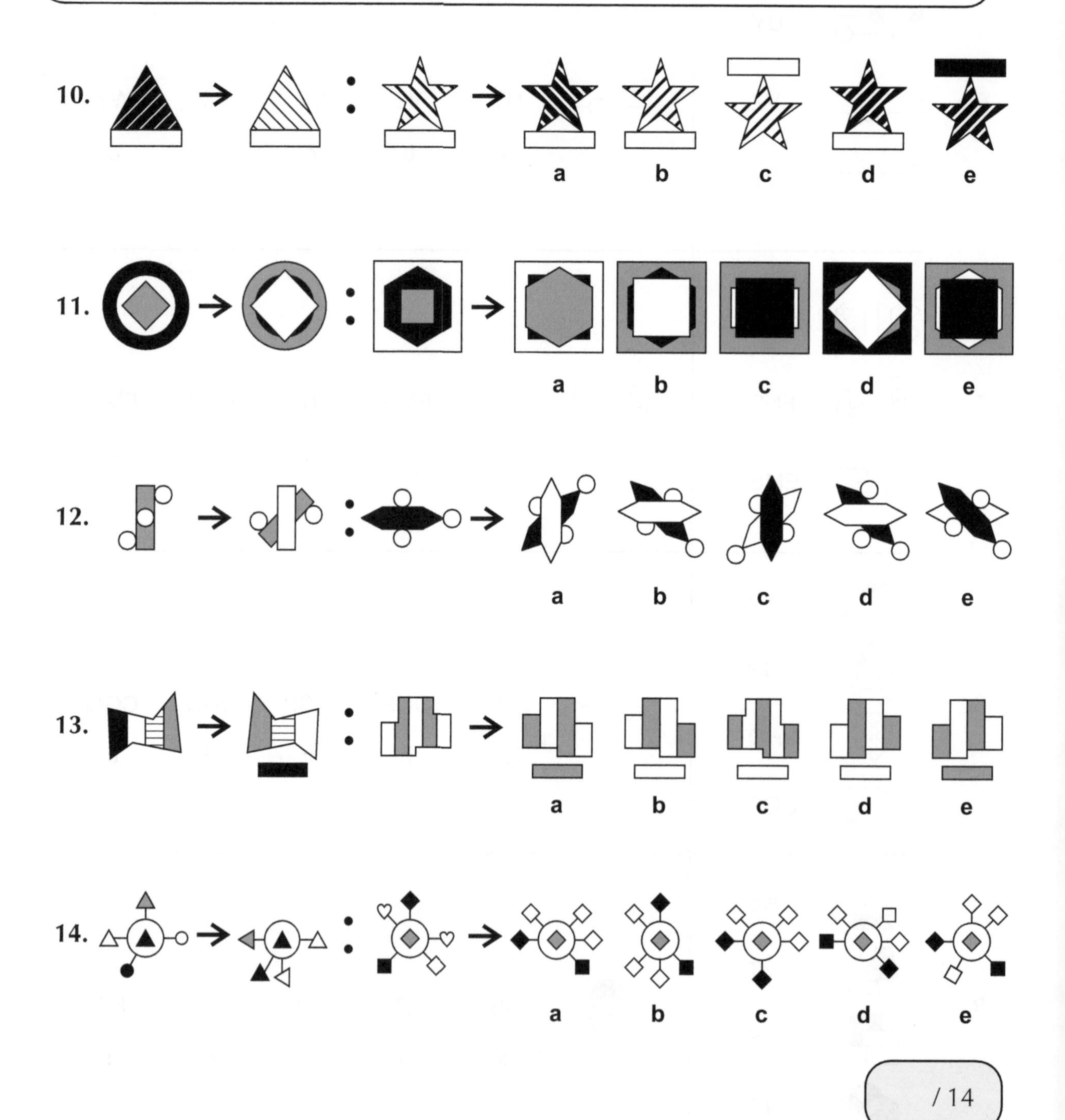

/ 14

Puzzles 5

Break time! These puzzles are a great way to practise **spotting patterns** and **sequences**.

Teacup Conundrum

Ayla collects teacups, but she's mixed up her collection.
There should only be four teacups in the set below.
The teacup that isn't part of the set is the one that's least like the others.
Which one is it?

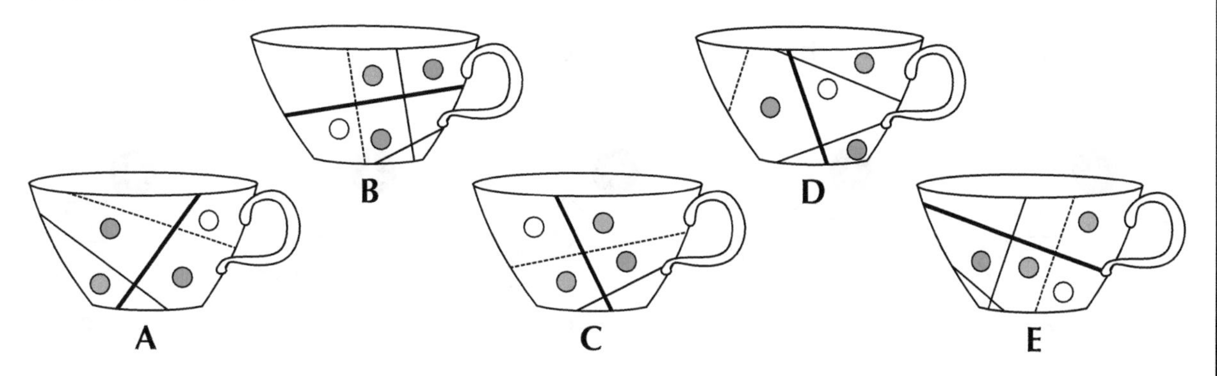

Permitted Path

A treasure hunter wants to get to the jewel at the centre of a maze. A map of the maze is shown on the right.
The only safe path through the maze is marked by symbols that follow a sequence.
Draw a line that passes through the symbols in the correct sequence to show the path that the treasure hunter should take.

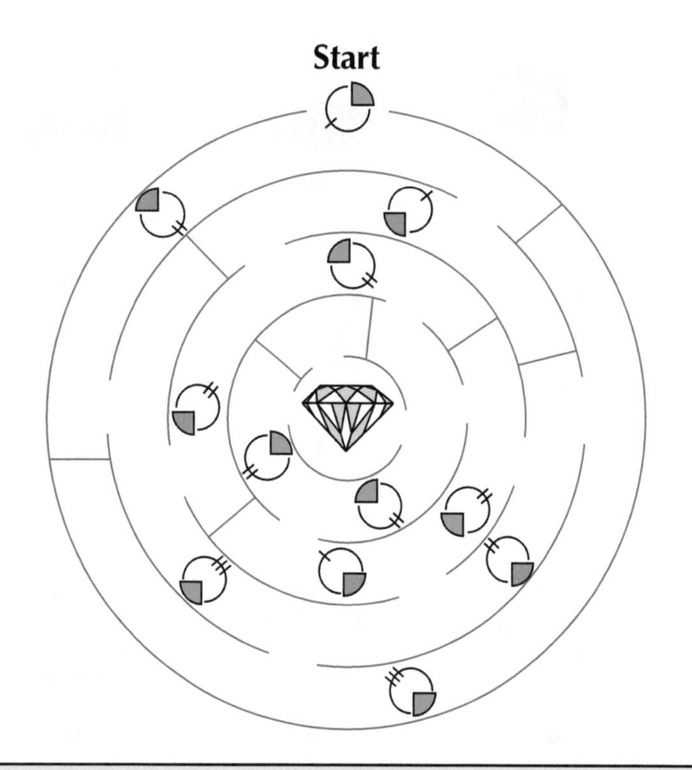

Test 16

You have **10 minutes** to do this test. Circle the letter underneath each correct answer.

Each of the questions below has five figures.
Find which figure in each row is most unlike the others.

1.

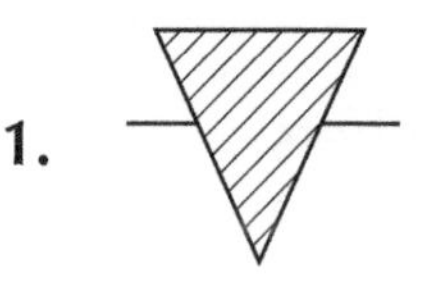
a

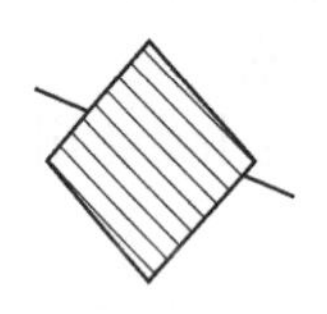
b

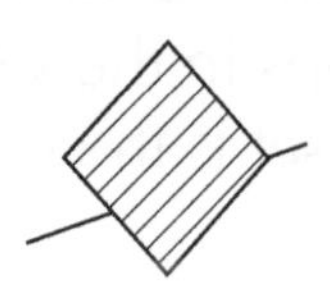
c

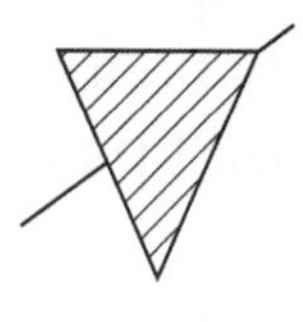
d

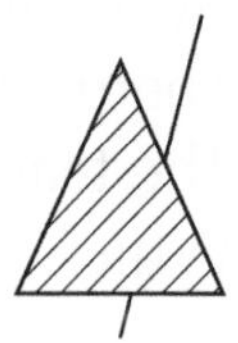
e

2.

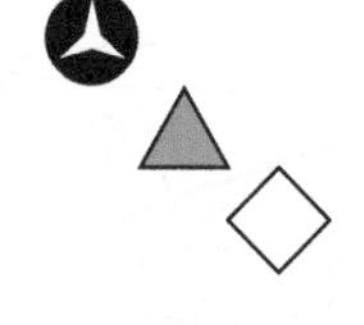
a

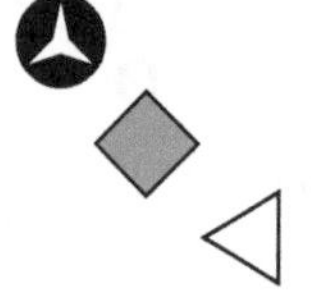
b

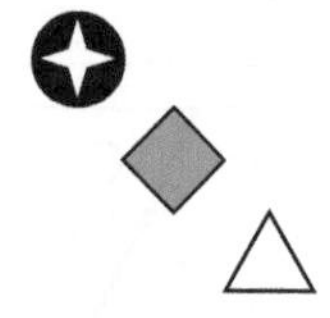
c

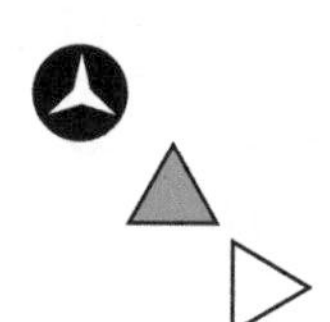
d

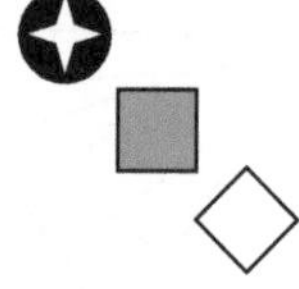
e

3.

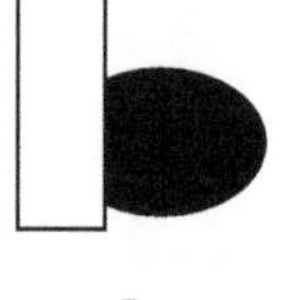
a

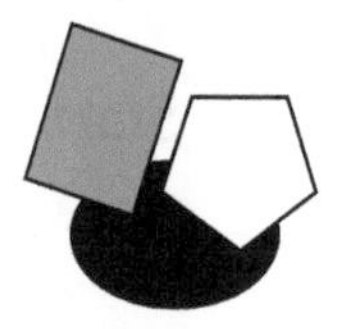
b

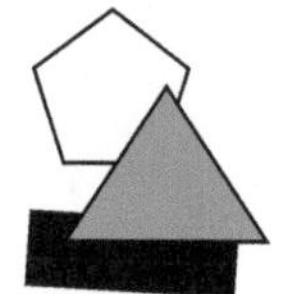
c

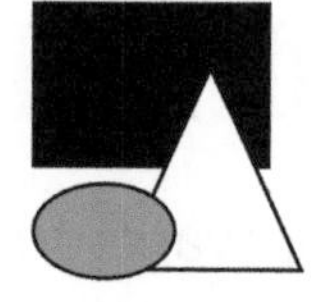
d

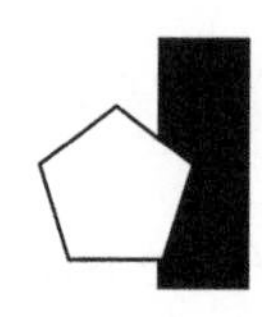
e

4.

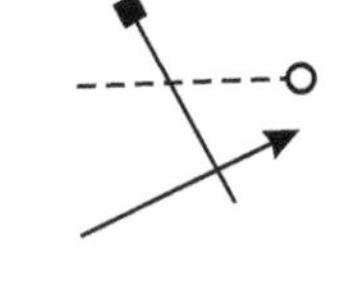
a

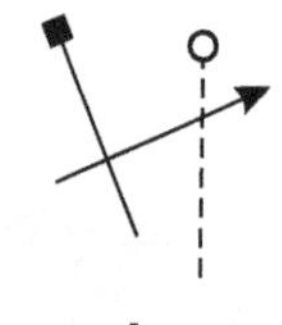
b

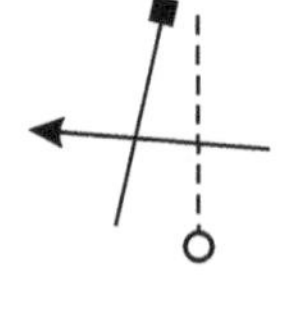
c

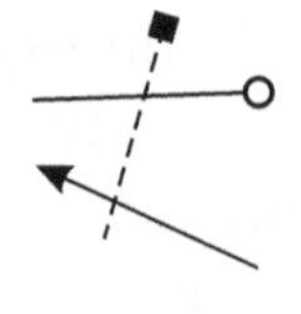
d

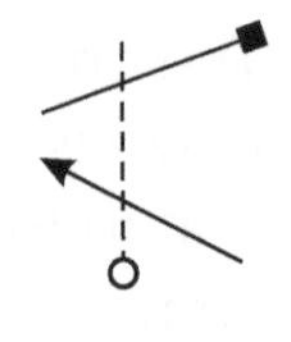
e

5.

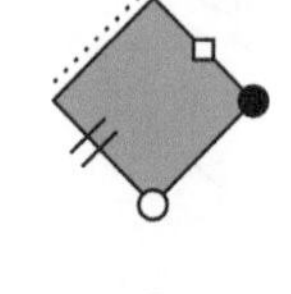
a

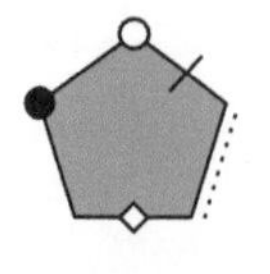
b

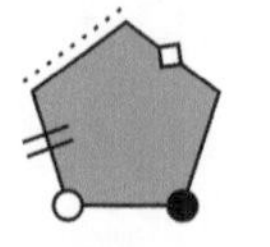
c

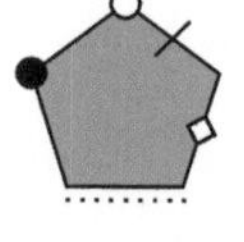
d

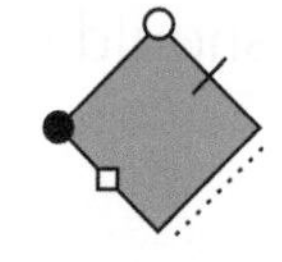
e

On the left of each question below is a big square with one small empty square. Find which of the five squares on the right should replace the empty square.

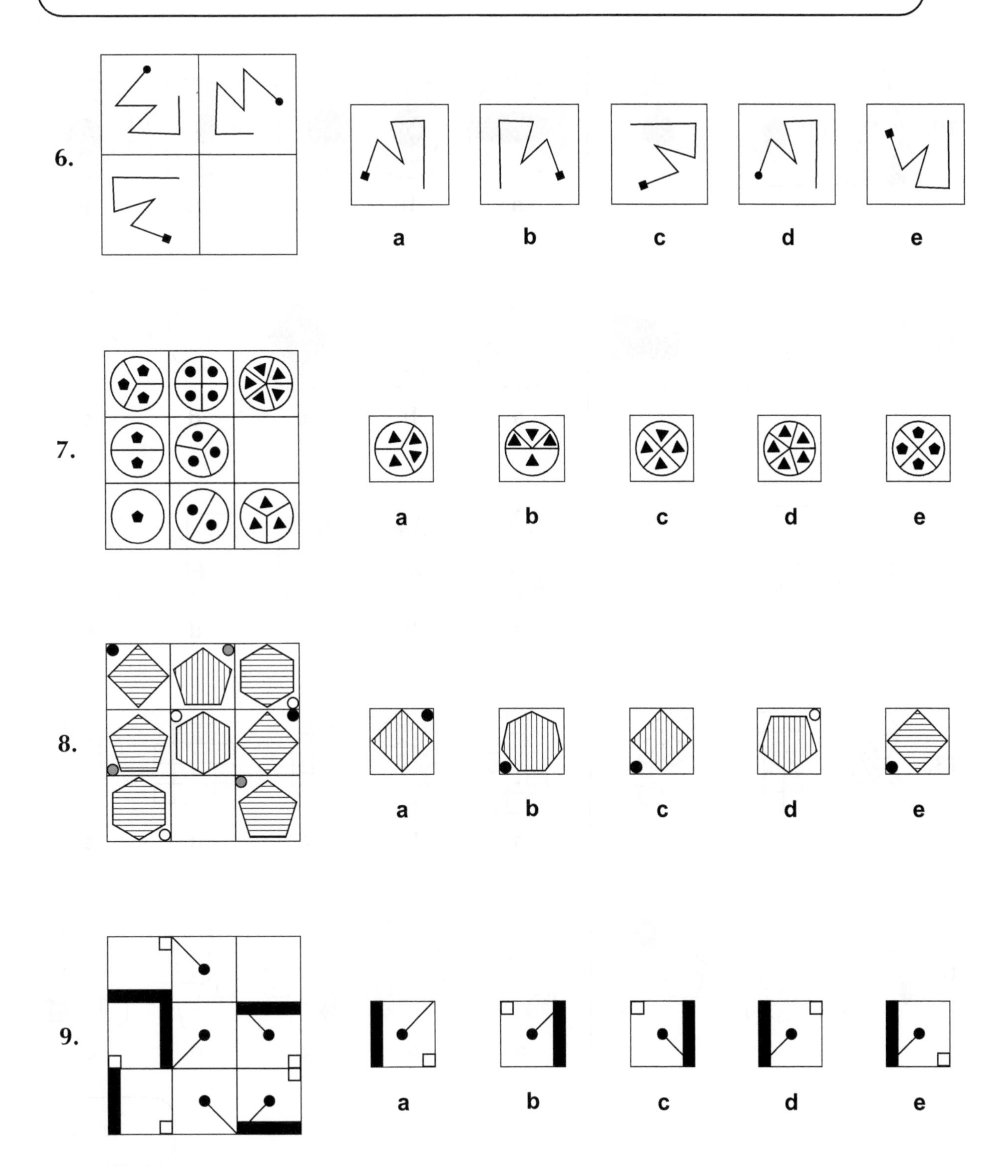

For each of the questions below there are three figures that are like each other in some way. Find which of the five figures on the right is most like the three figures on the left.

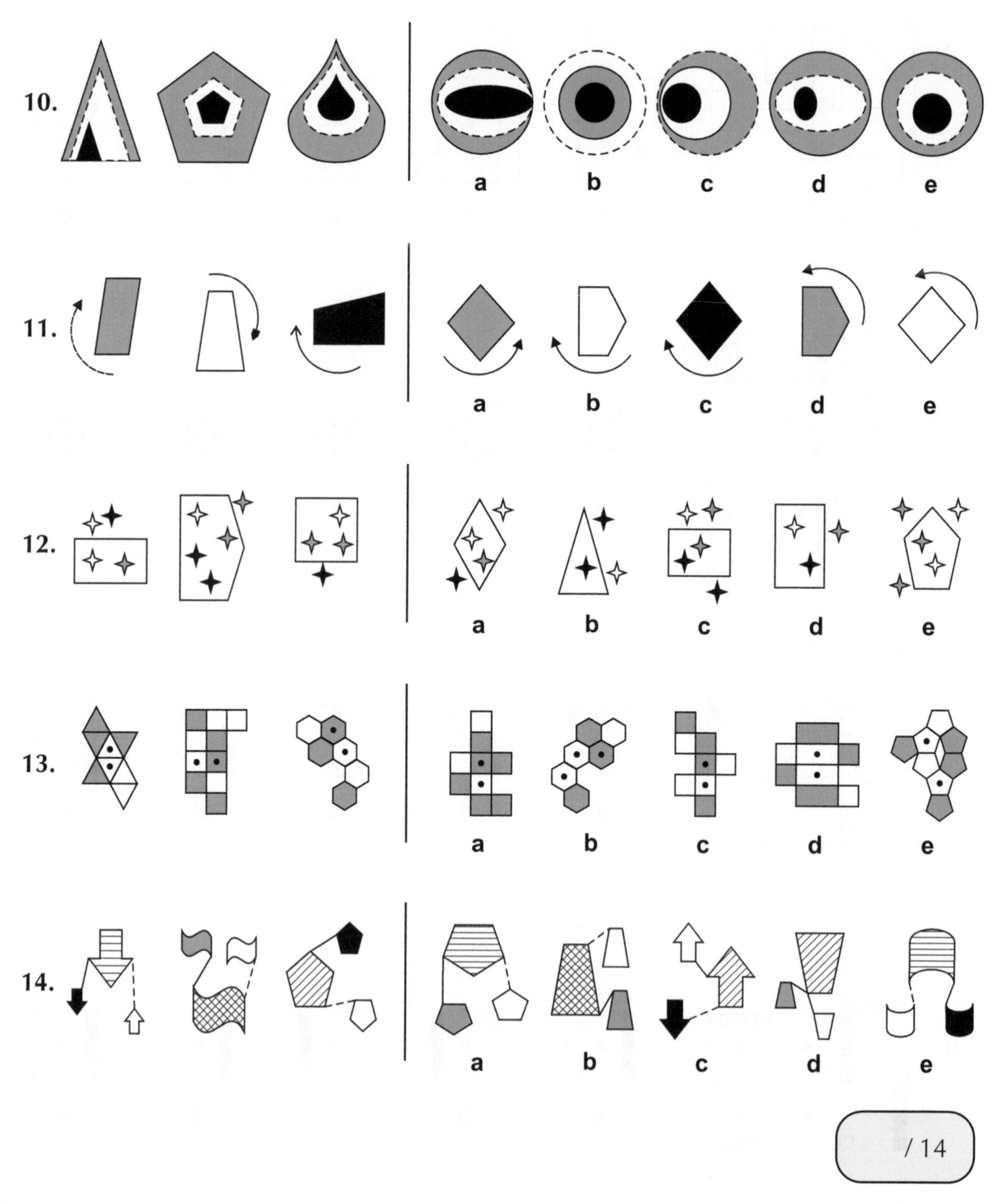

/ 14

Test 17

You have **10 minutes** to do this test. Circle the letter underneath each correct answer.

In the boxes on the left are shapes with code letters. The top letters have a different meaning to the bottom ones. Work out how the letters go with the shapes and then find the code for the new shape from the five codes on the right.

1.

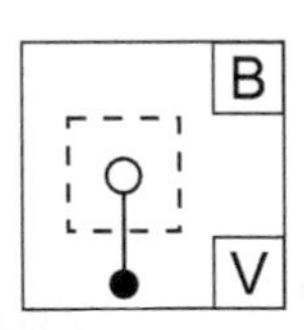
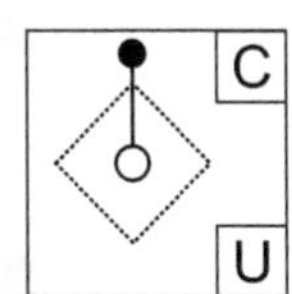
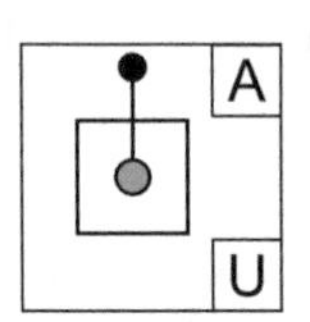
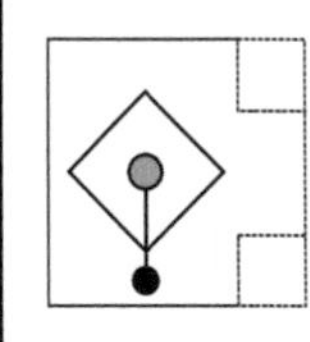
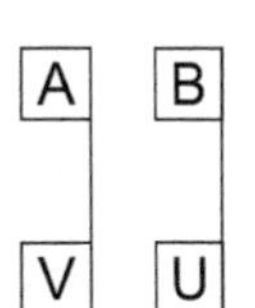

2.

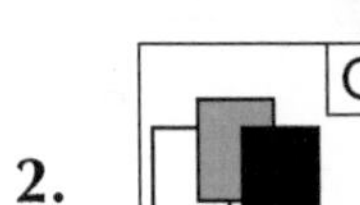
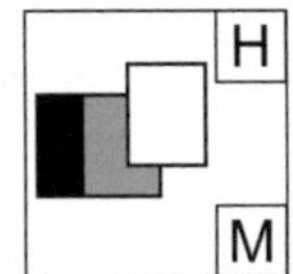
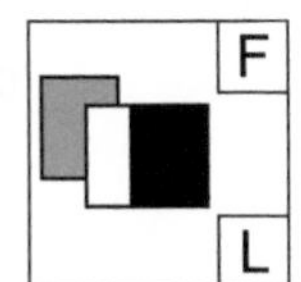
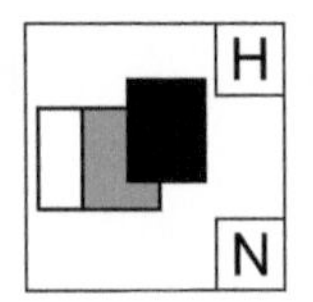
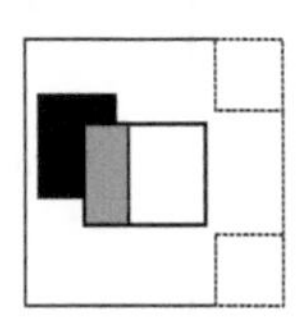
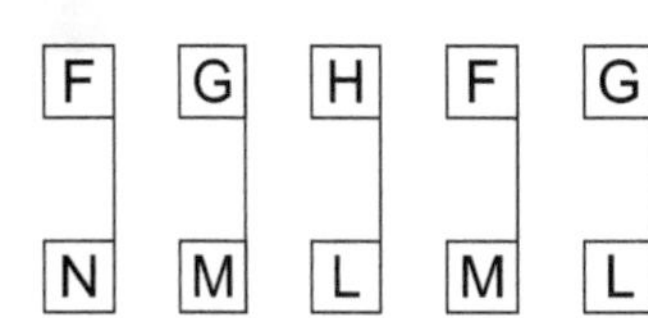
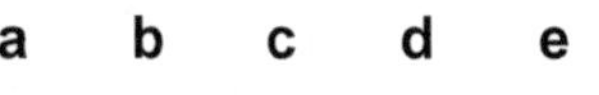

3.

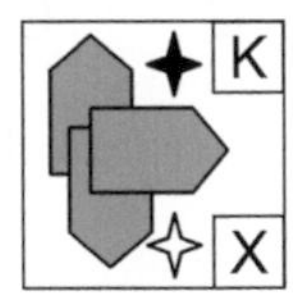
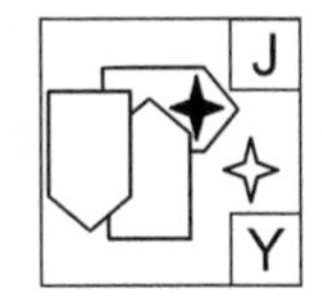
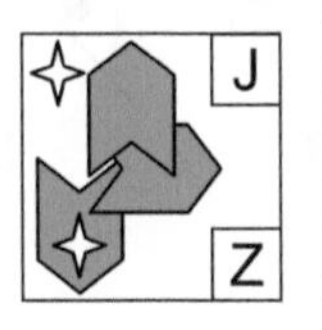
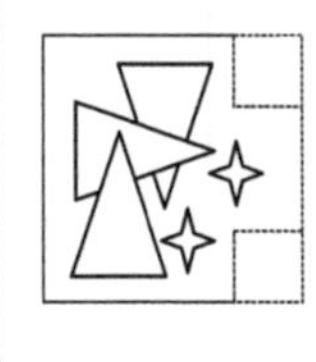
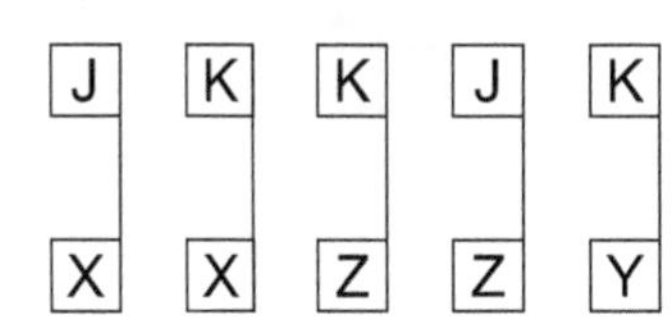

4.

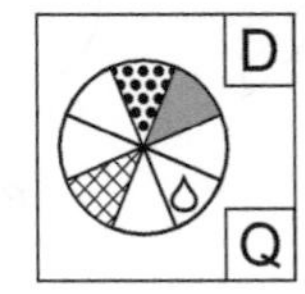

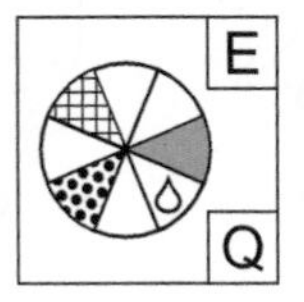
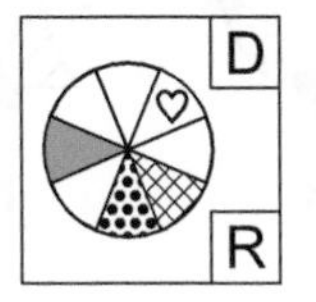
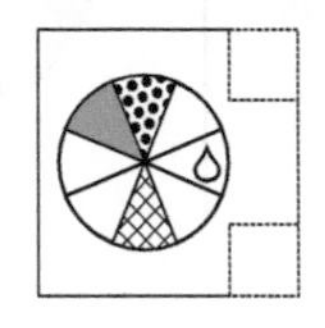
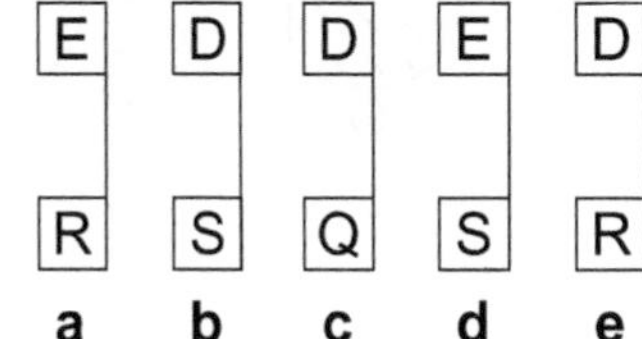

5.

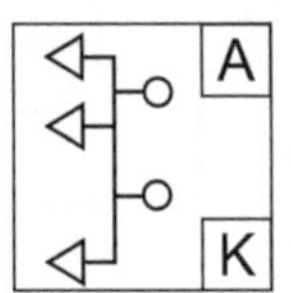
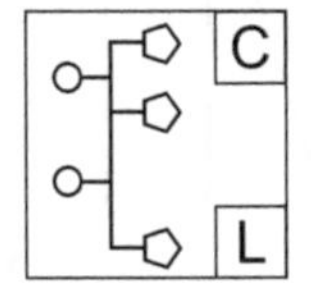
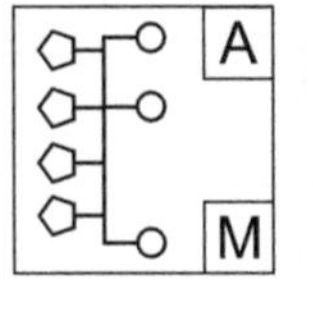
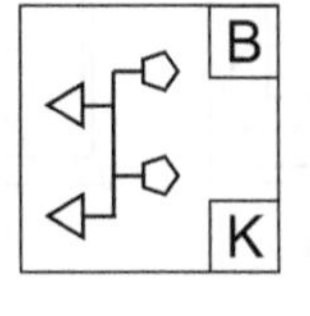
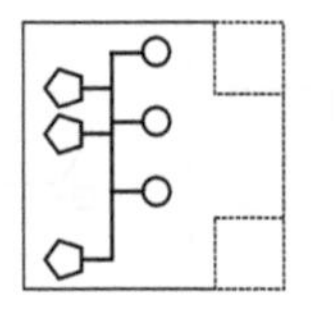
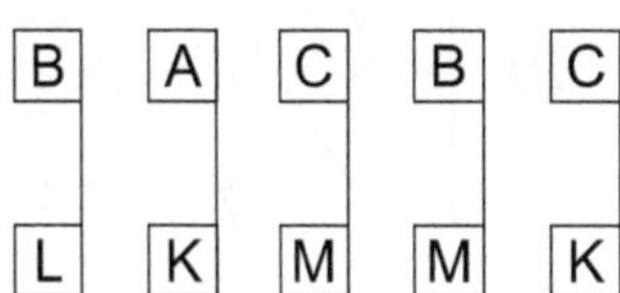

For each question below there are two figures that are like each other in some way.
Find which of the five figures on the right is most like the two figures on the left.

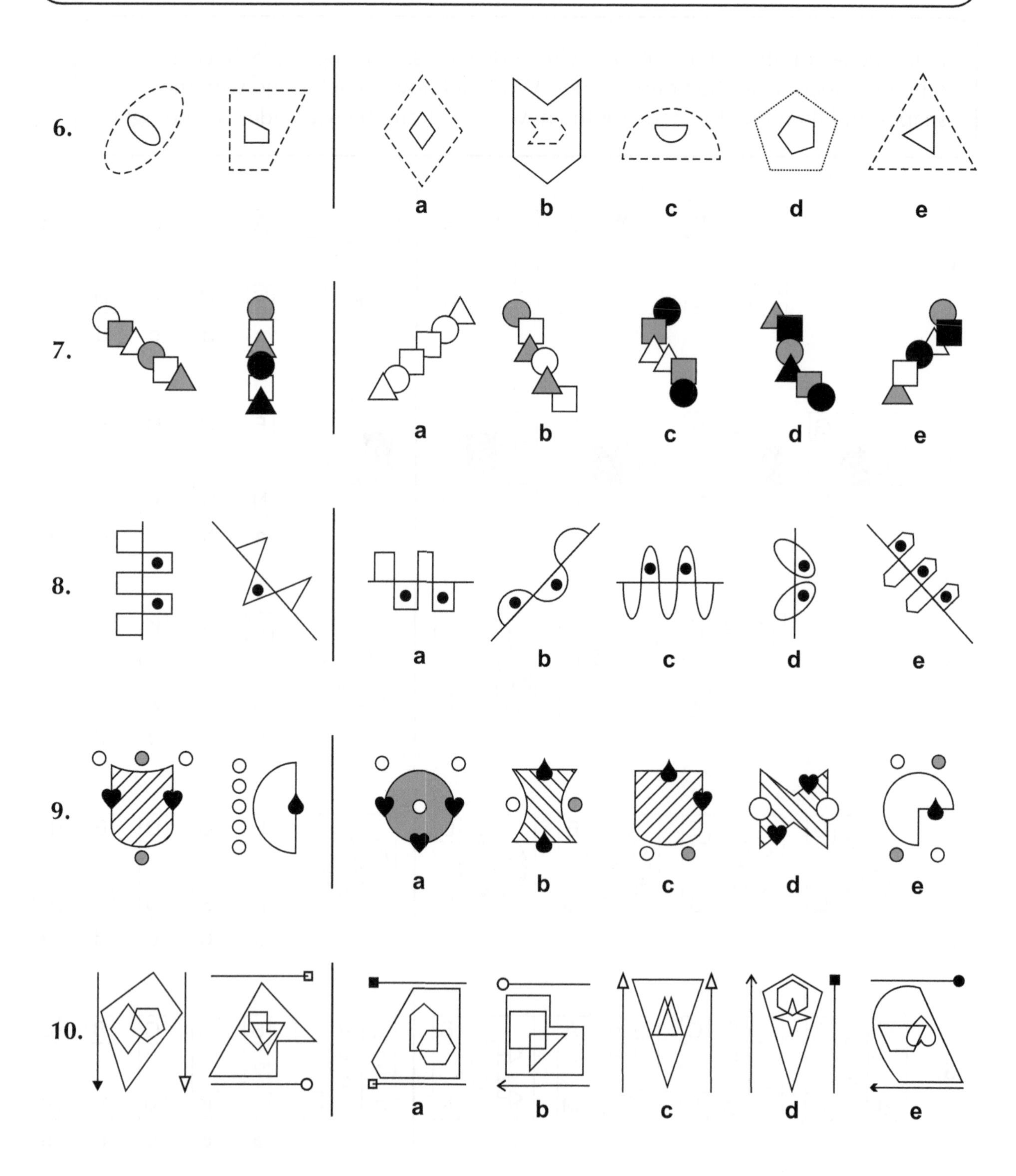

Each of these questions has five squares on the left that are arranged in order.
One of the squares is missing. One of the squares on the right should go in its place.
Find which one of the five squares on the right should go in place of the empty square.

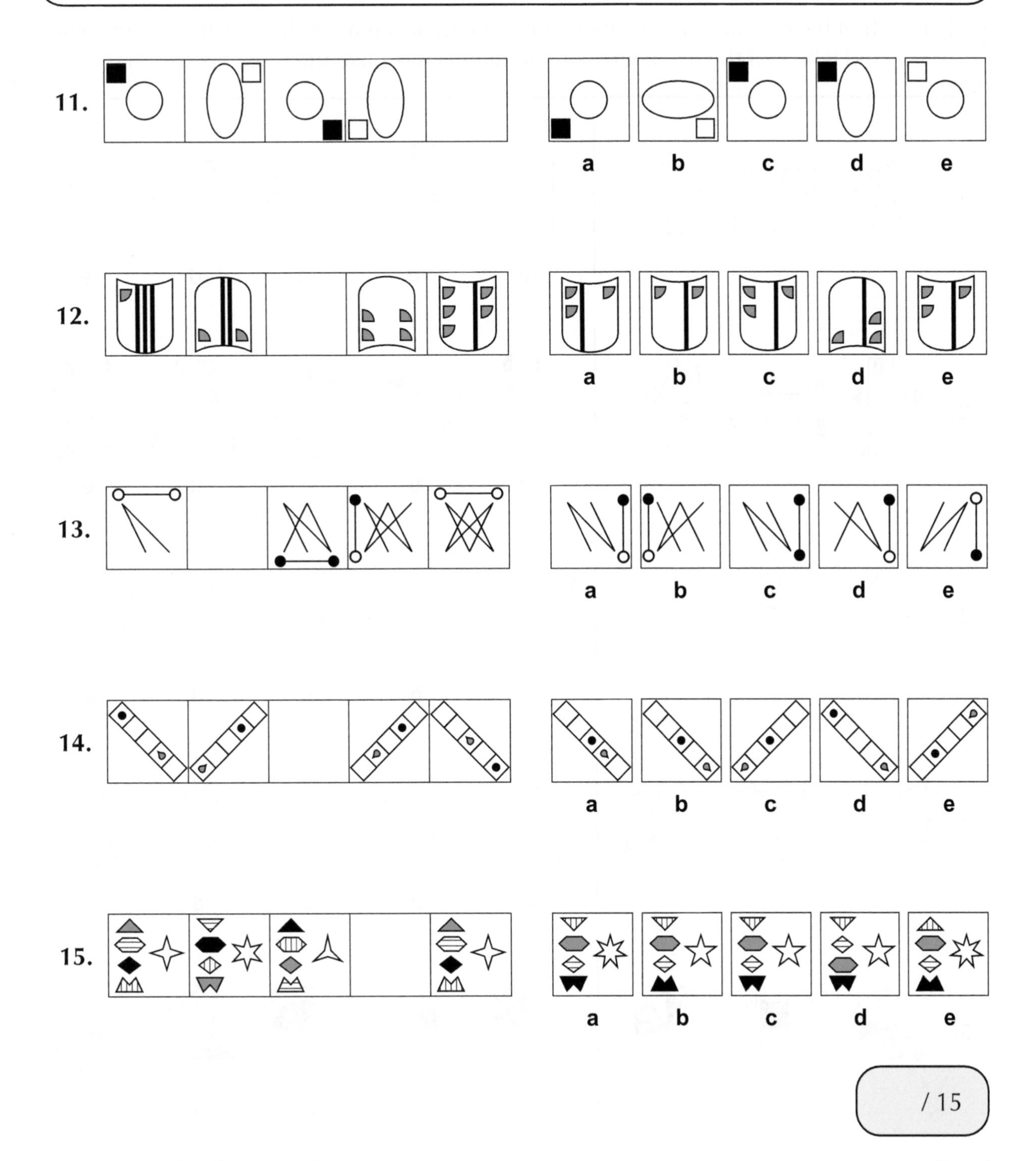

/ 15

Test 18

You have **10 minutes** to do this test. Circle the letter underneath each correct answer.

For each of the questions below there are three figures that are like each other in some way. Find which of the five figures on the right is most like the three figures on the left.

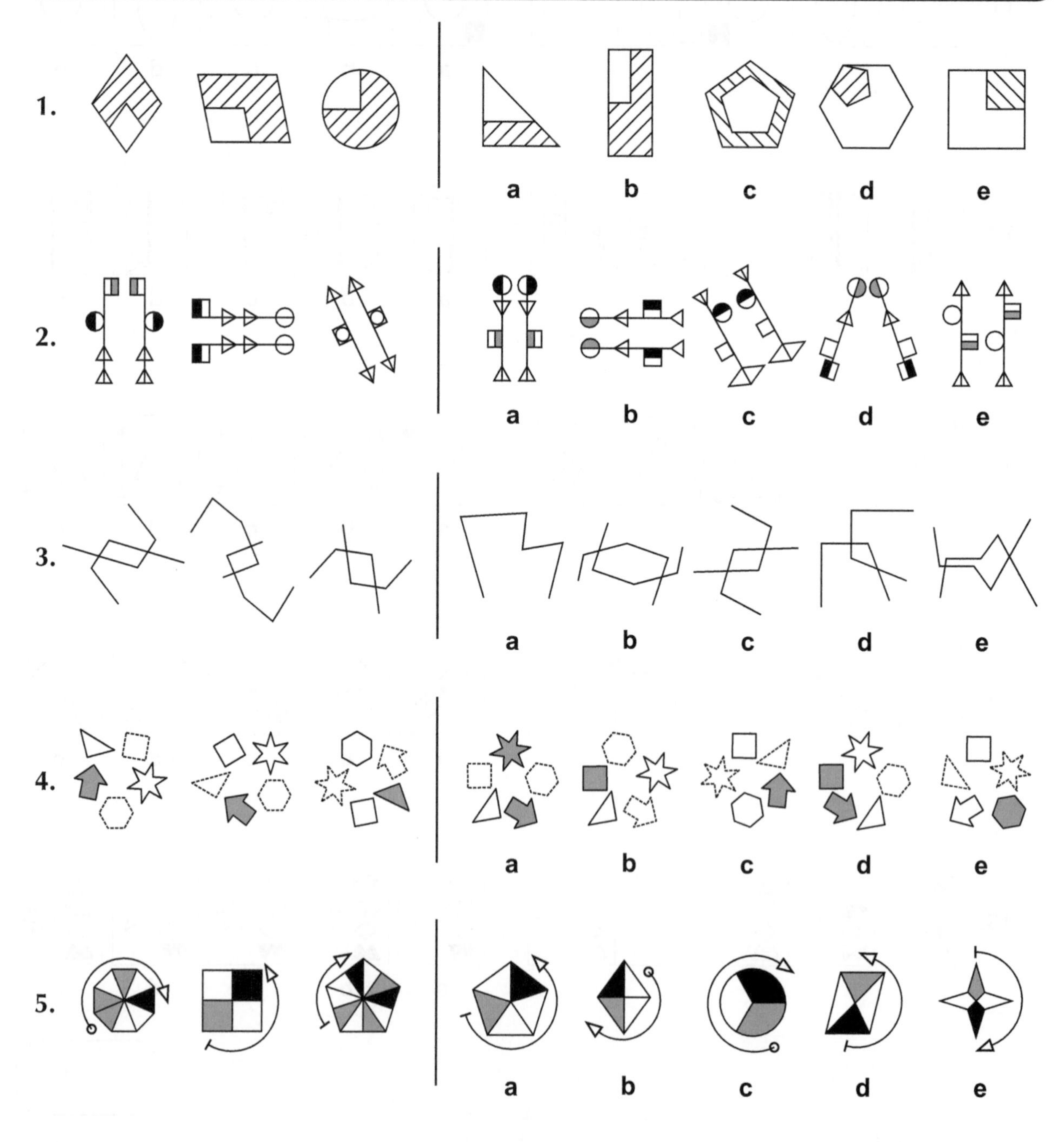

Each question has some shapes on the left with code letters that describe them. You need to work out what the code letters mean. There is then a shape on its own next to a choice of five codes. Work out which code describes this shape.

6.

XAM

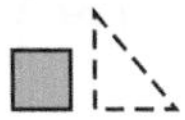

YBM

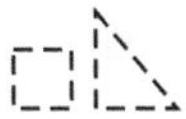

ZBN

XAN	YAM	ZAN	YBM	YAN
a	**b**	**c**	**d**	**e**

7.

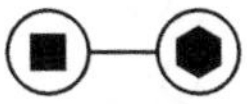

DP

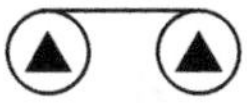

EQ

DR

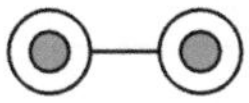

EP

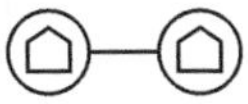

DR	DP	EP	EQ	ER
a	**b**	**c**	**d**	**e**

8.

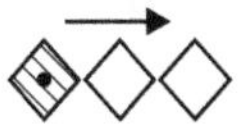

GJ

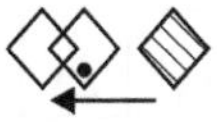

GK

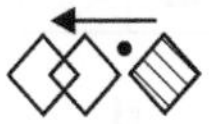

HJ

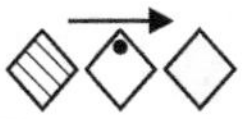

HJ	GJ	HK	GL	GK
a	**b**	**c**	**d**	**e**

9.

SBW

SCX

TBX

UBY

SCW	TCX	UBW	TCW	SBY
a	**b**	**c**	**d**	**e**

Each question has two shapes on the left with an arrow between them.
The first shape is changed in some way to become the second. There is then a third shape followed by an arrow and a choice of five shapes. Choose the shape on the right that relates to the third shape like the second does to the first.

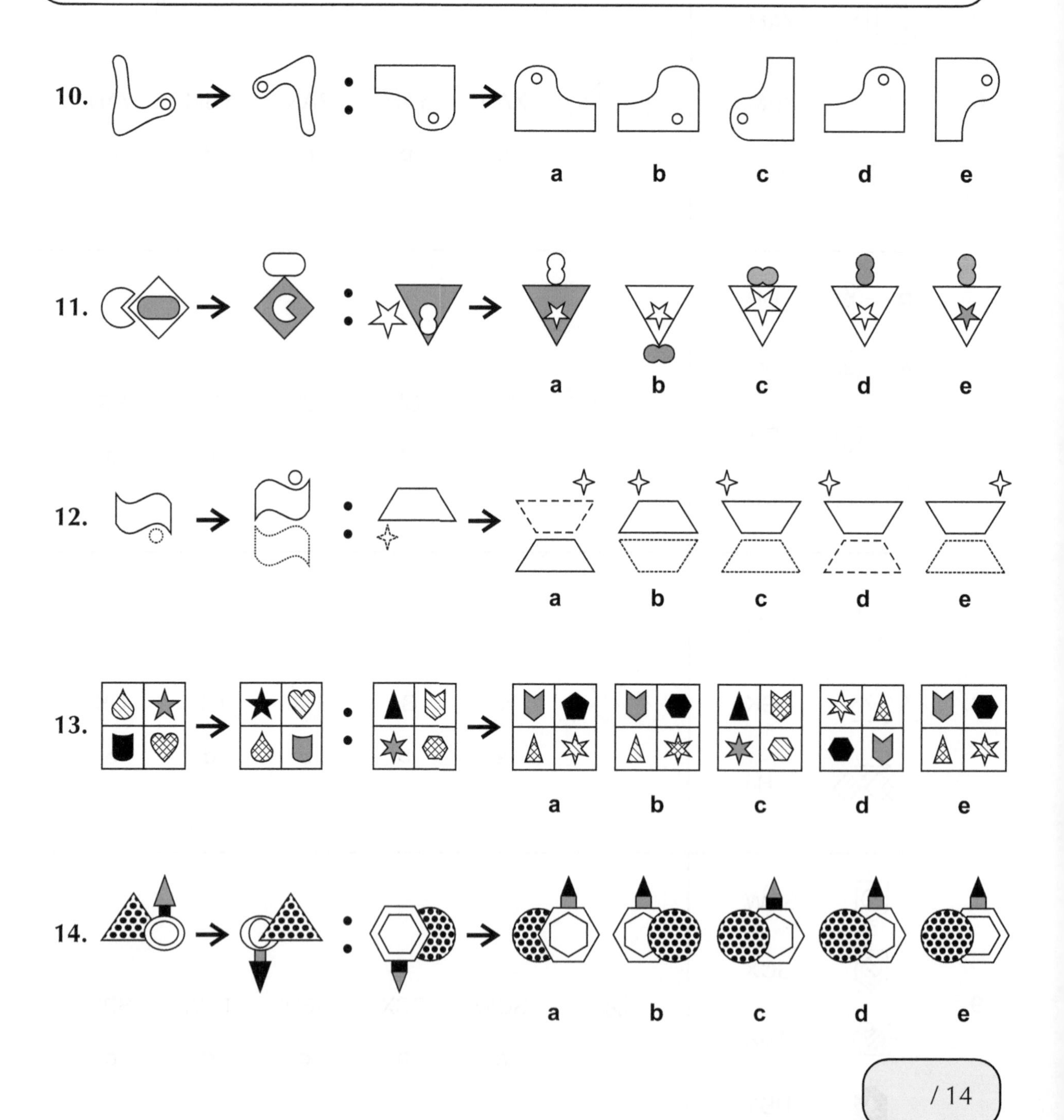

/ 14

Puzzles 6

Time for some puzzles! This page should help with **spotting connections** and **coding**.

Related Robots

In Robot City, the batteries needed to power the robots are related to the appearance of the robots. Match each robot below to its battery.

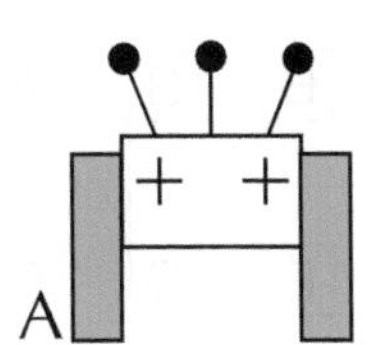

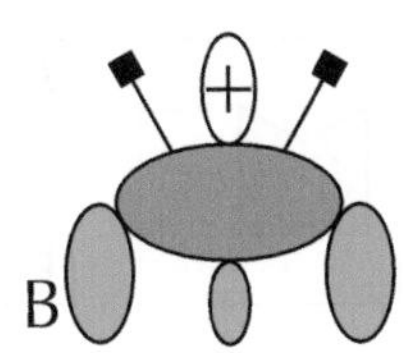

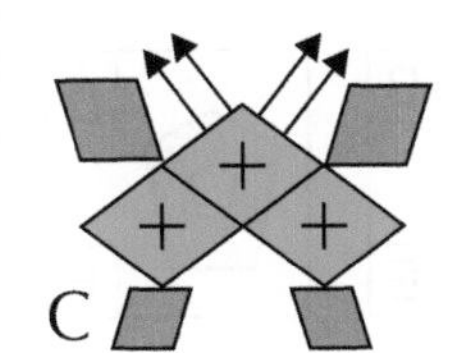

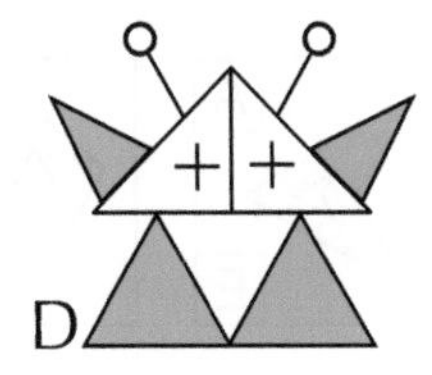

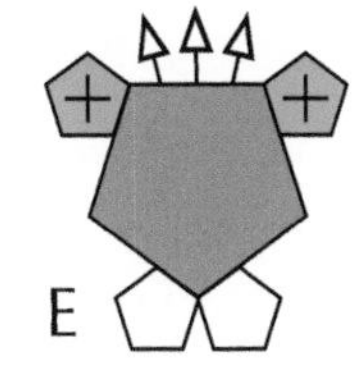

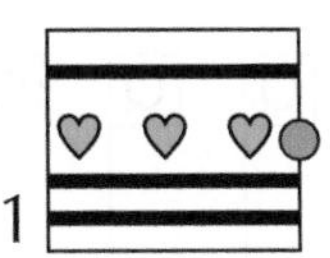

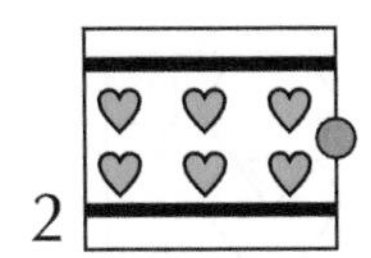

Cracked Code

A sculpture was knocked over and it broke. Use the codes to fill in each large square on the right and put the sculpture together again.

Code

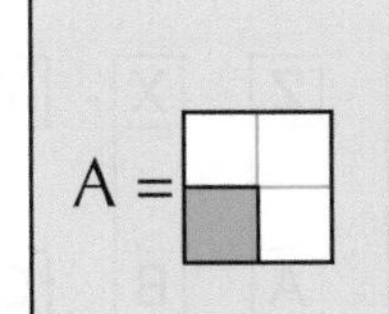

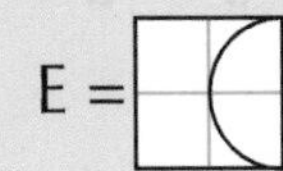

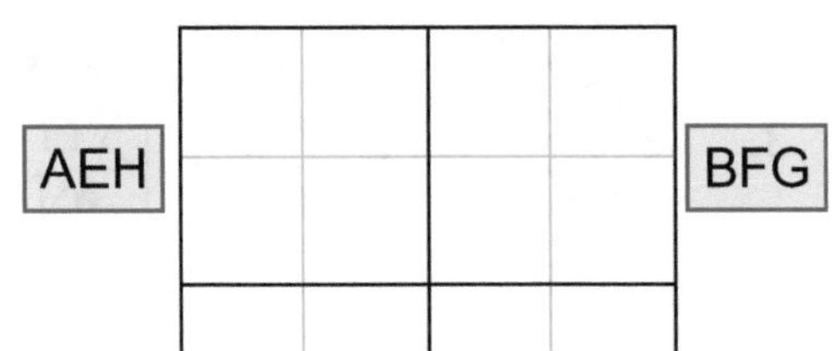

Test 19

You have **10 minutes** to do this test. Circle the letter underneath each correct answer.

In the boxes on the left are shapes with code letters. The top letters have a different meaning to the bottom ones. Work out how the letters go with the shapes and then find the code for the new shape from the five codes on the right.

1.

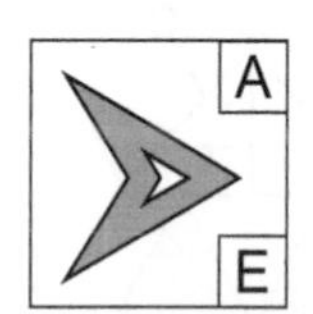 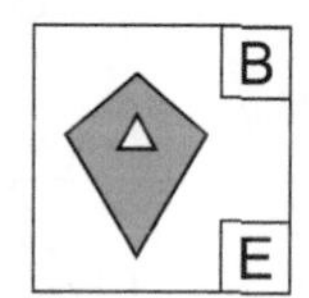 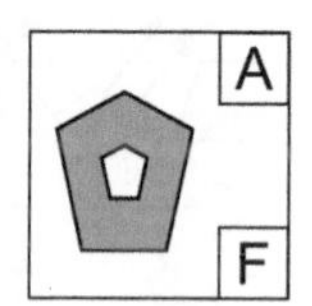 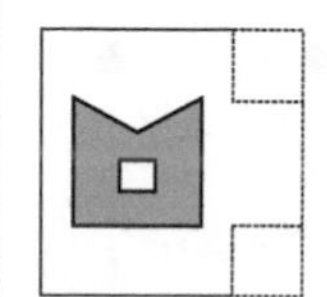 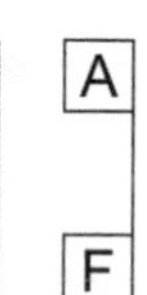 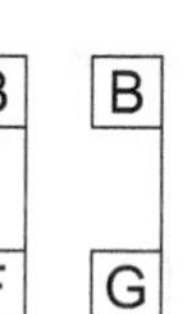 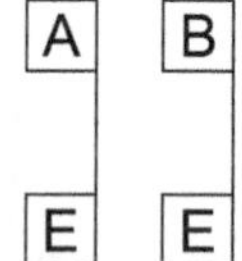

a	b	c	d	e
AF	BF	BG	AE	BE

2.

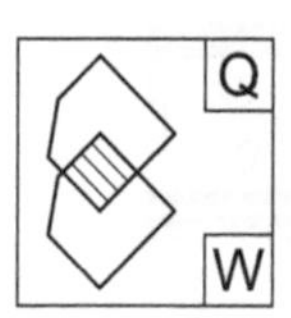 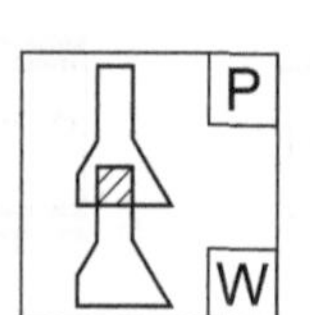   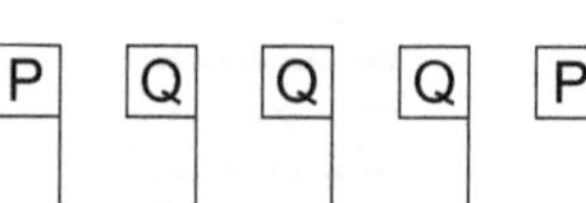

a	b	c	d	e
PW	QX	QW	QY	PX

3.

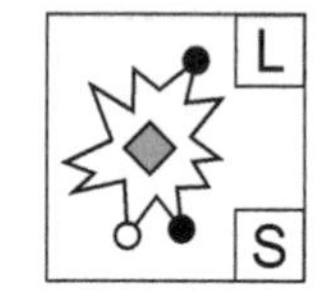 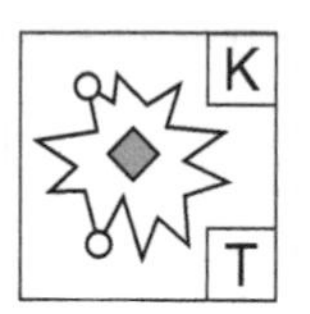 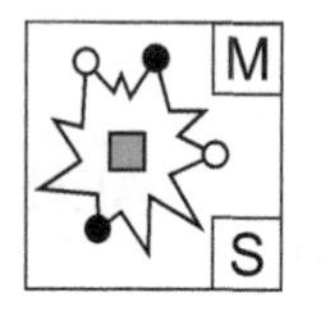 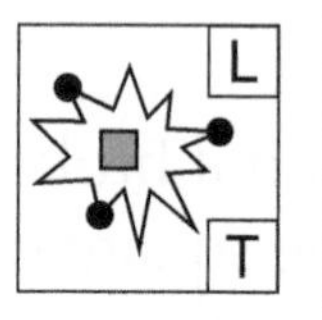 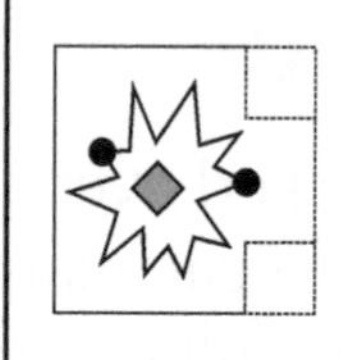 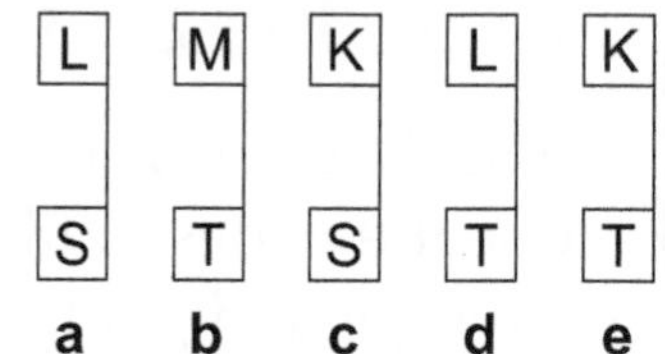

a	b	c	d	e
LS	MT	KS	LT	KT

4.

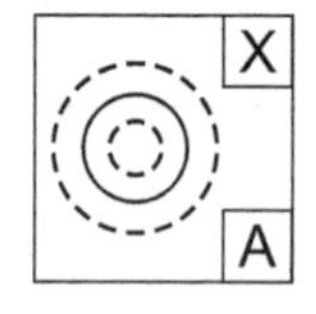 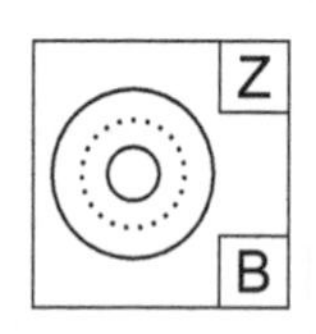 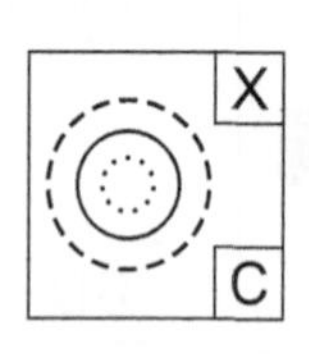 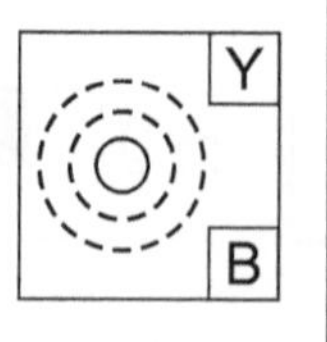 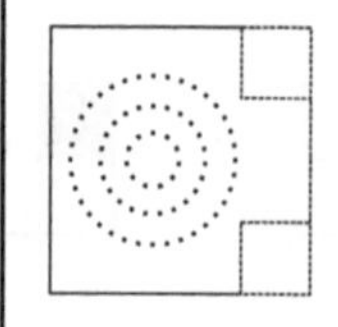 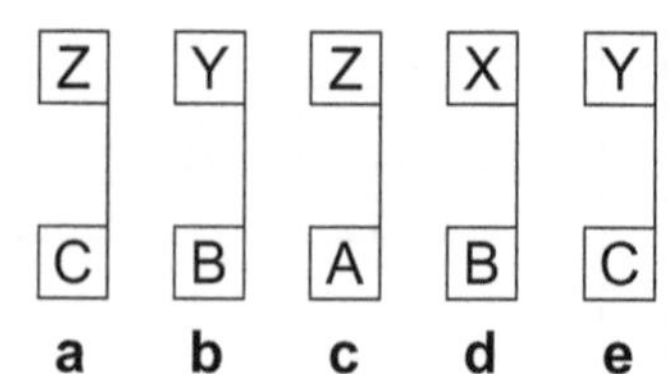

a	b	c	d	e
ZC	YB	ZA	XB	YC

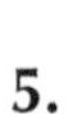

5.

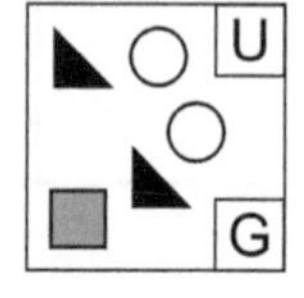 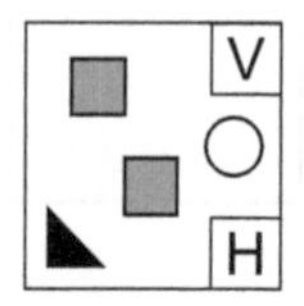 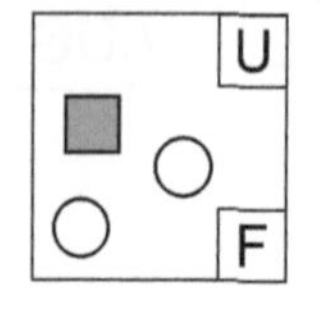 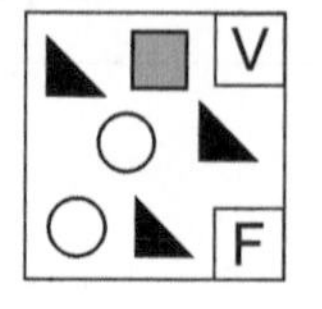 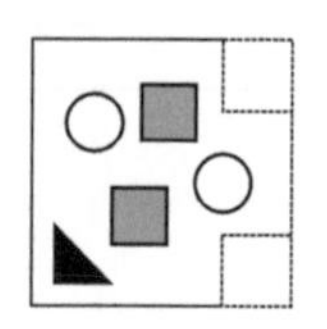 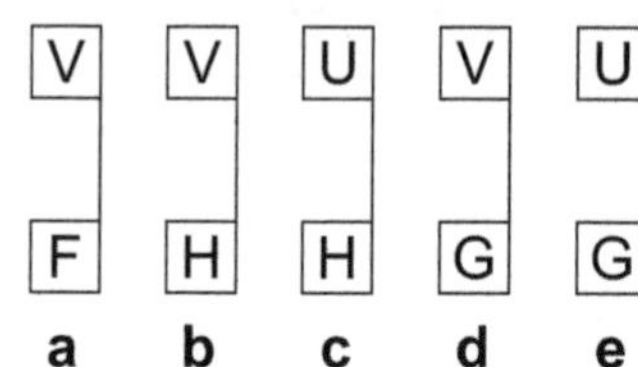

a	b	c	d	e
VF	VH	UH	VG	UG

For each question below there are two figures that are like each other in some way.
Find which of the five figures on the right is most like the two figures on the left.

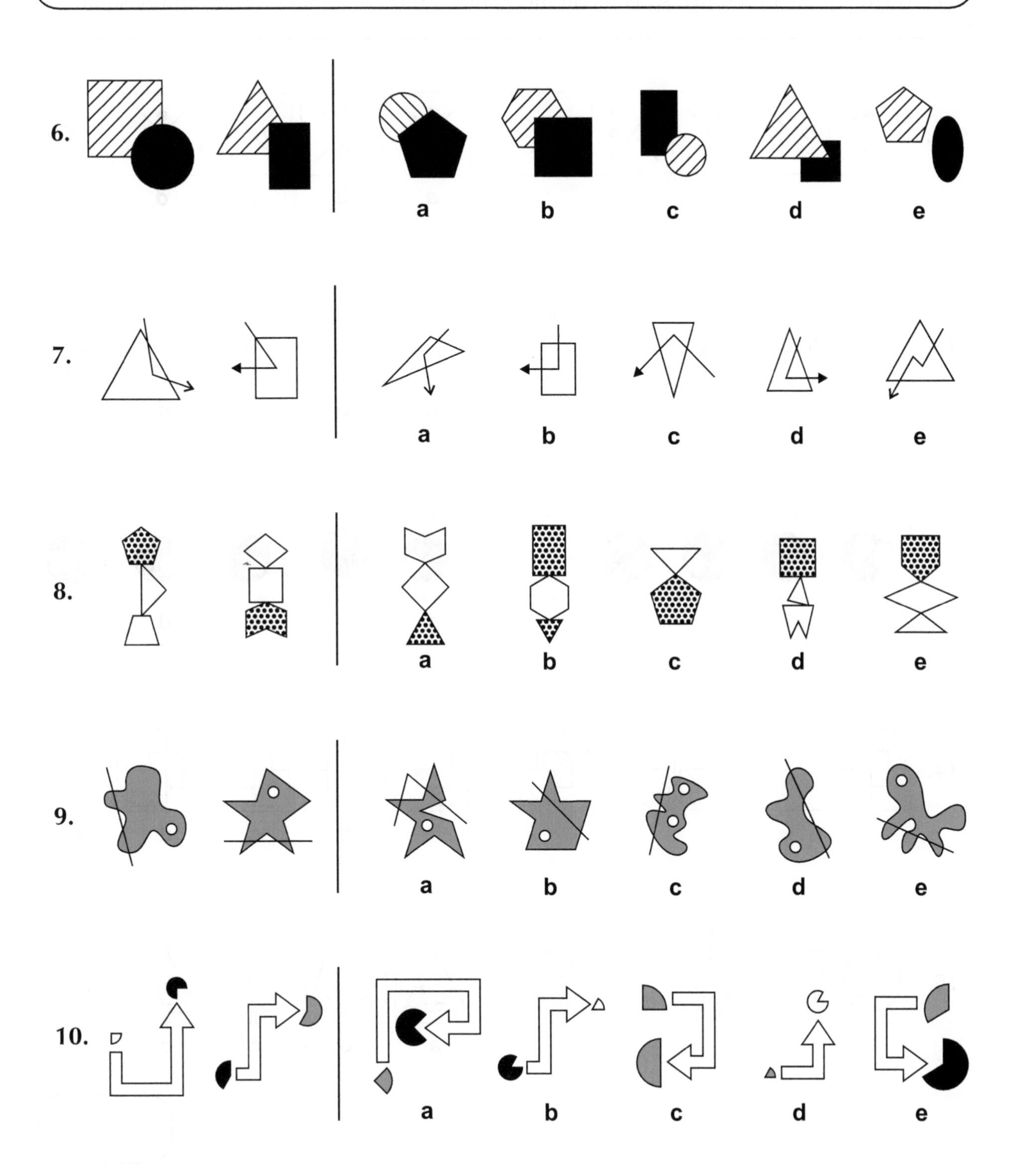

Each of these questions has five squares on the left that are arranged in order.
One of the squares is missing. One of the squares on the right should go in its place.
Find which one of the five squares on the right should go in place of the empty square.

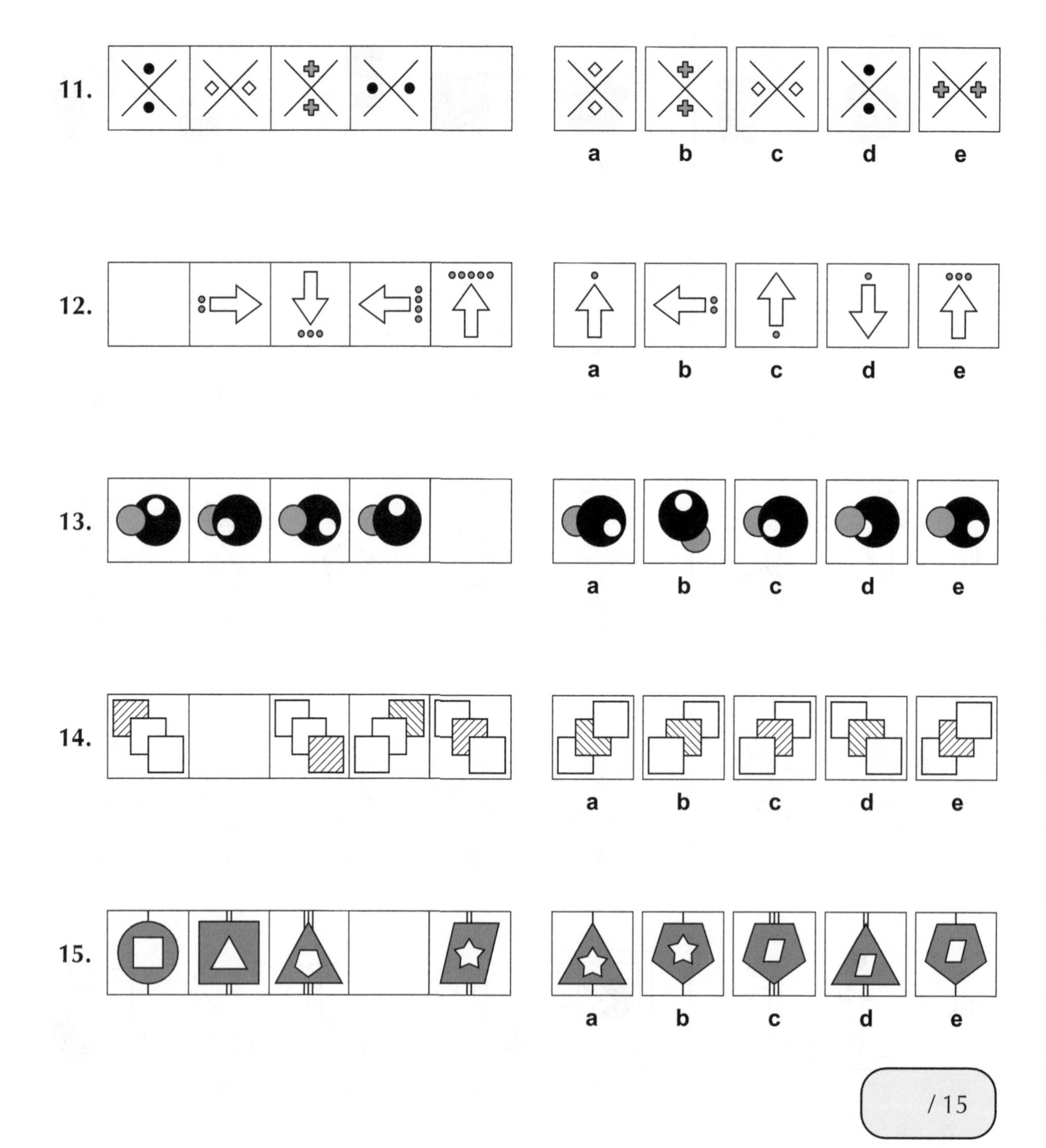

/ 15

Test 20

You have **10 minutes** to do this test. Circle the letter underneath each correct answer.

Each question has two shapes on the left with an arrow between them.
The first shape is changed in some way to become the second. There is then a third shape followed by an arrow and a choice of five shapes. Choose the shape on the right that relates to the third shape like the second does to the first.

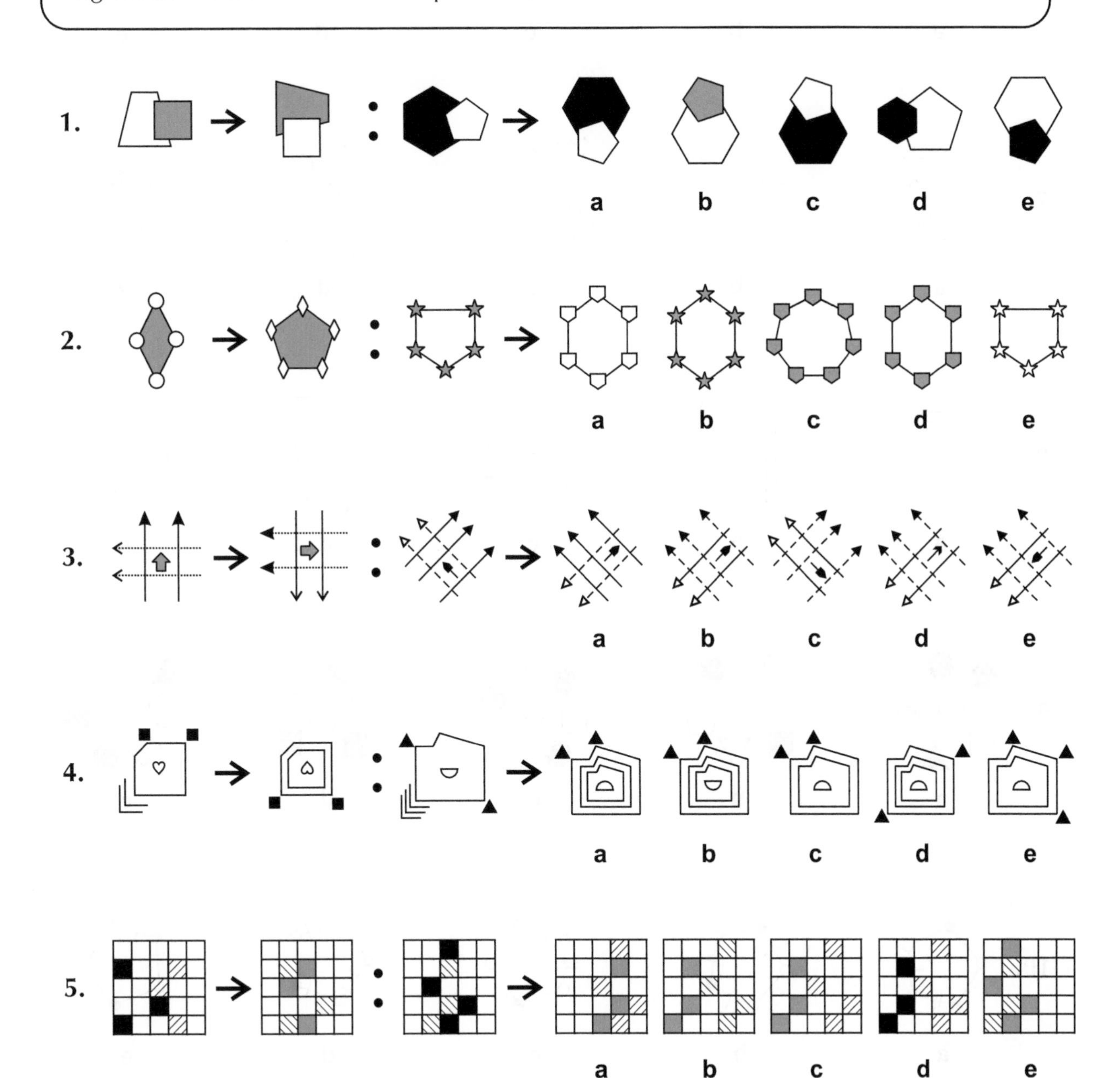

Each of the questions below has five figures.
Find which figure in each row is most unlike the others.

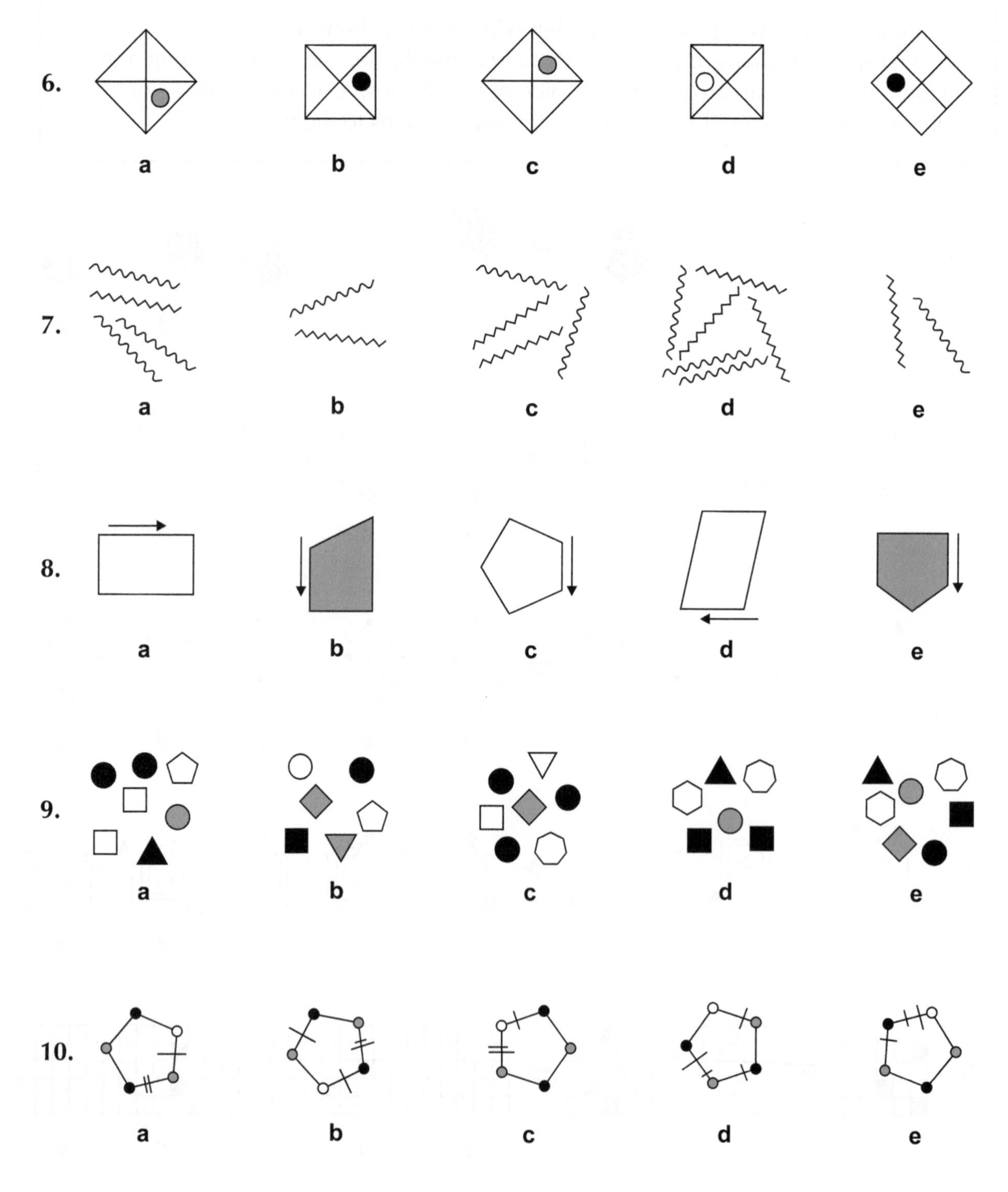

On the left of each question below is a big square with one small empty square. Find which of the five squares on the right should replace the empty square.

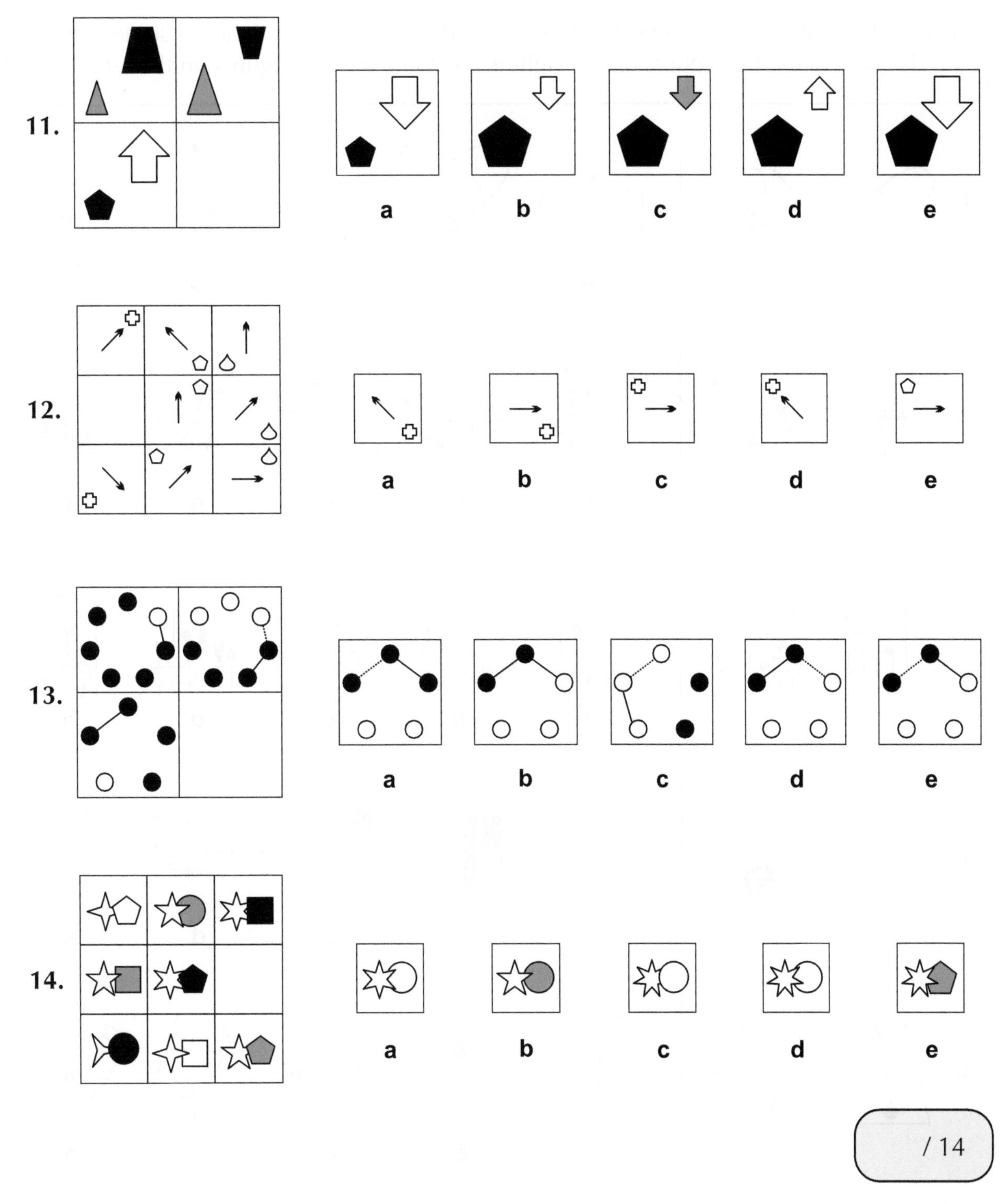

/ 14

Test 21

You have **10 minutes** to do this test. Circle the letter underneath each correct answer.

For each question below there are two figures that are like each other in some way. Find which of the five figures on the right is most like the two figures on the left.

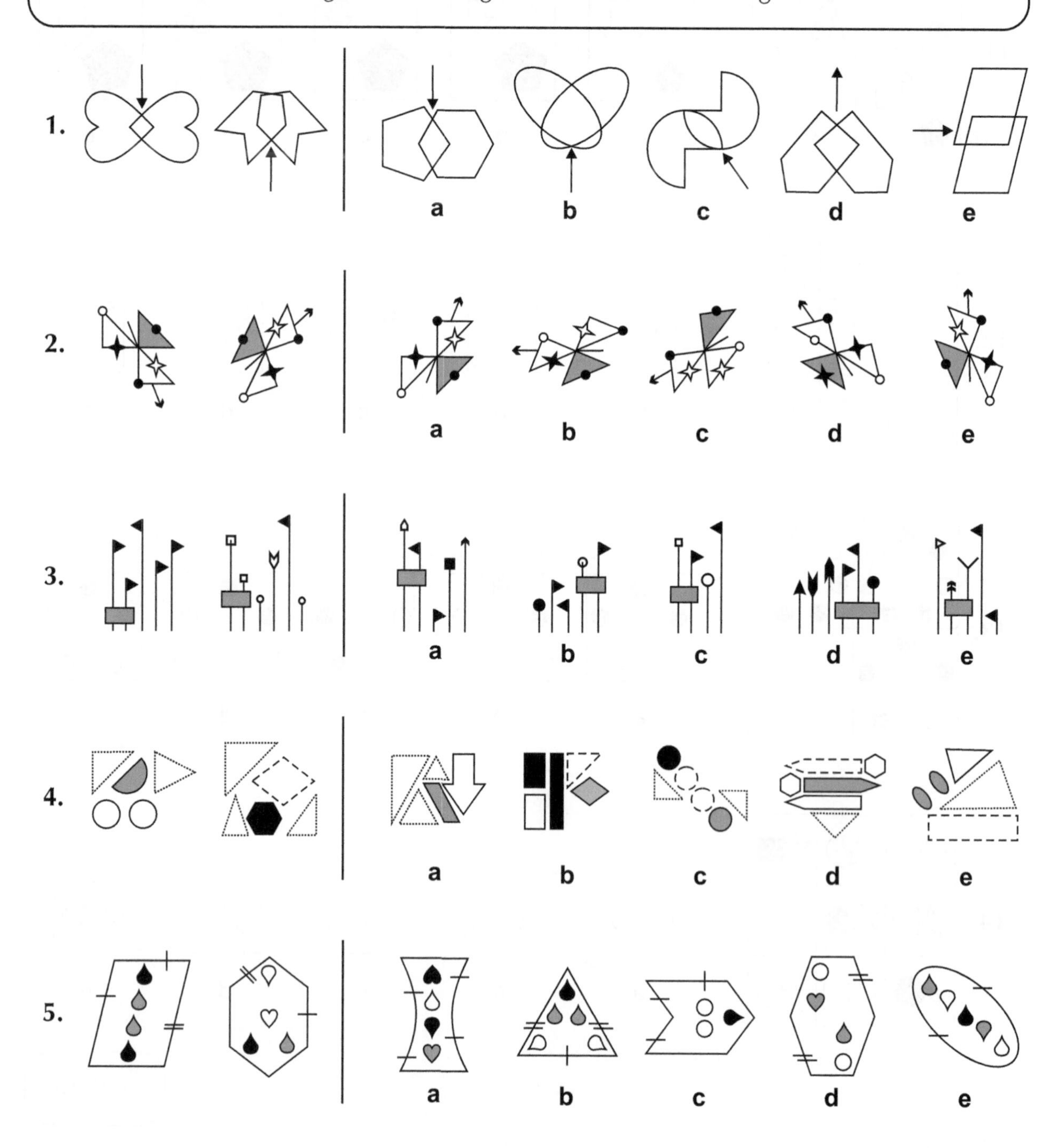

Each question has some shapes on the left with code letters that describe them. You need to work out what the code letters mean. There is then a shape on its own next to a choice of five codes. Work out which code describes this shape.

6.

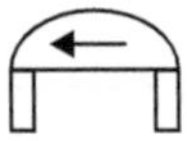

RJ

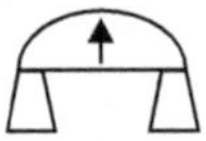

SK

RL

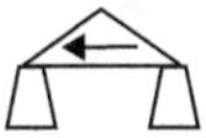

SL	RJ	SK	SJ	RL
a	b	c	d	e

7.

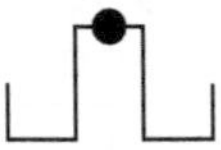

ET

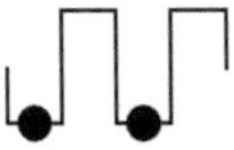

FV

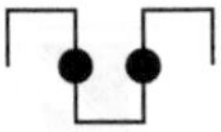

EU

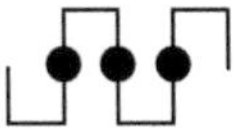

FT	FU	EV	EU	FV
a	b	c	d	e

8.

AX

BY

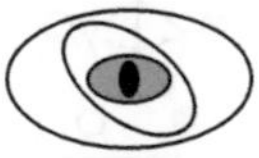

AY

CZ

CX	BX	AZ	BZ	CY
a	b	c	d	e

9.

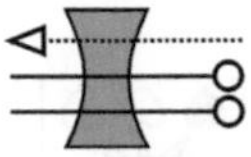

GMU

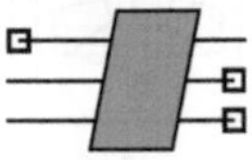

HMS

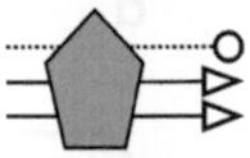

HNU

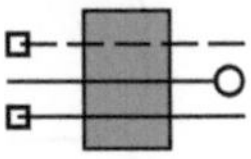

GLT

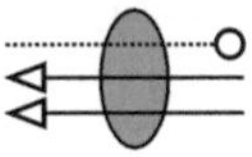

GLU	GMS	HLS	HNT	GNU
a	b	c	d	e

Each of these questions has five squares on the left that are arranged in order.
One of the squares is missing. One of the squares on the right should go in its place.
Find which one of the five squares on the right should go in place of the empty square.

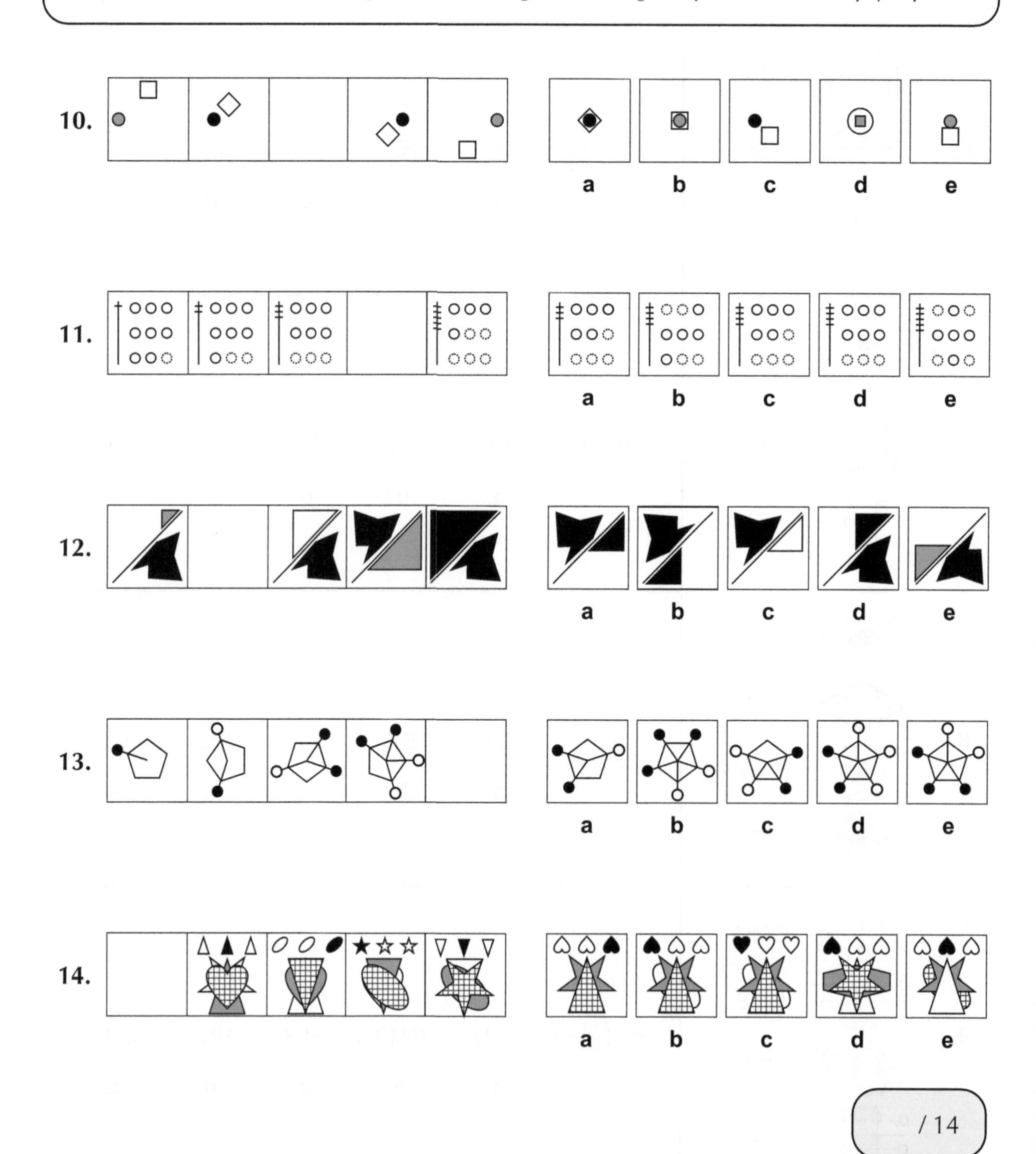

/ 14

Puzzles 7

Give these puzzles a go! They'll help you practise **spotting patterns** and **similarities.**

Pumpkin Patterns

Five of the pumpkins below form a sequence.
Write their numbers in the correct order. The first two have been done for you.

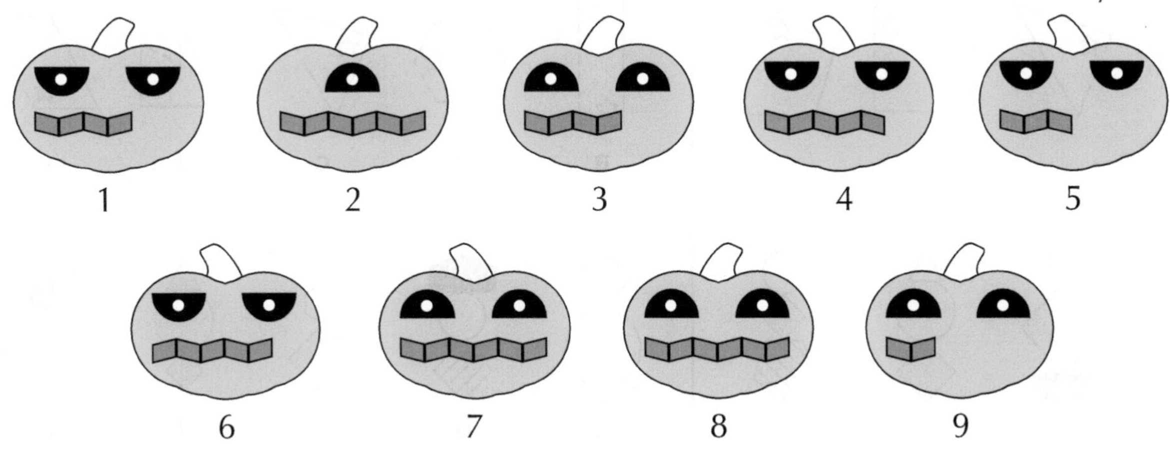

Sequence: 9 , 5 , __ , __ , __

Haunted House

The house whose chimney smoke looks the most different from the others is haunted. Draw a circle around the haunted house.

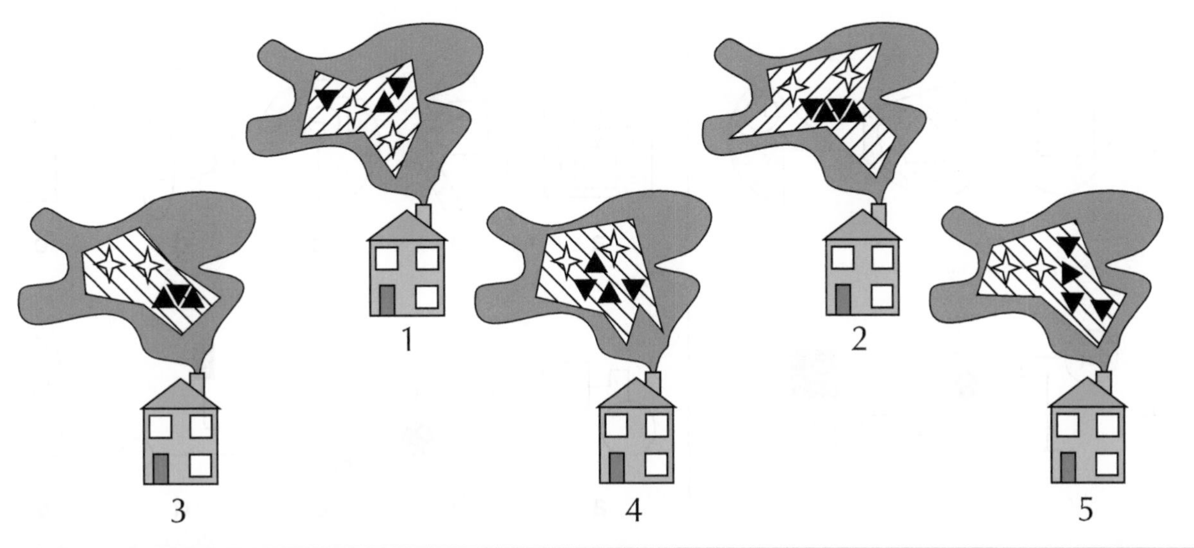

Test 22

You have **10 minutes** to do this test. Circle the letter underneath each correct answer.

For each of the questions below there are three figures that are like each other in some way. Find which of the five figures on the right is most like the three figures on the left.

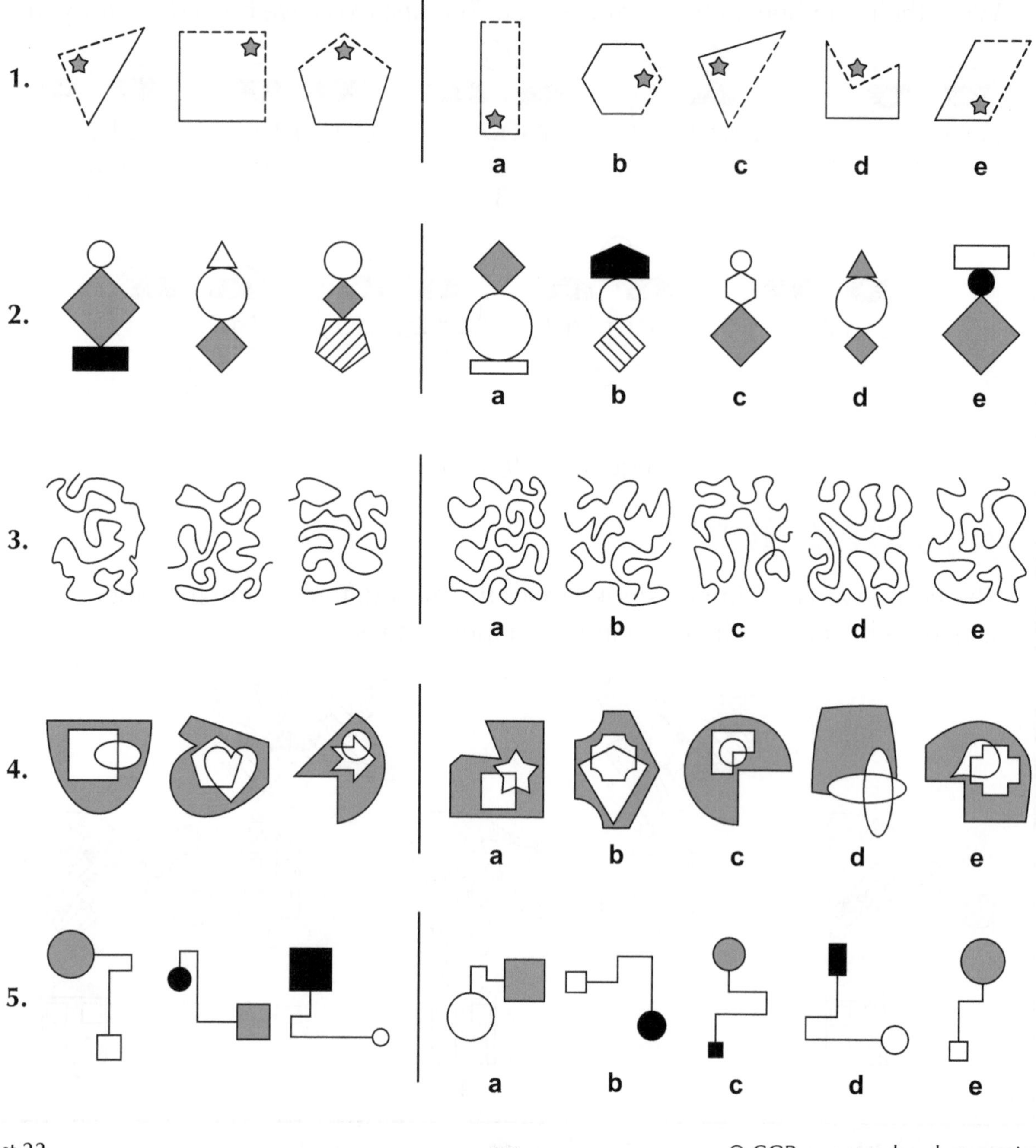

Each of the questions below has five figures.
Find which figure in each row is most unlike the others.

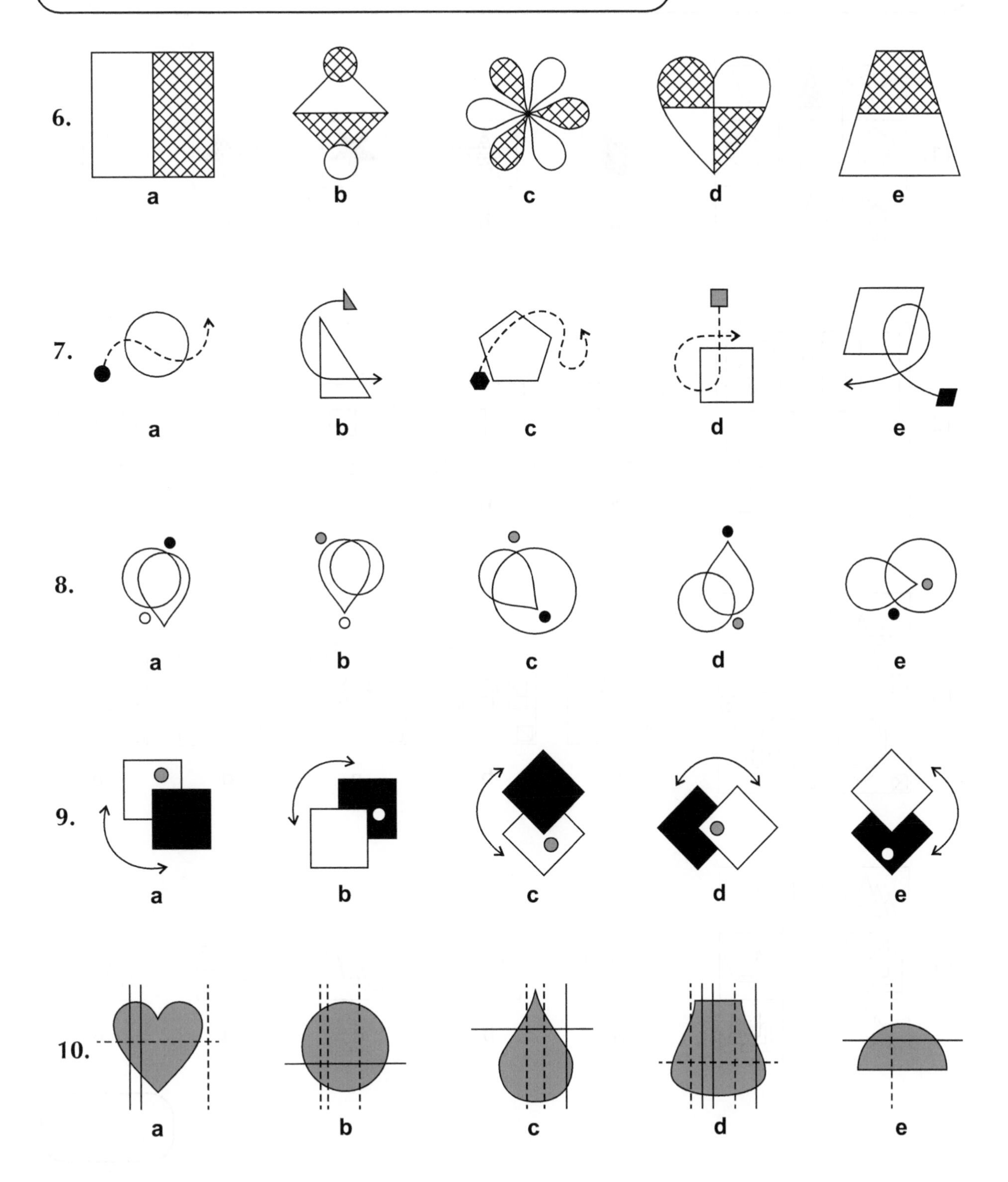

On the left of each question below is a big square with one small empty square. Find which of the five squares on the right should replace the empty square.

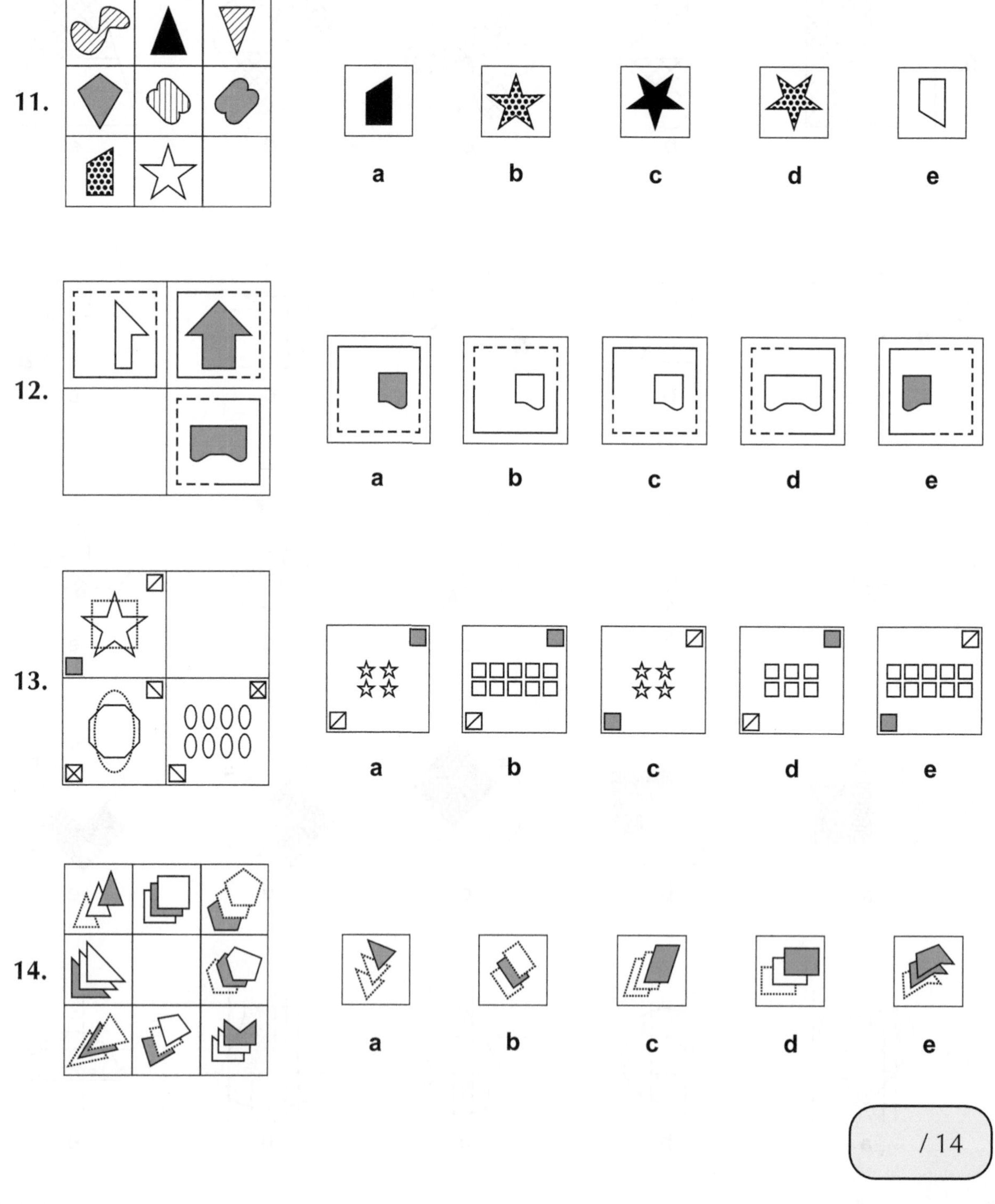

/ 14

Test 23

You have **10 minutes** to do this test. Circle the letter underneath each correct answer.

In the boxes on the left are shapes with code letters. The top letters have a different meaning to the bottom ones. Work out how the letters go with the shapes and then find the code for the new shape from the five codes on the right.

1.

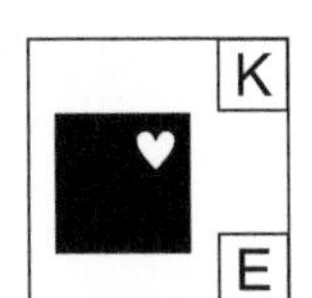

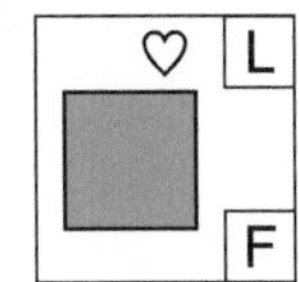

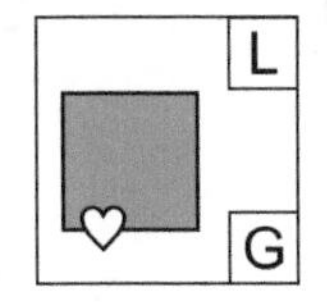

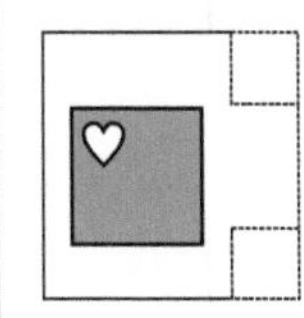
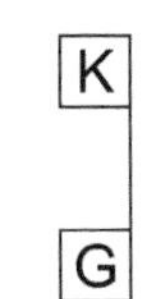
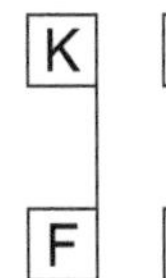
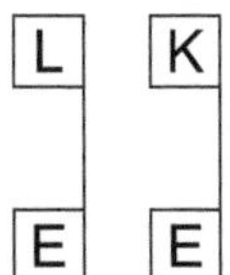

a b c d e

2.

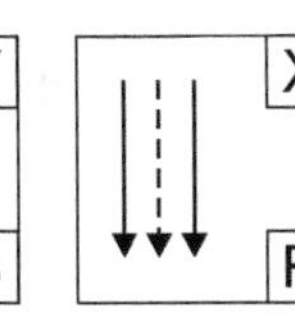

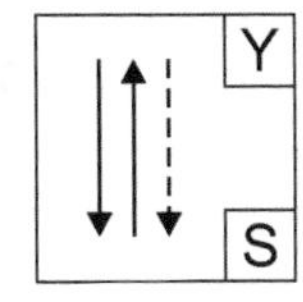

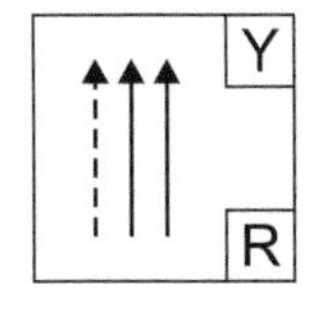

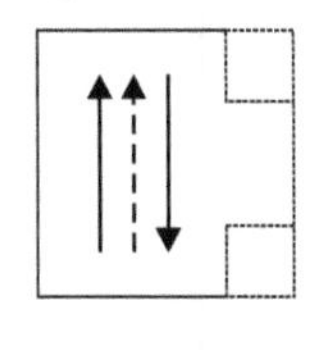
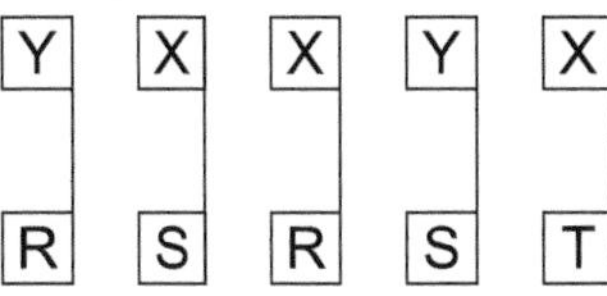

a b c d e

3.

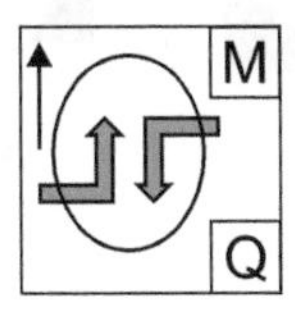

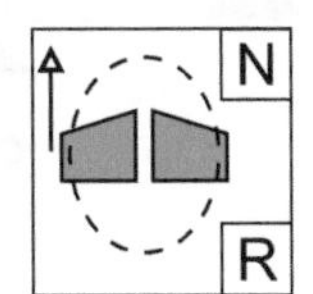

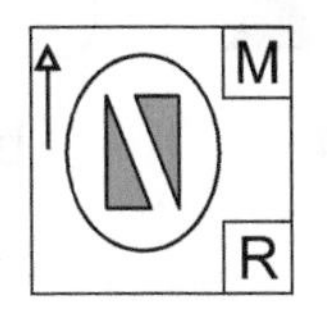

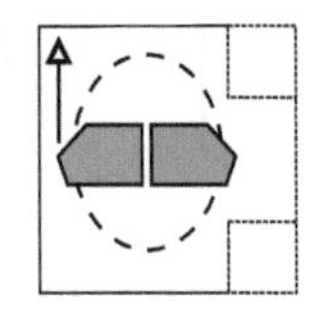
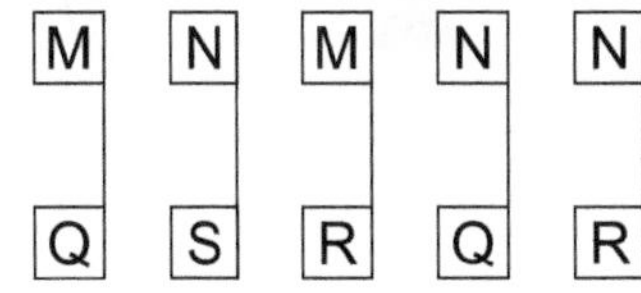

a b c d e

4.

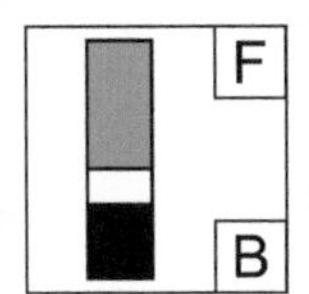

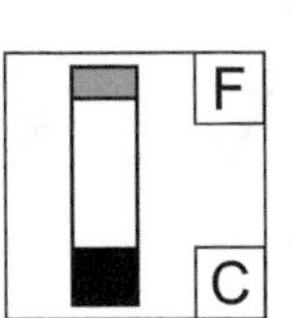

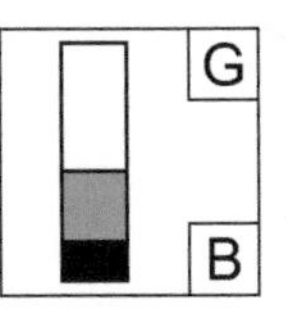

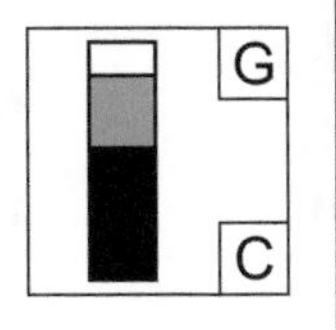

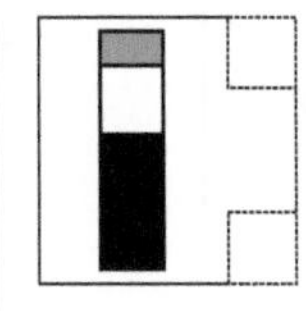
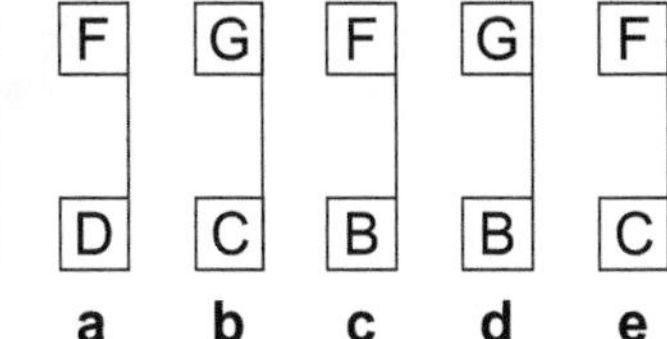

a b c d e

5.

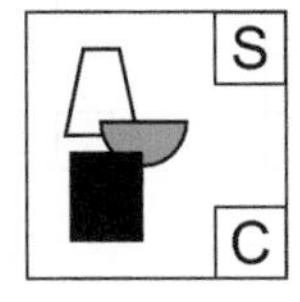

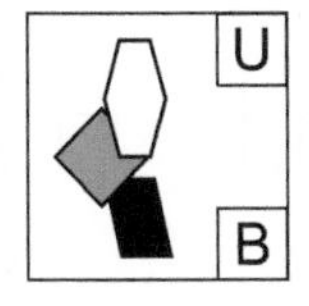

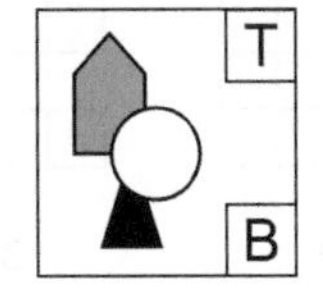

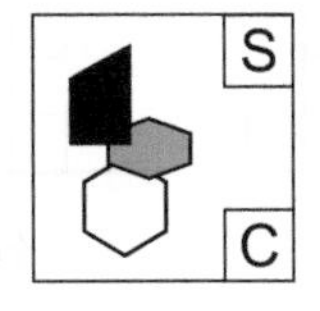

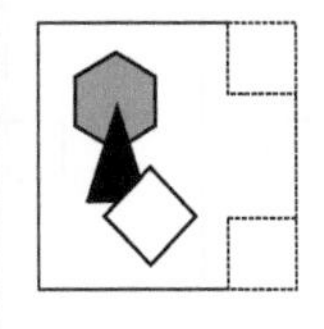
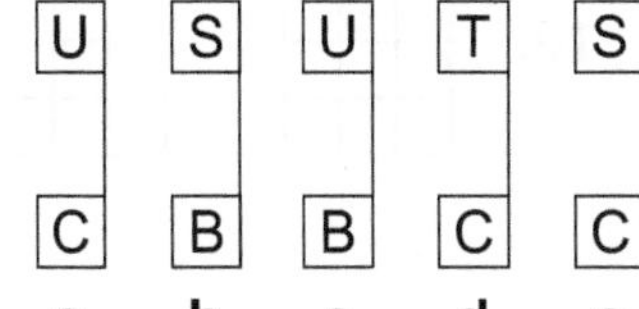

a b c d e

For each question below there are two figures that are like each other in some way.
Find which of the five figures on the right is most like the two figures on the left.

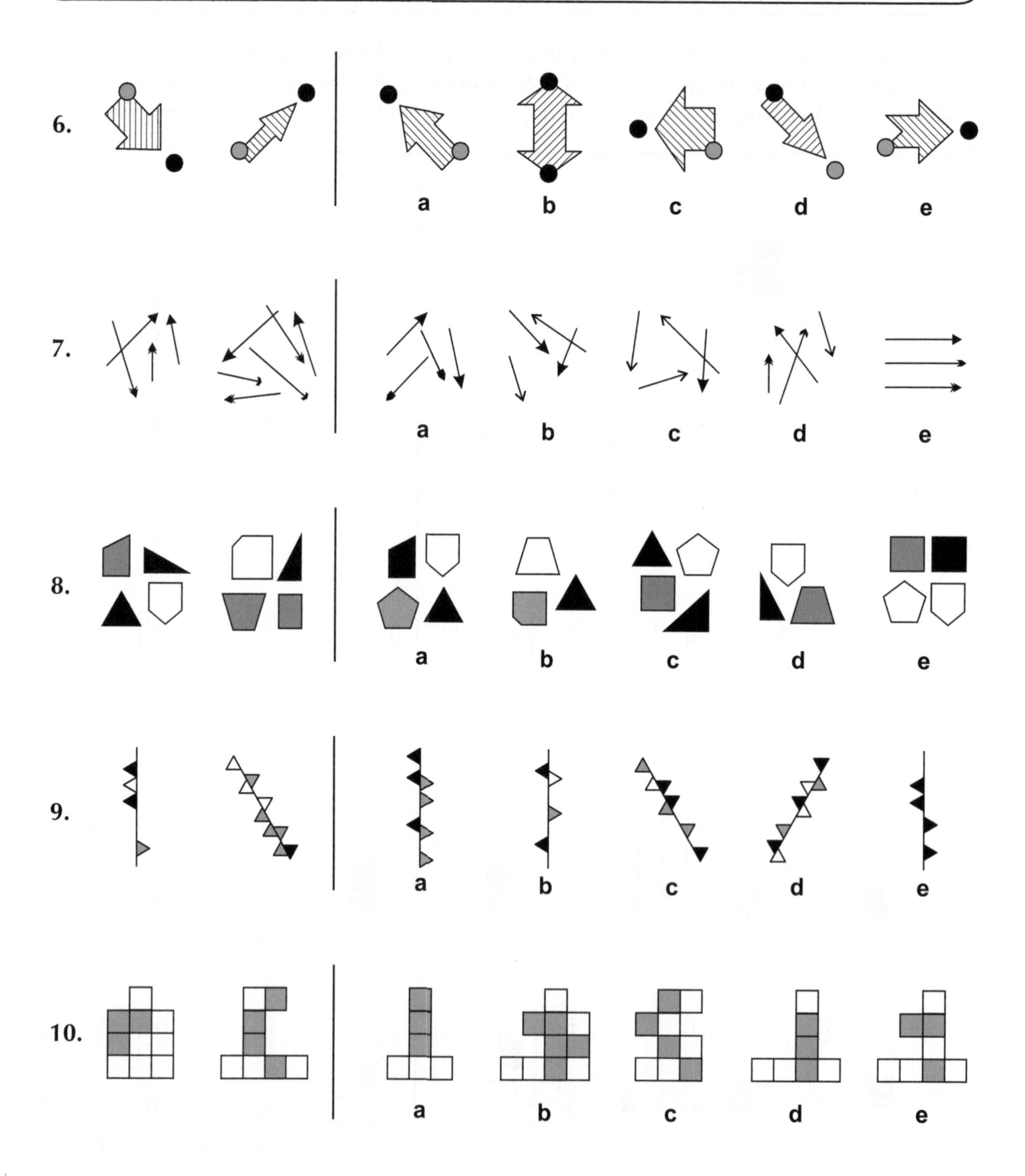

Each question has two shapes on the left with an arrow between them.
The first shape is changed in some way to become the second. There is then a third shape followed by an arrow and a choice of five shapes. Choose the shape on the right that relates to the third shape like the second does to the first.

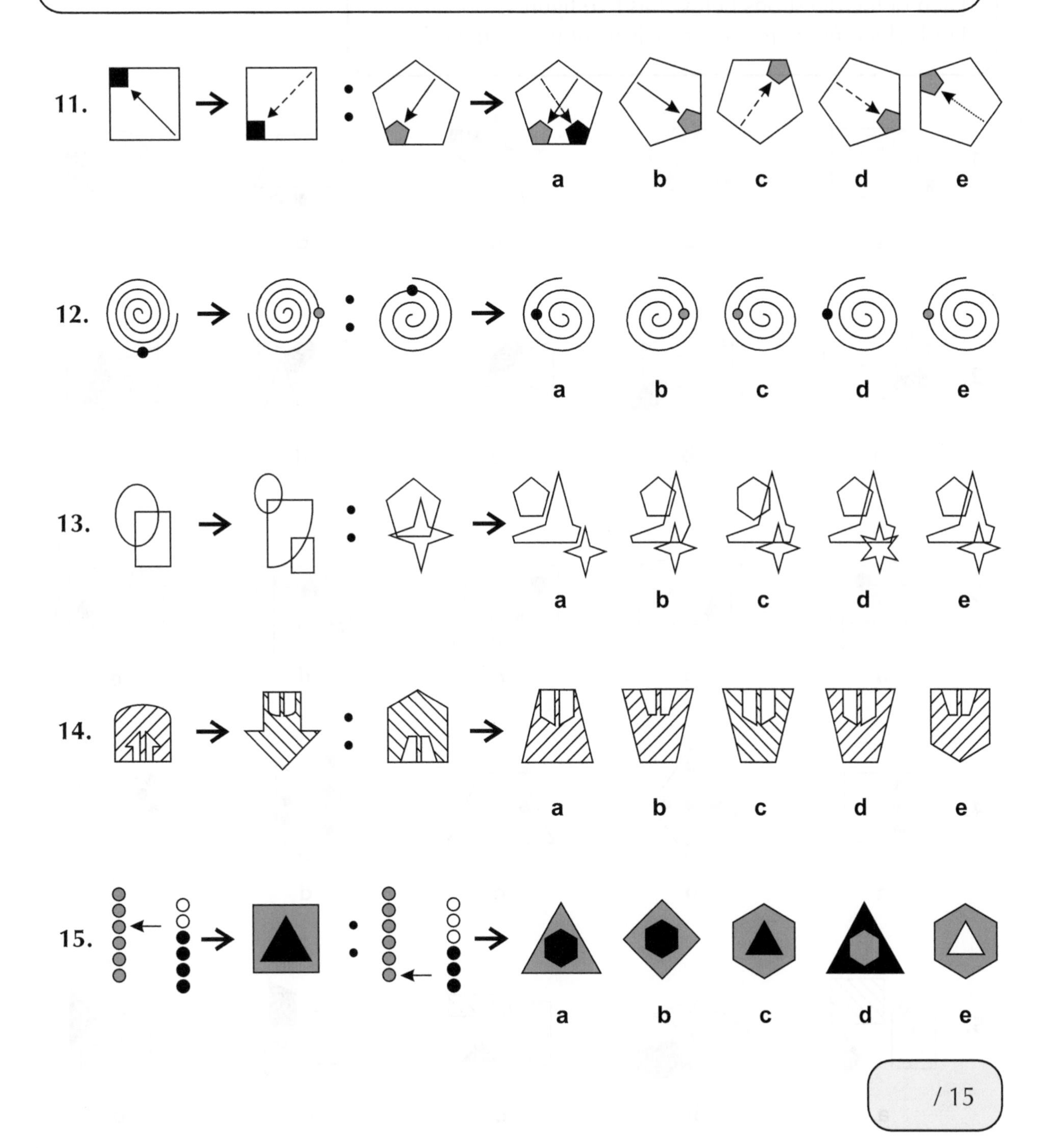

/ 15

Test 24

You have **10 minutes** to do this test. Circle the letter underneath each correct answer.

Each of the questions below has five figures.
Find which figure in each row is most unlike the others.

1.

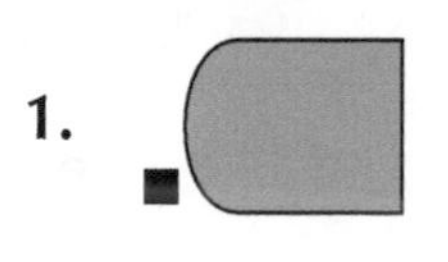

a

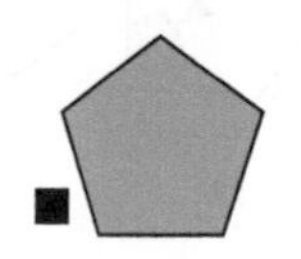

b

c

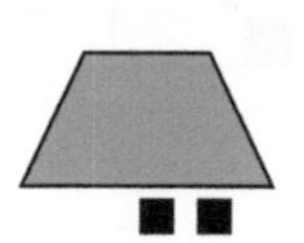

d

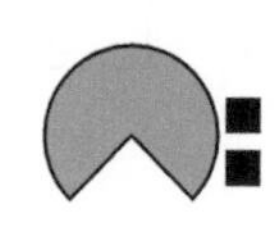

e

2.

a

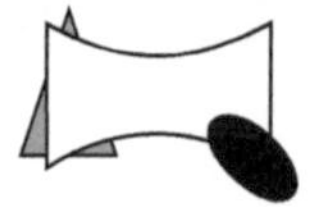

b

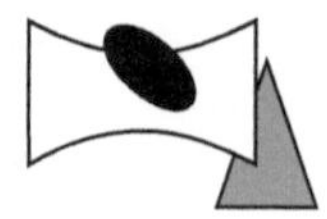

c

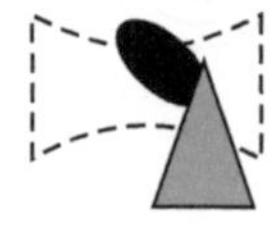

d

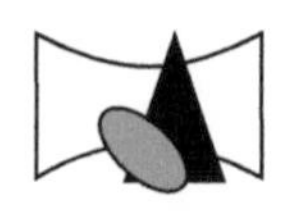

e

3.

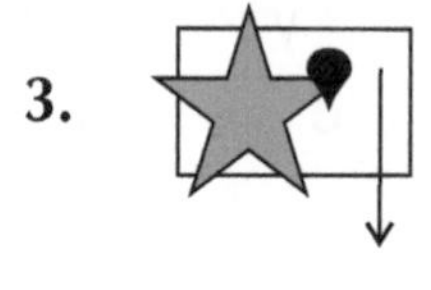

a

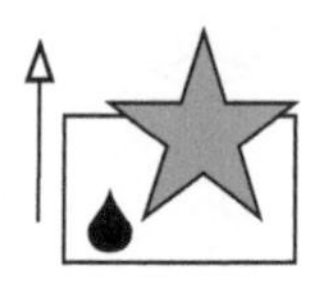

b

c

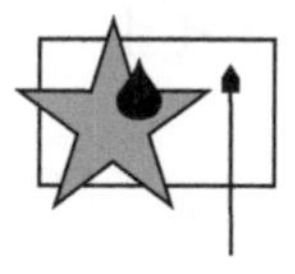

d

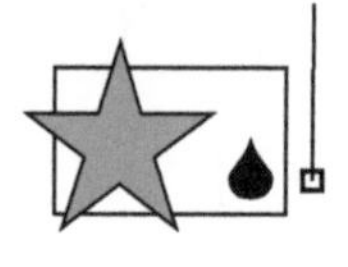

e

4.

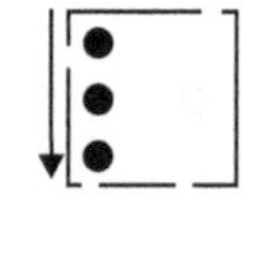

a

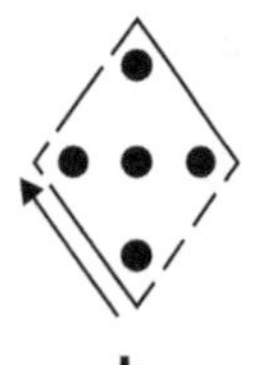

b

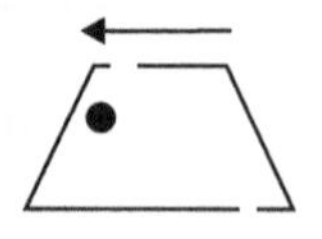

c

d

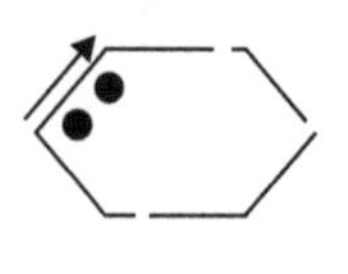

e

5.

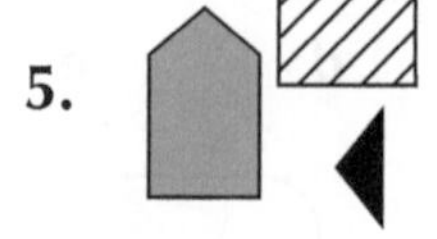

a

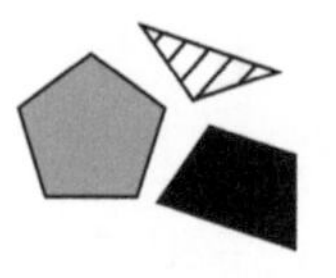

b

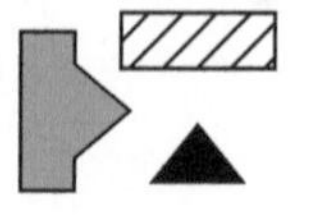

c

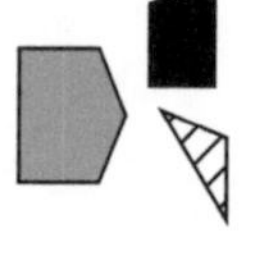

d

e

Each question has some shapes on the left with code letters that describe them. You need to work out what the code letters mean. There is then a shape on its own next to a choice of five codes. Work out which code describes this shape.

6.

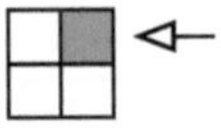

BK

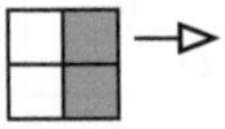

CL

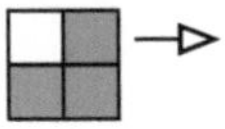

CM

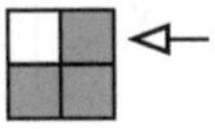

BL	BM	CK	CM	BK
a	**b**	**c**	**d**	**e**

7.

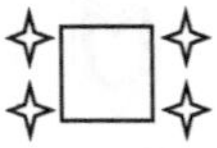

ER

ES

FS

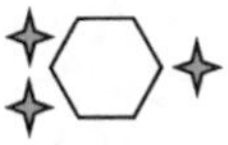

FT

ET	ER	FS	FR	ES
a	**b**	**c**	**d**	**e**

8.

ZWH

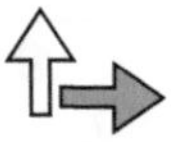

YWG

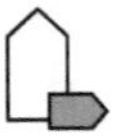

ZVG

ZWG	ZVG	YVG	YWH	YWG
a	**b**	**c**	**d**	**e**

9.

AMR

BLR

ALR

BMQ

BMR	BLQ	BLR	AMR	ALQ
a	**b**	**c**	**d**	**e**

Each of these questions has five squares on the left that are arranged in order.
One of the squares is missing. One of the squares on the right should go in its place.
Find which one of the five squares on the right should go in place of the empty square.

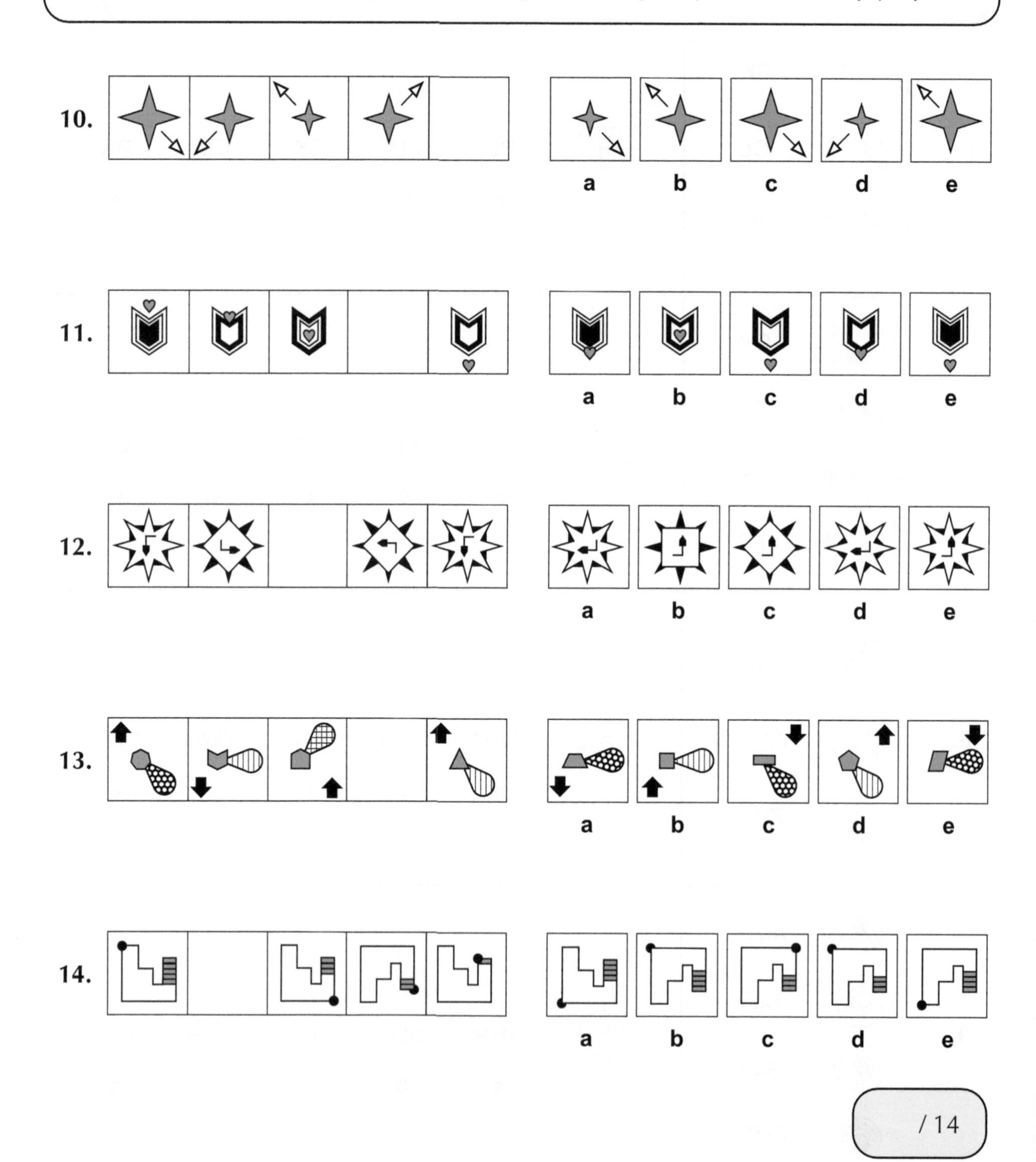

/ 14

Puzzles 8

Give these puzzles a go — they'll help you practise your **layering** skills.

Abra-card-abra

A magic trick uses five cards labelled A to E.

During the magic trick, the cards are always placed down on the table in the same order.

Two ways that the cards are laid out on the table are shown on the right.

Write down the order that the cards must be placed on the table.

______ 1st ______ 2nd ______ 3rd ______ 4th ______ 5th

Perplexing Post

A postal worker uses a rule to work out which piles of post to deliver one day. If a pile follows the rule, she will deliver it that day.

Here are some piles of post and whether or not they follow the rule.

This pile does follow the rule.

This pile does **not** follow the rule.

This pile does follow the rule.

This pile does follow the rule.

Which of the piles of post below should she deliver that day? Circle your answer.

A 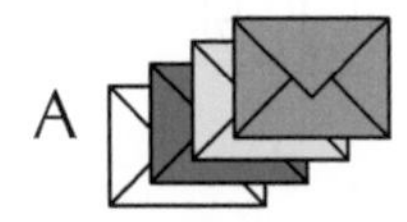

B 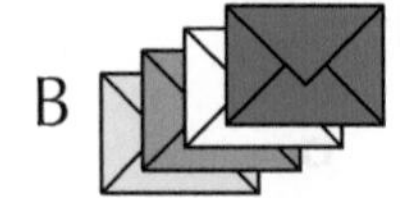

C 

Test 25

You have **10 minutes** to do this test. Circle the letter underneath each correct answer.

On the left of each question below is a big square with one small empty square. Find which of the five squares on the right should replace the empty square.

1. 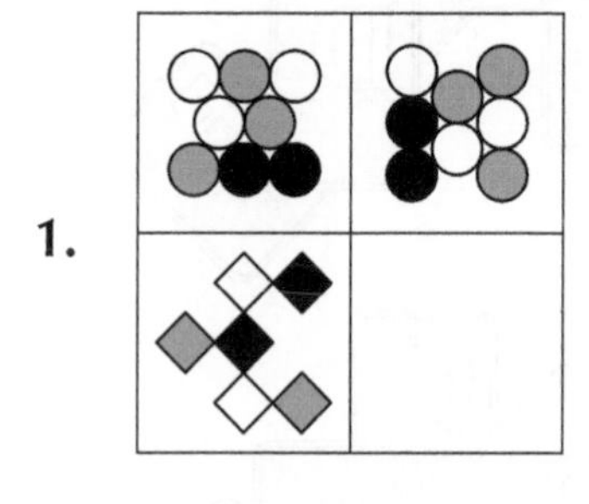

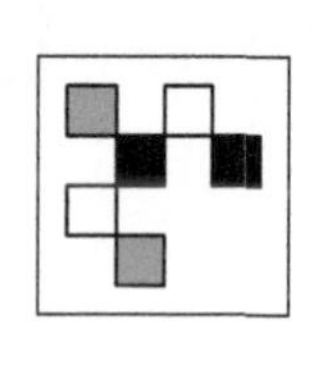 a  b  c  d 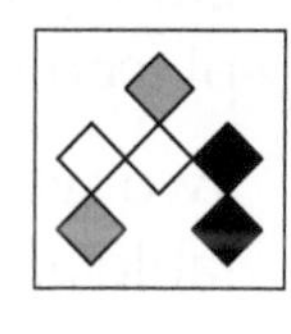 e

2. 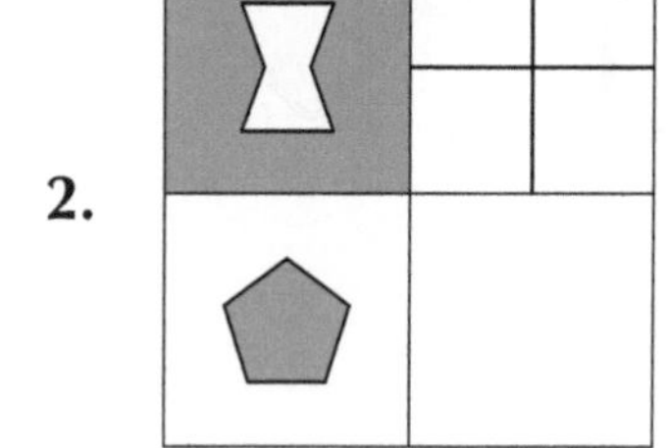

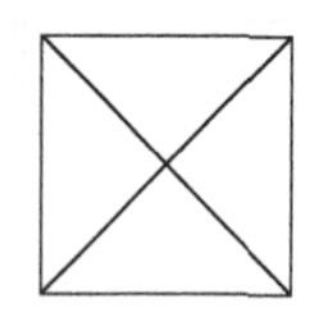 a 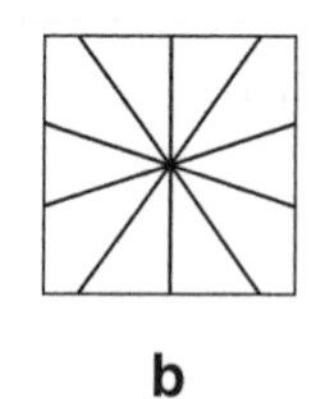 b 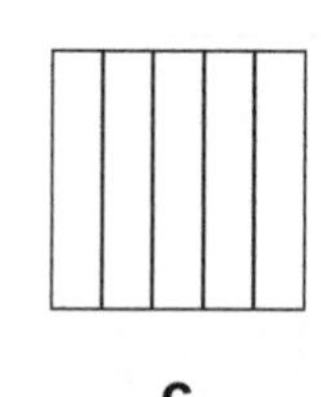 c 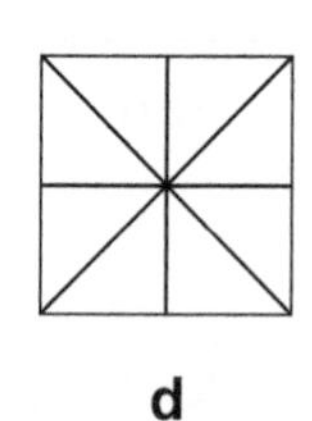 d 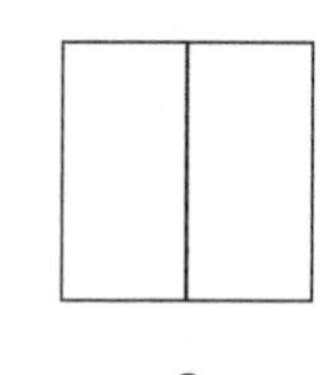 e

3. 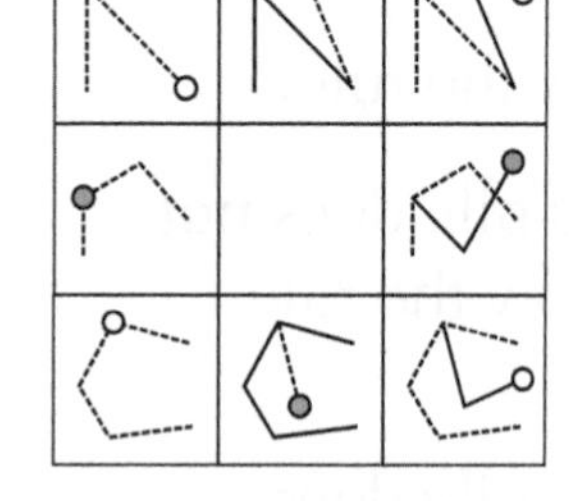

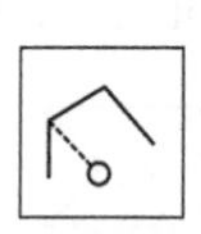 a 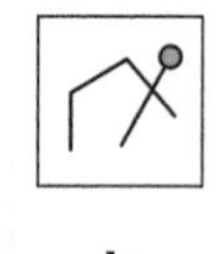 b  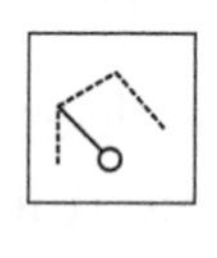 c 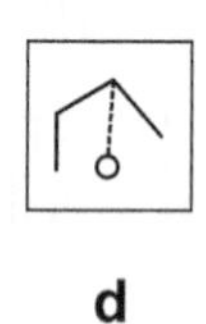 d  e

4. 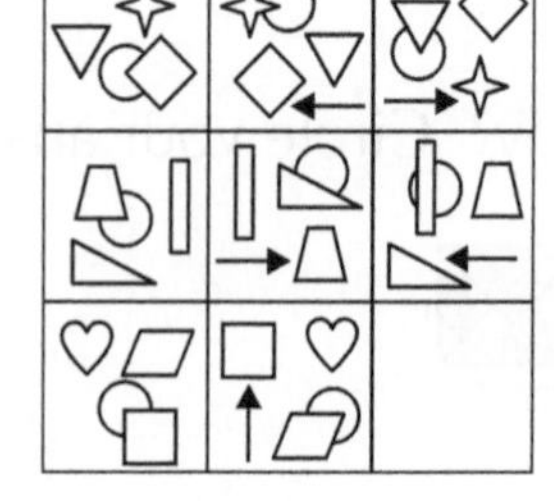

 a  b c 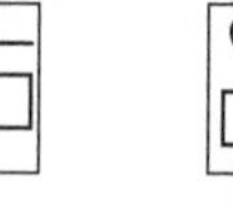 d 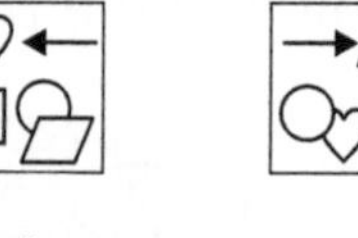 e

In the boxes on the left are shapes with code letters. The top letters have a different meaning to the bottom ones. Work out how the letters go with the shapes and then find the code for the new shape from the five codes on the right.

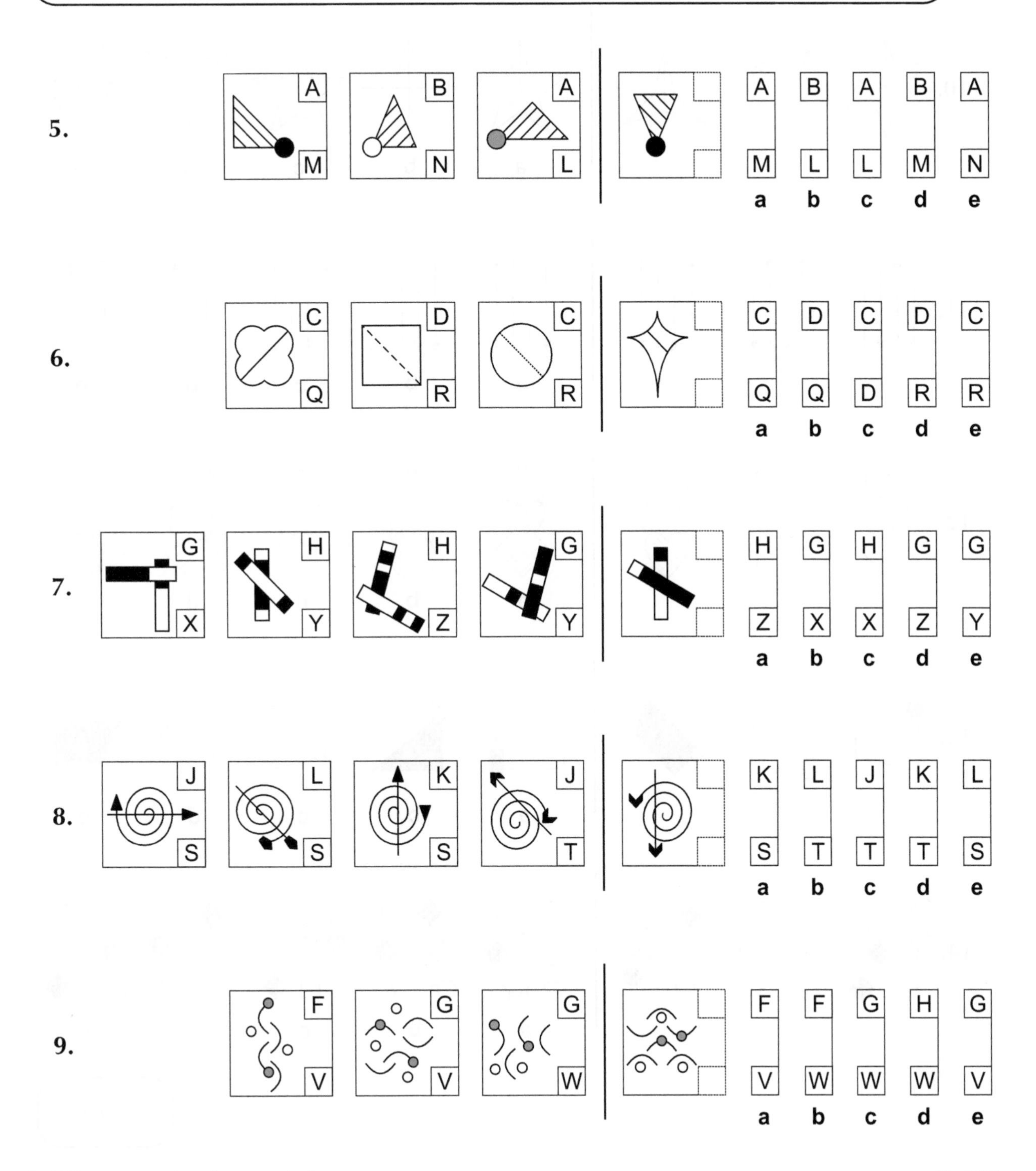

For each of the questions below there are three figures that are like each other in some way. Find which of the five figures on the right is most like the three figures on the left.

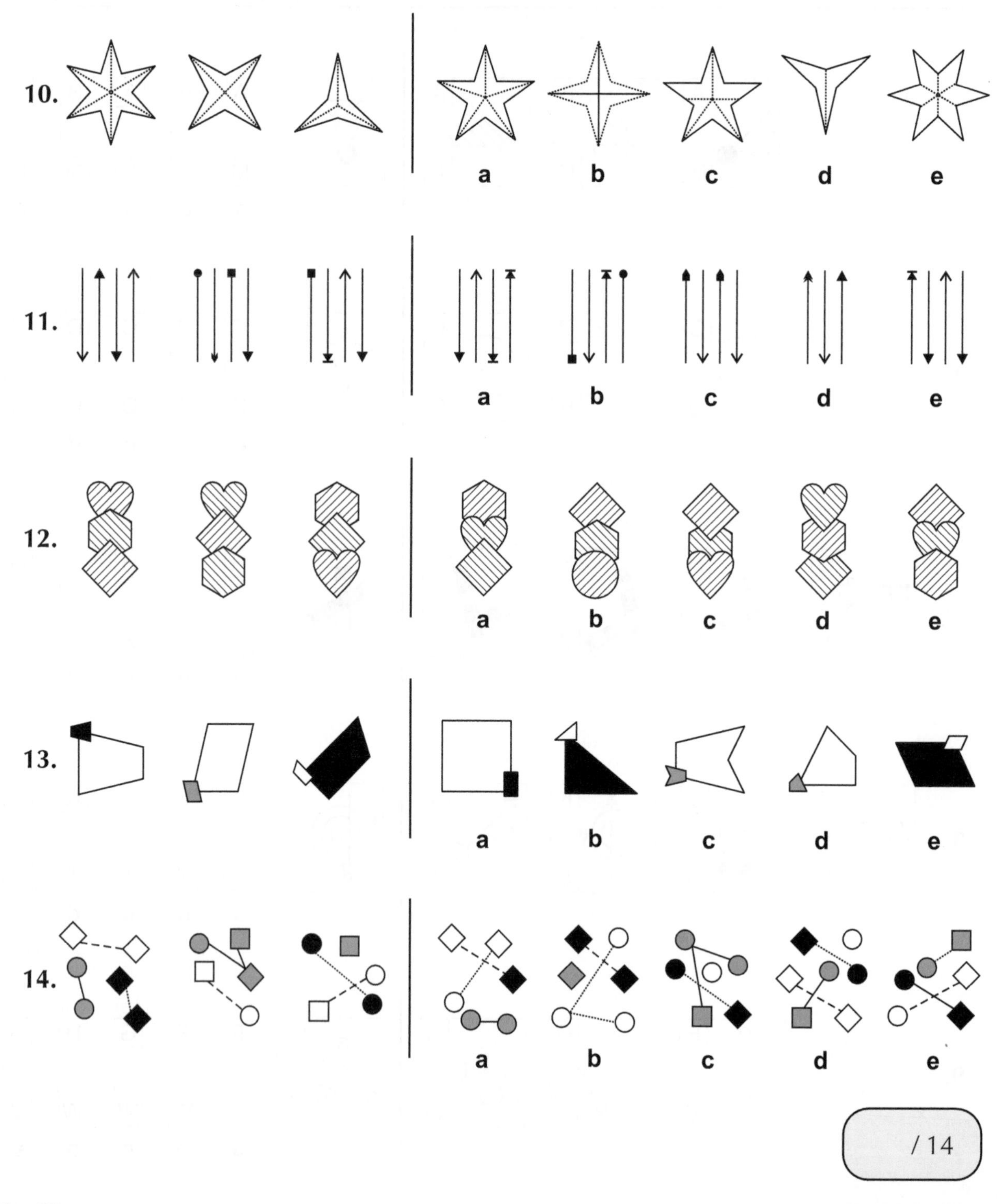

/ 14

Test 26

You have **10 minutes** to do this test. Circle the letter underneath each correct answer.

Each question has two shapes on the left with an arrow between them.
The first shape is changed in some way to become the second. There is then a third shape followed by an arrow and a choice of five shapes. Choose the shape on the right that relates to the third shape like the second does to the first.

1. 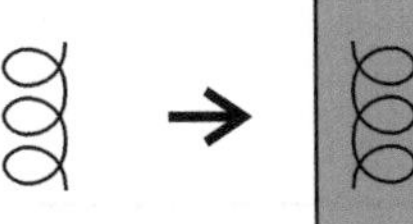 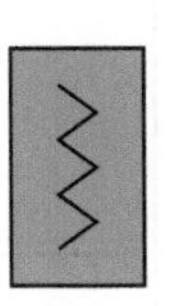 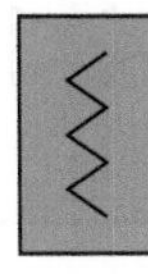 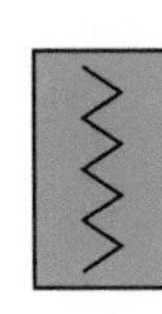

a b c d e

2. 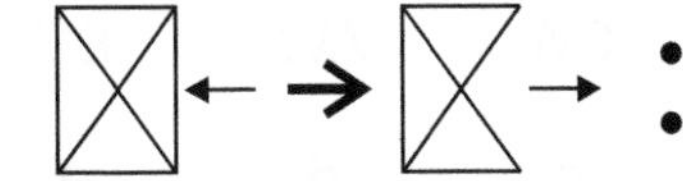 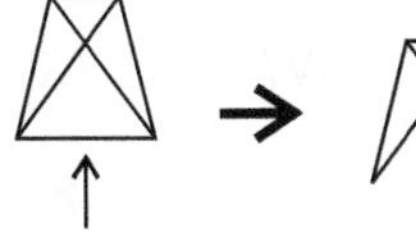 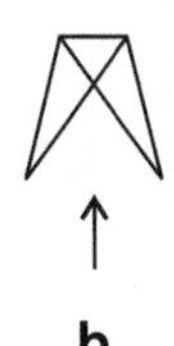 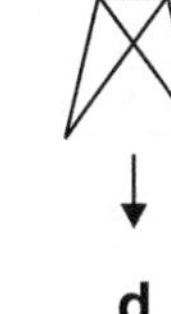

a b c d e

3. 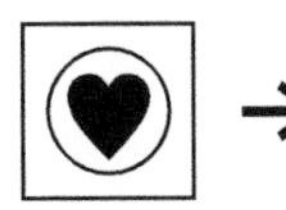 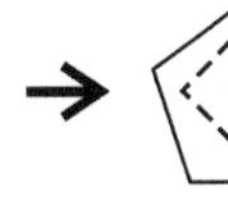  

a b c d e

4. 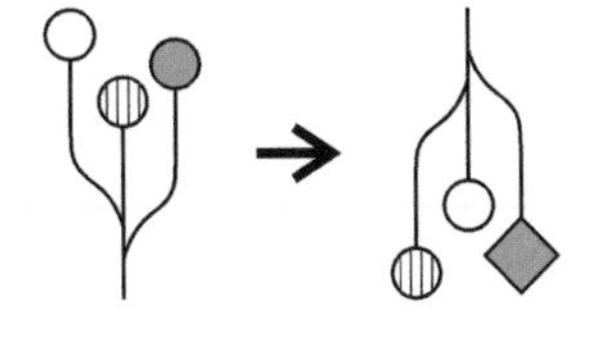 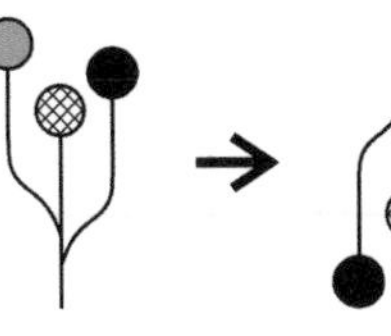 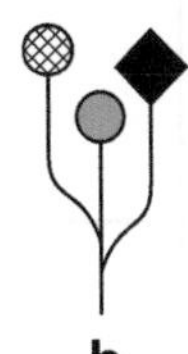 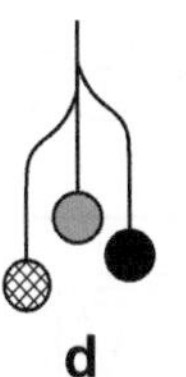 

a b c d e

5.  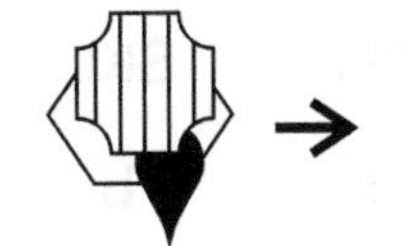 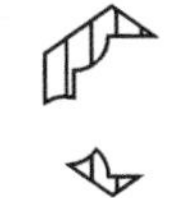    

a b c d e

Each question has some shapes on the left with code letters that describe them. You need to work out what the code letters mean. There is then a shape on its own next to a choice of five codes. Work out which code describes this shape.

6.

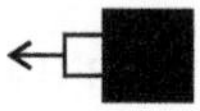

EMY

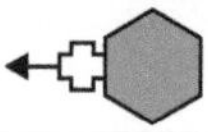

ENX

FMX

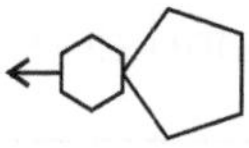

ENY	FNX	FMY	ENX	FNY
a	b	c	d	e

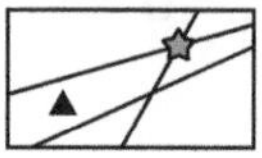

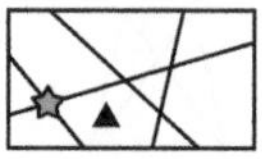

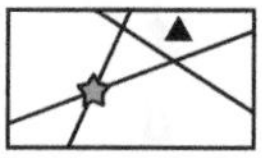

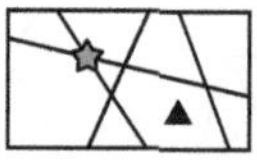

7.

AV

BV

AW

BW	AV	CW	AW	BV
a	b	c	d	e

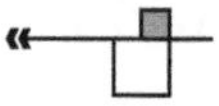

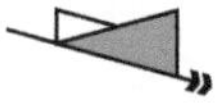

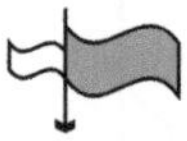

8.

GR

GQ

HQ

HP

HQ	GR	HP	GQ	GP
a	b	c	d	e

9.

SLC

TKD

SJD

TKC

SLD	SKC	SLC	TJD	TLC
a	b	c	d	e

For each question below there are two figures that are like each other in some way. Find which of the five figures on the right is most like the two figures on the left.

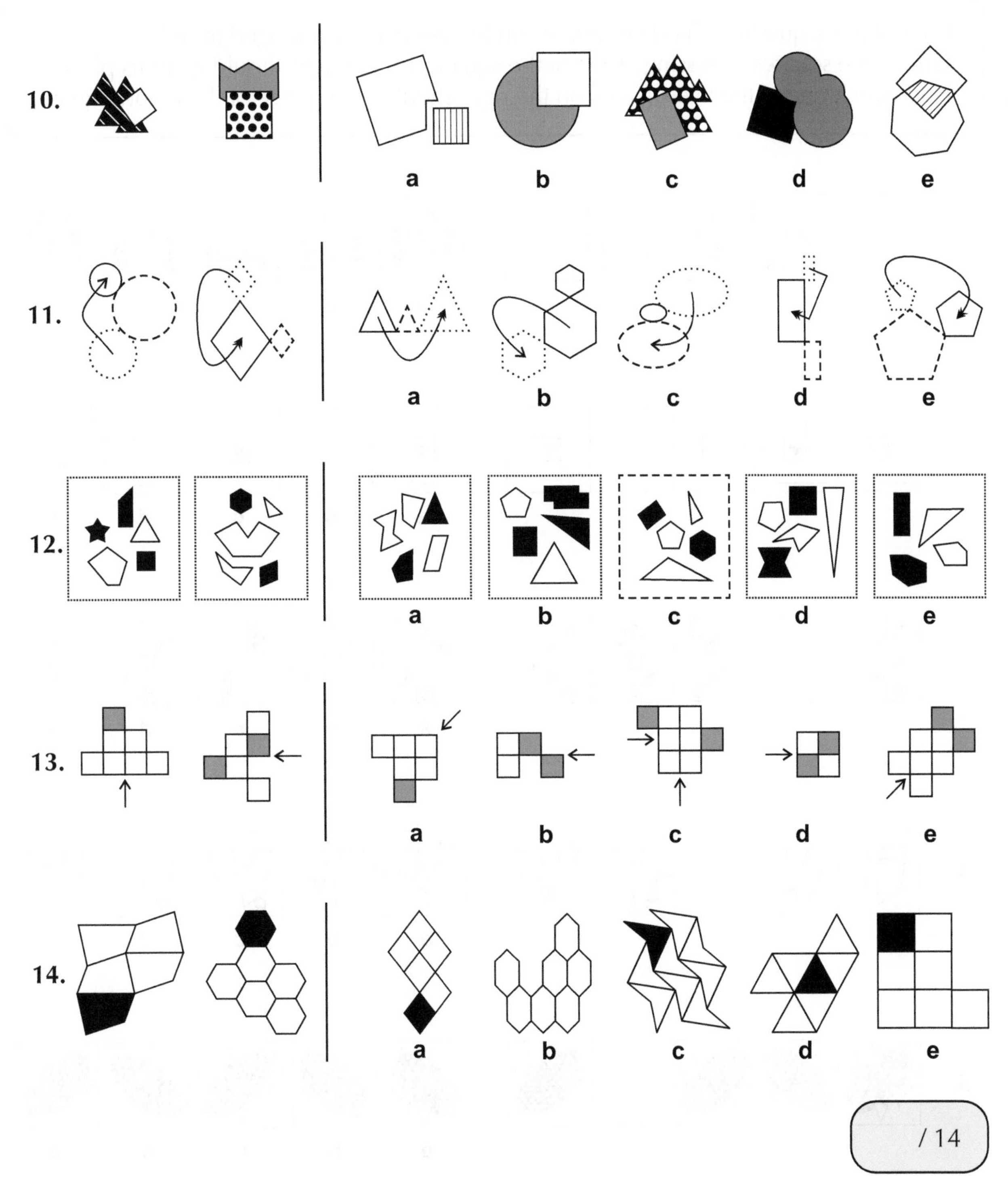

/ 14

Test 27

You have **10 minutes** to do this test. Circle the letter underneath each correct answer.

Each of these questions has five squares on the left that are arranged in order.
One of the squares is missing. One of the squares on the right should go in its place.
Find which one of the five squares on the right should go in place of the empty square.

1. 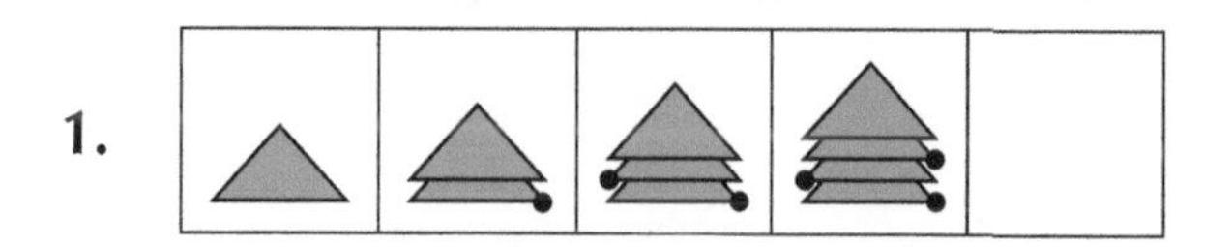 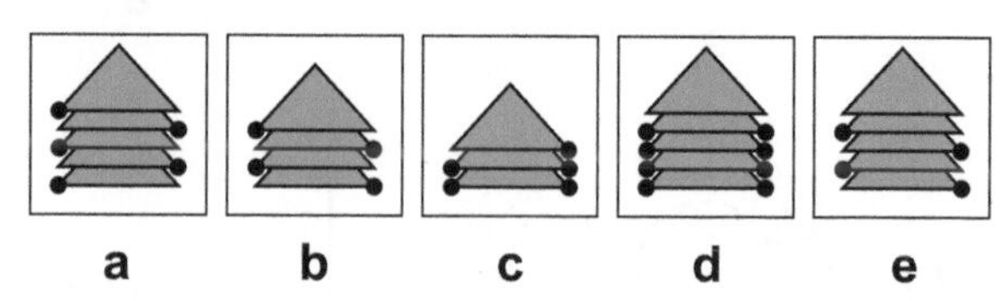

a b c d e

2. 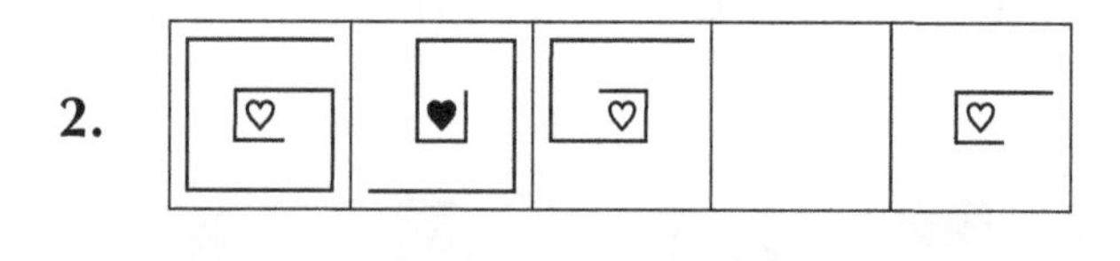 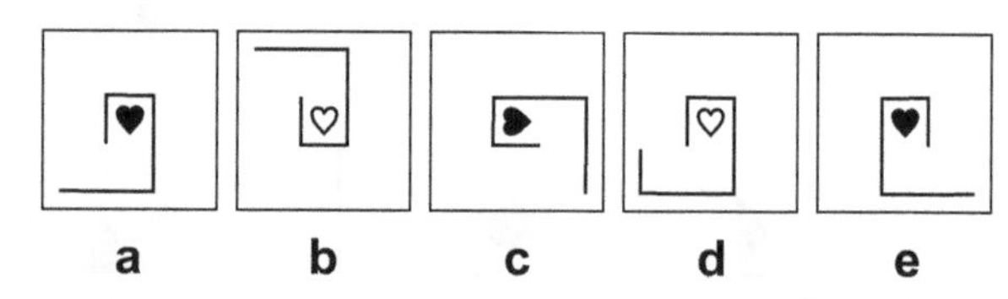

a b c d e

3. 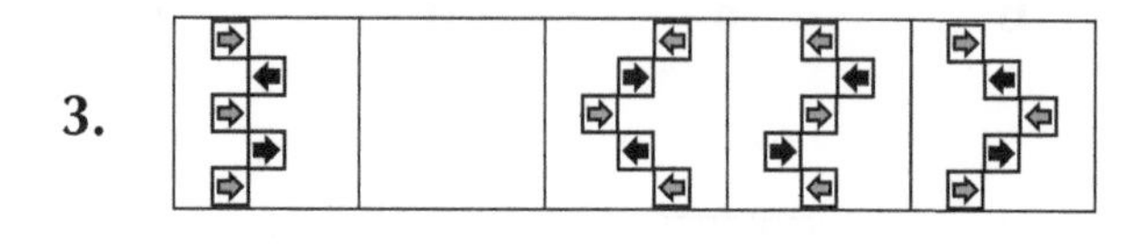 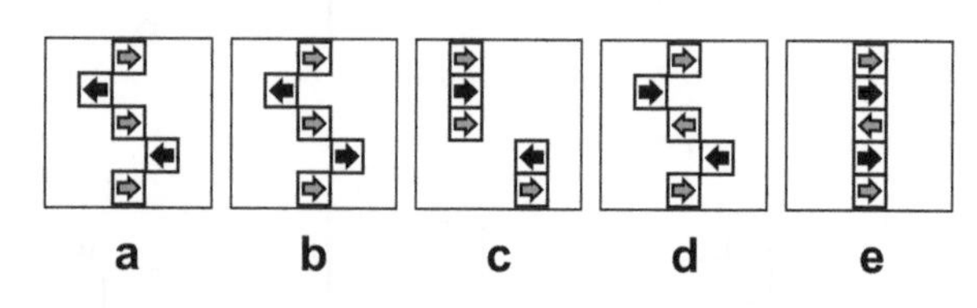

a b c d e

4. 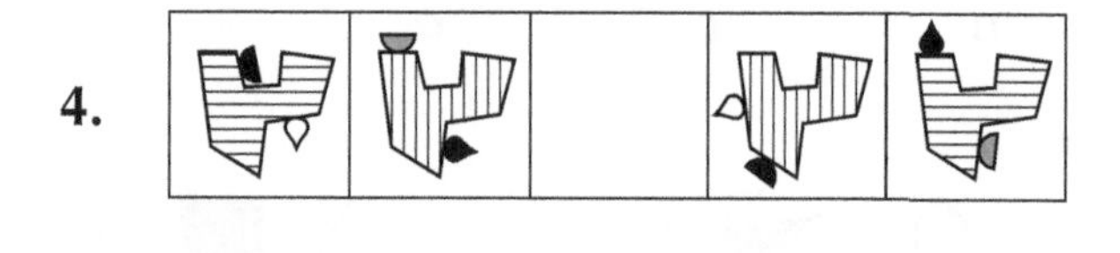 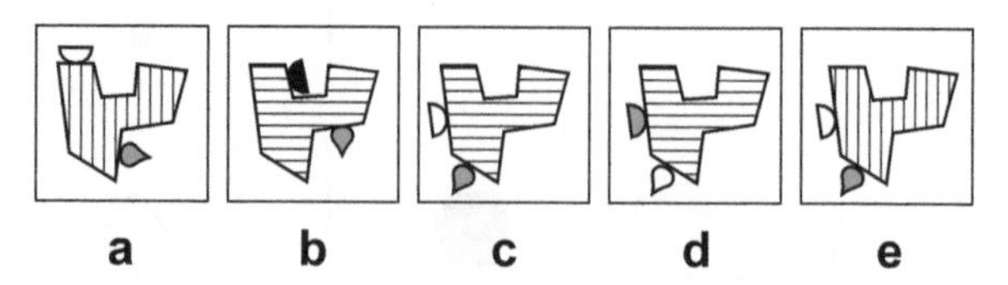

a b c d e

5. 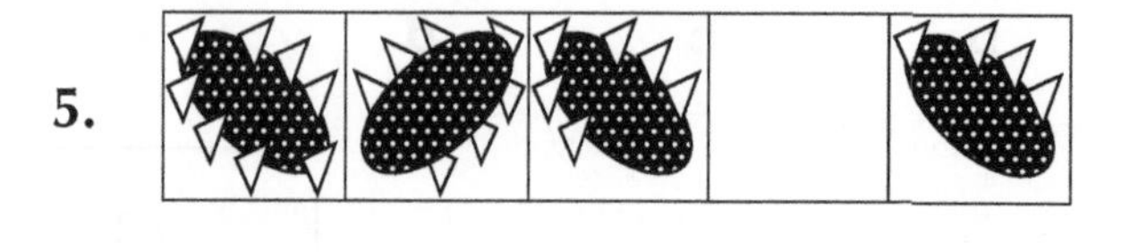 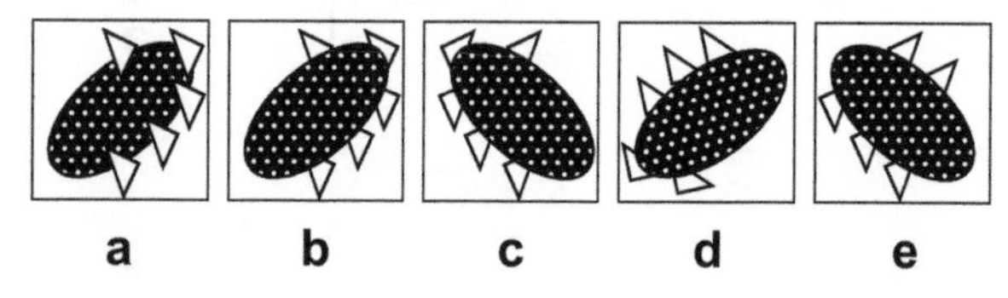

a b c d e

In the boxes on the left are shapes with code letters. The top letters have a different meaning to the bottom ones. Work out how the letters go with the shapes and then find the code for the new shape from the five codes on the right.

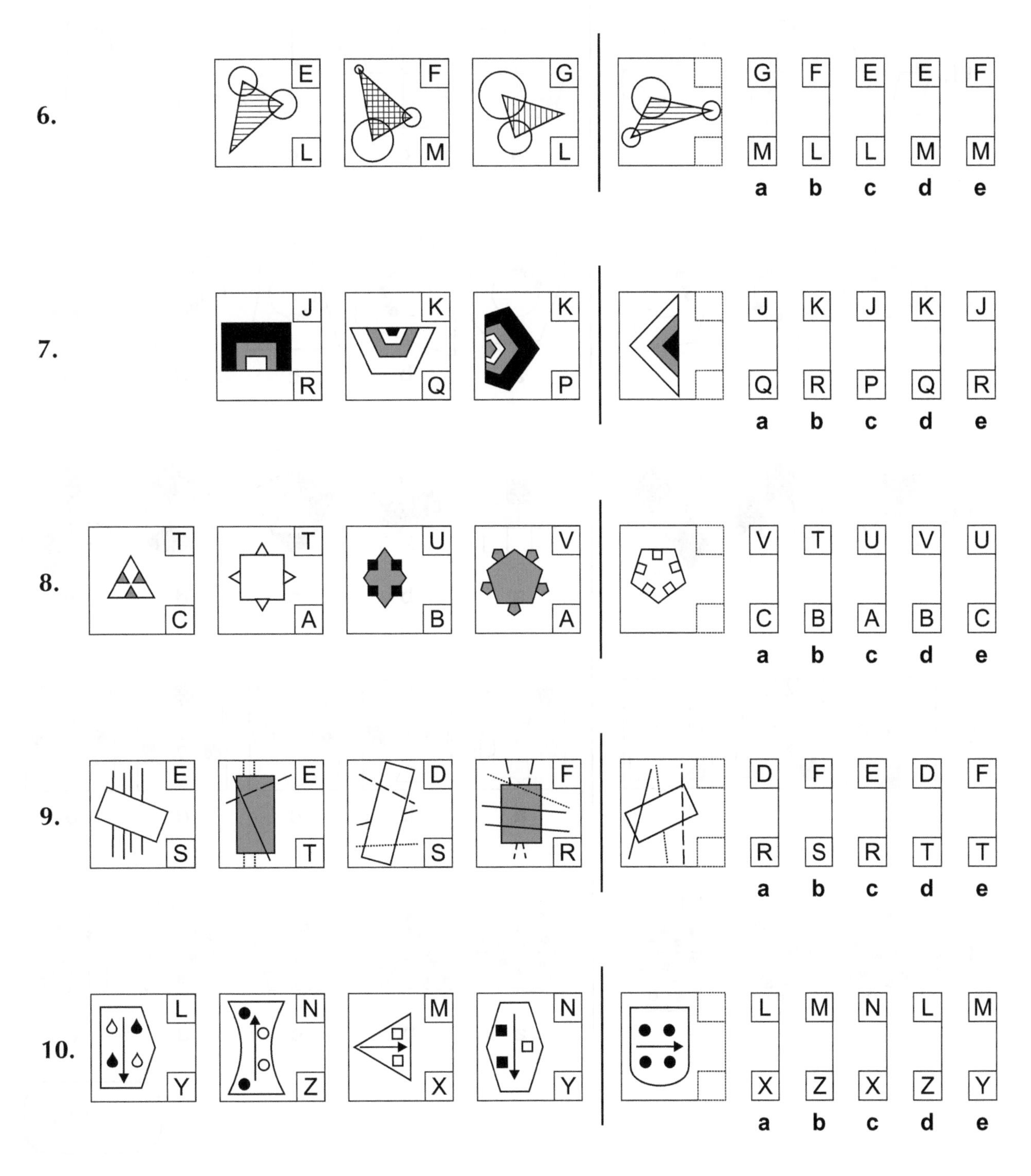

For each of the questions below there are three figures that are like each other in some way. Find which of the five figures on the right is most like the three figures on the left.

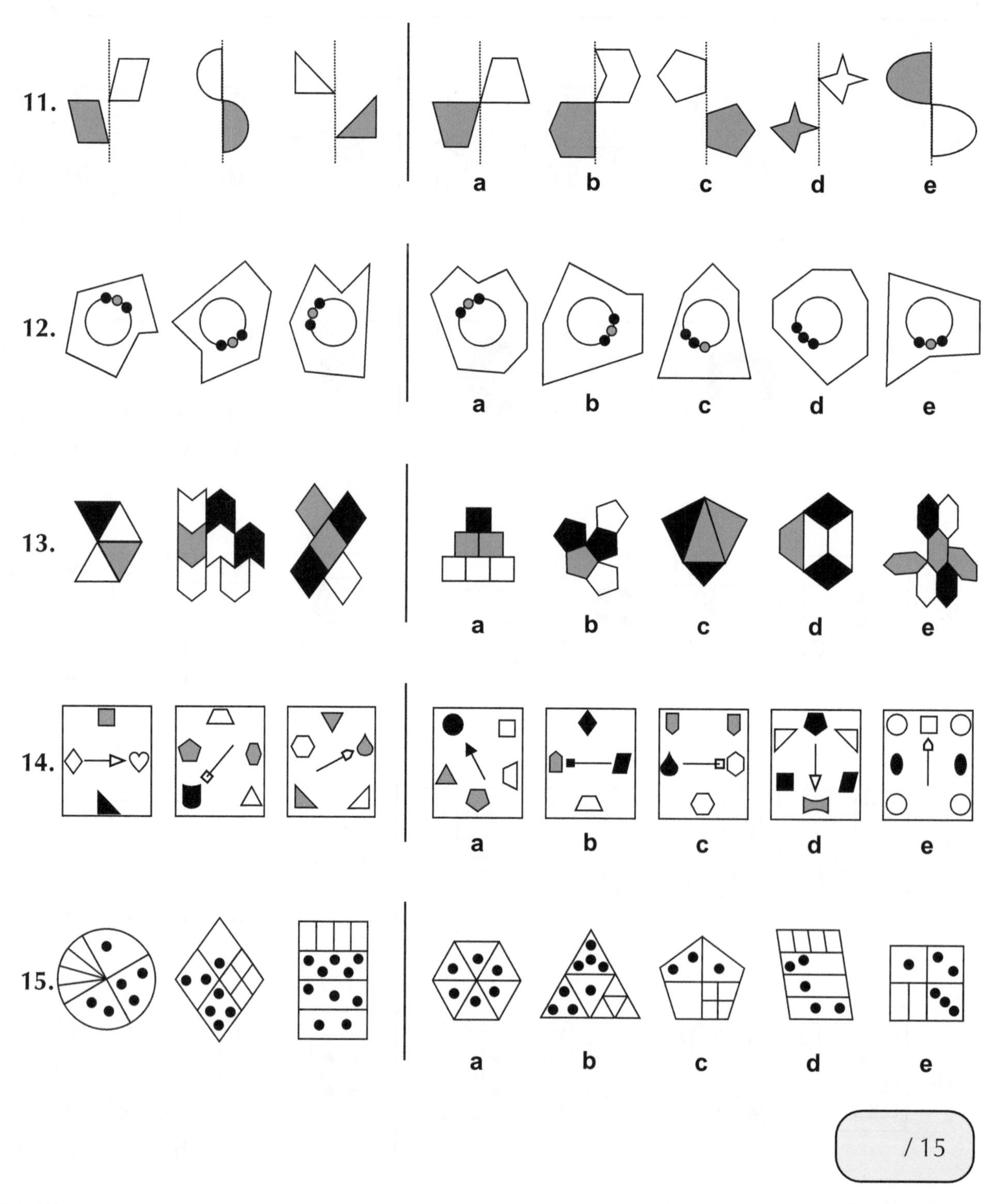

/ 15

Puzzles 9

Time to practise your **shape** and **coding** skills with this puzzle break.

Puzzling Pairs

In this grid, there are some shapes that appear twice and some that only appear once.

None of the shapes are rotated or reflected.

Shade in any squares that contain matching shapes to reveal the hidden pattern.

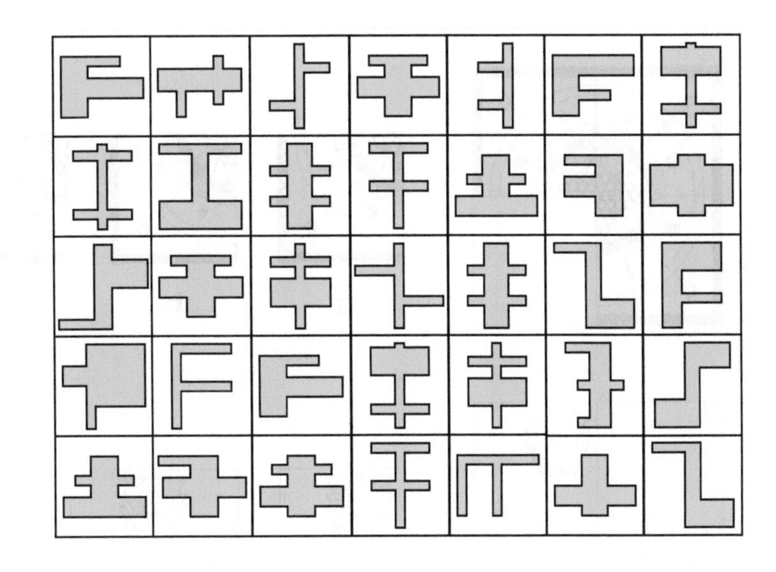

Decode the Bug

Barry the beekeeper sorts his bees into hives depending on three of their features. Each hive has a three-letter code that describes the bees in it.

The figures below show the codes for four different hives. Work out the code for the hive that the bee on the right should go in.

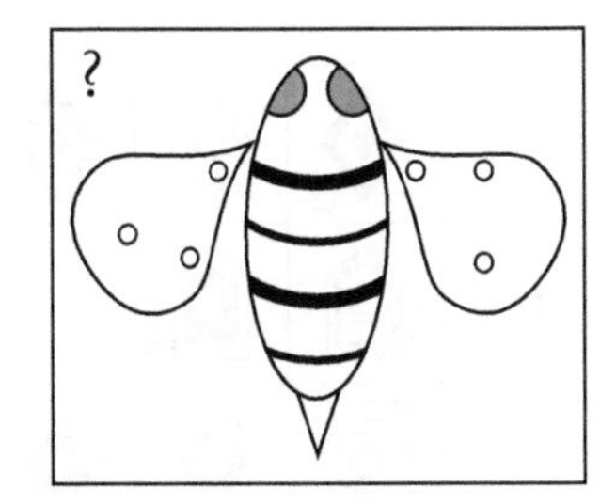

The hive code is: __ __ __

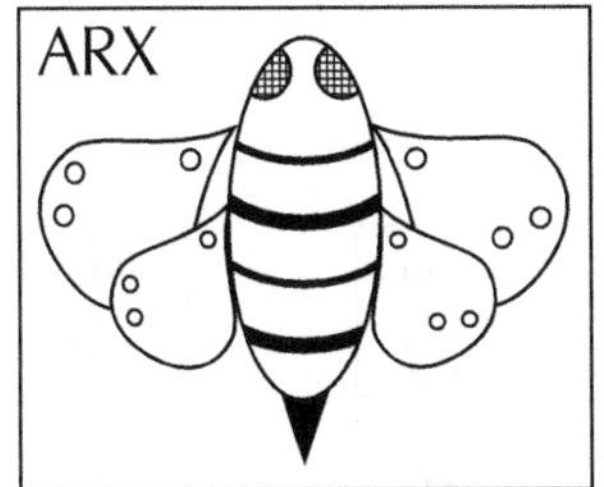

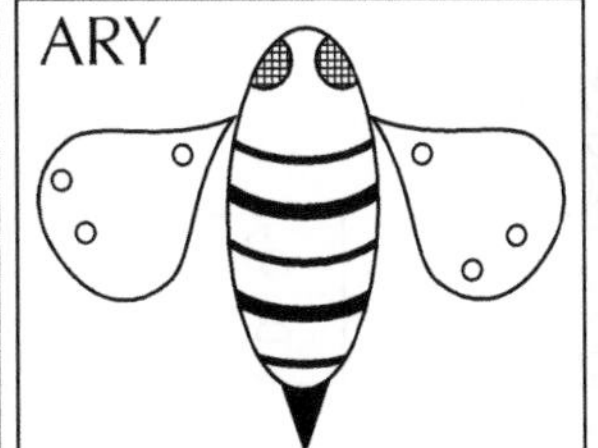

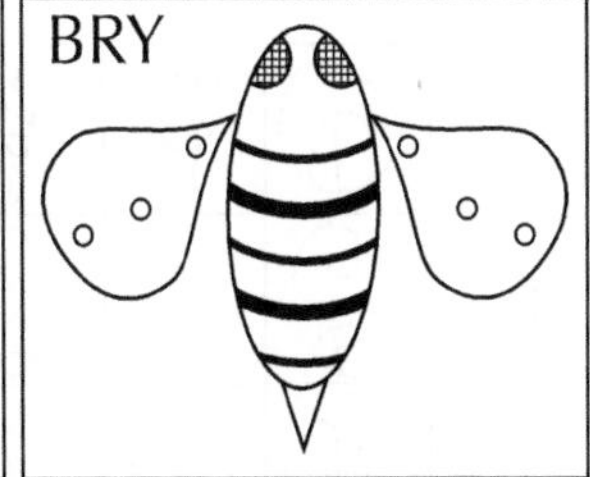

Test 28

You have **10 minutes** to do this test. Circle the letter underneath each correct answer.

On the left of each question below is a big square with one small empty square. Find which of the five squares on the right should replace the empty square.

1.

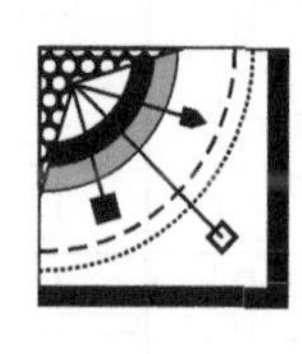
a

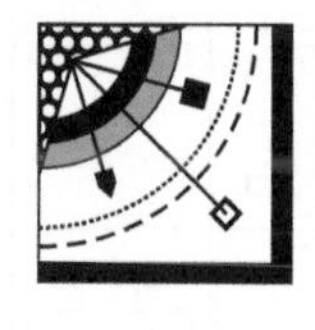
b

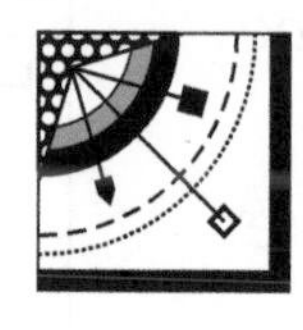
c

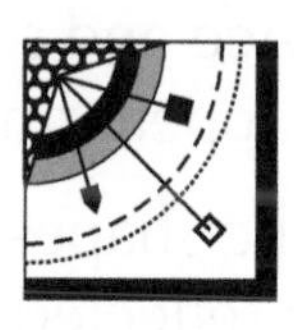
d

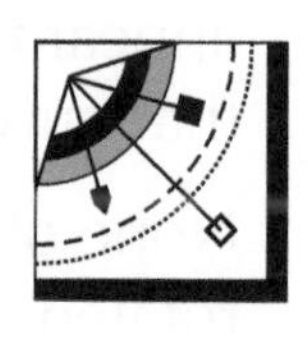
e

2.

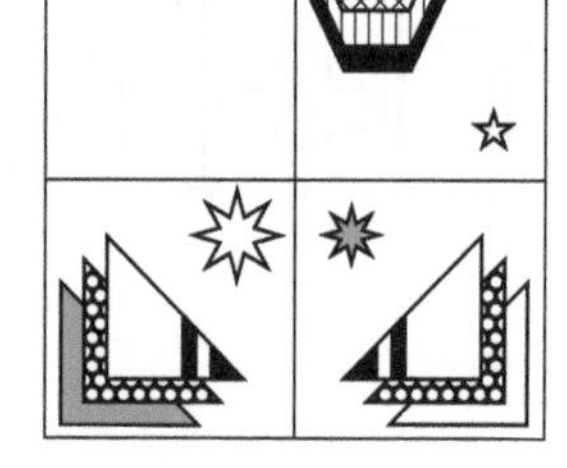

a

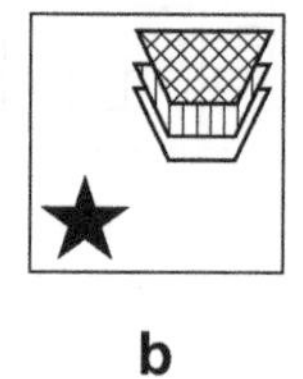
b

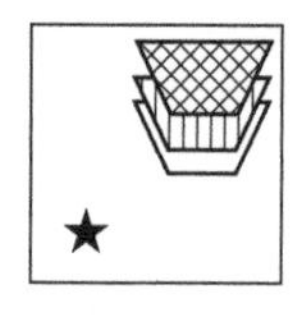
c

d

e

3.

a

b

c

d

e

4.

a

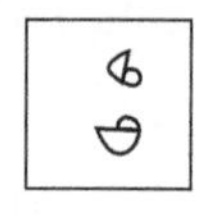
b

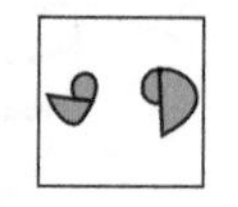
c

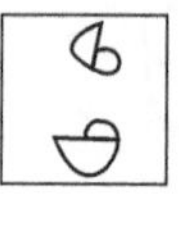
d

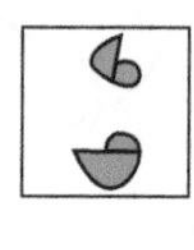
e

For each of the questions below there are three figures that are like each other in some way. Find which of the five figures on the right is most like the three figures on the left.

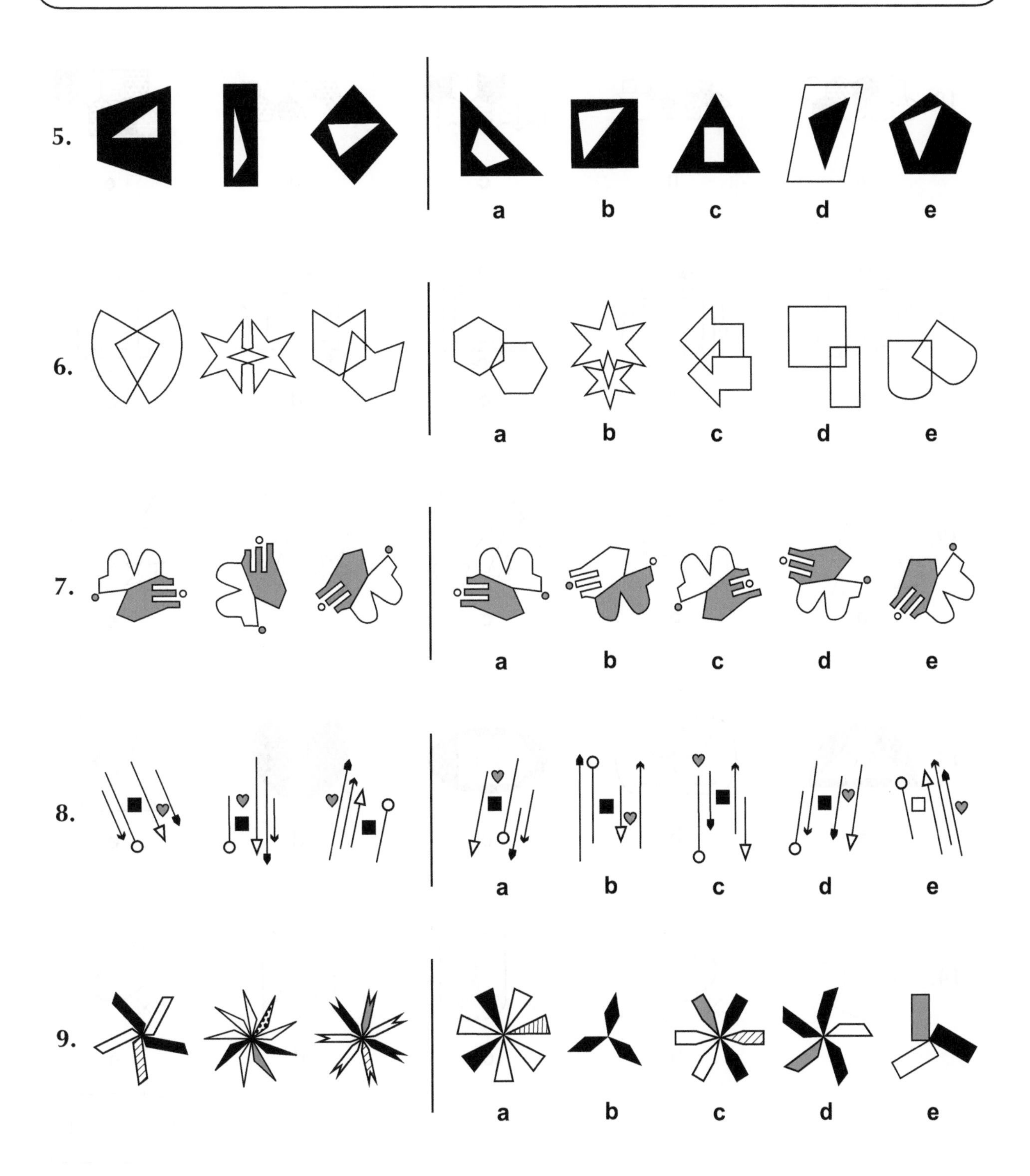

Each of the questions below has five figures.
Find which figure in each row is most unlike the others.

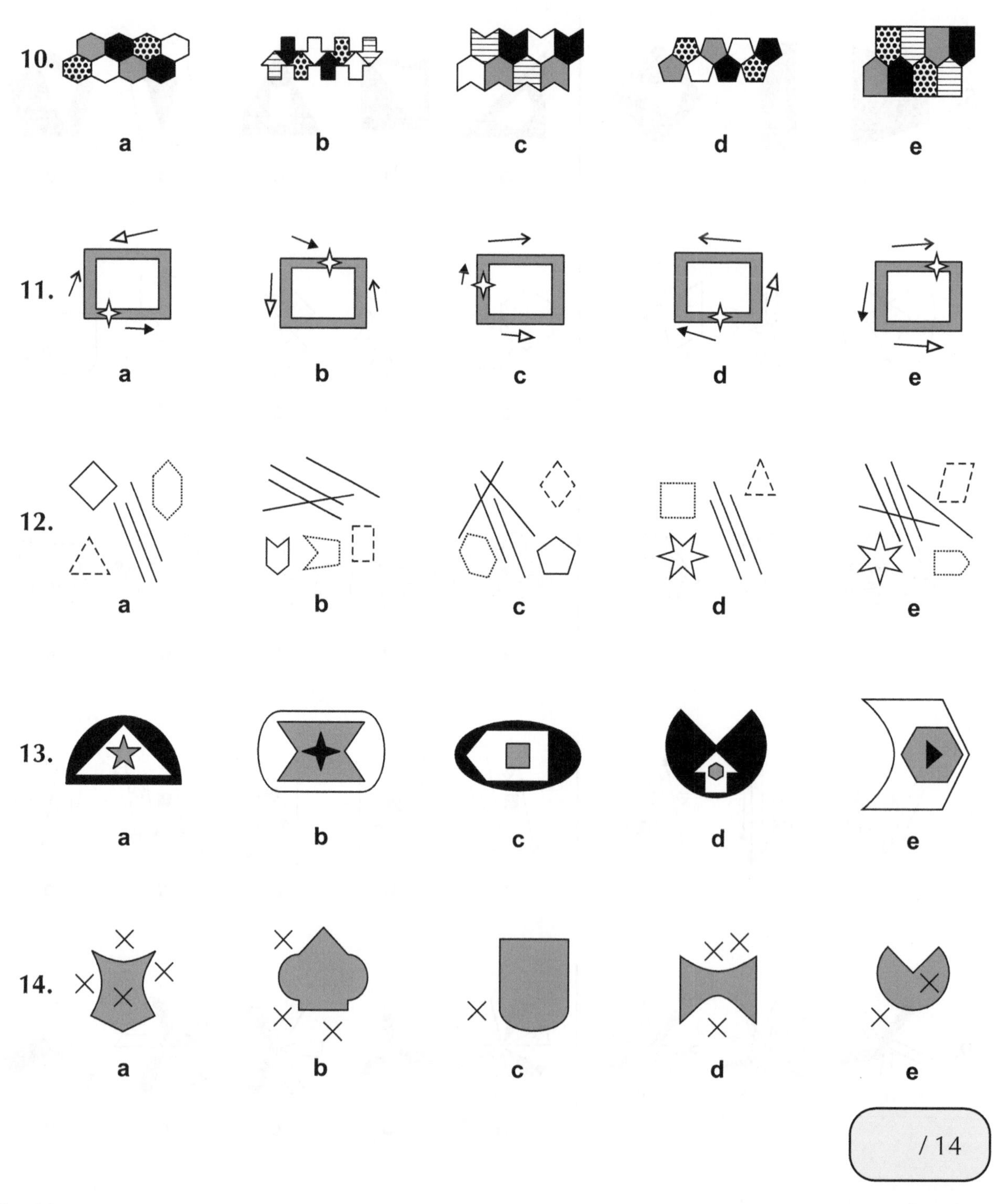

/ 14

Test 29

10

You have **10 minutes** to do this test. Circle the letter underneath each correct answer.

Each of these questions has five squares on the left that are arranged in order.
One of the squares is missing. One of the squares on the right should go in its place.
Find which one of the five squares on the right should go in place of the empty square.

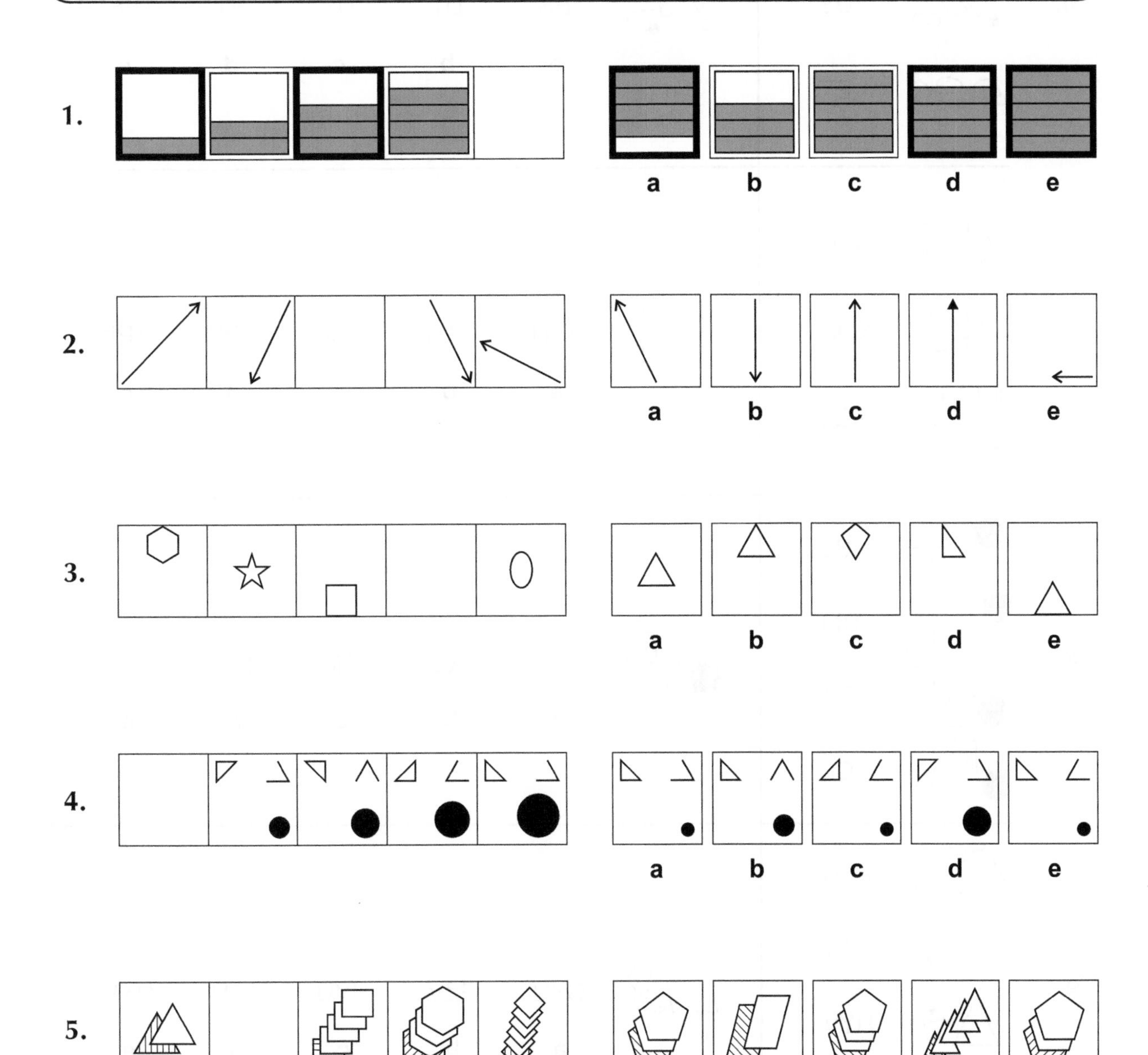

Each question has some shapes on the left with code letters that describe them. You need to work out what the code letters mean. There is then a shape on its own next to a choice of five codes. Work out which code describes this shape.

6.

Shape	Code
	DT
	DS
	ET

ES	DT	DS	ET	FS
a	b	c	d	e

7.

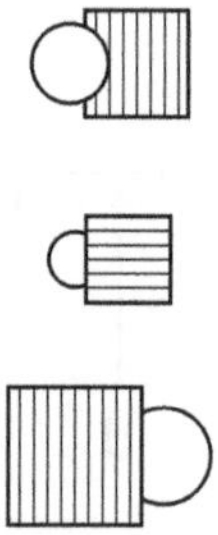

Shape	Code
	XPJ
	XQK
	YQJ

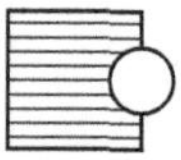

YQJ	XPJ	YQK	XPK	YPK
a	b	c	d	e

8.

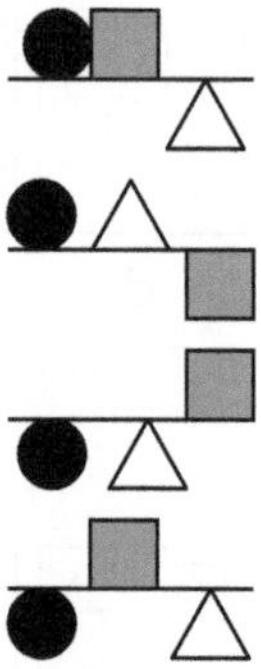

Shape	Code
	BL
	BM
	CM
	CL

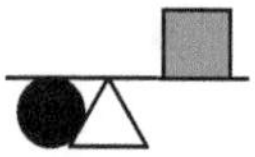

BL	AL	CM	BM	CL
a	b	c	d	e

9.

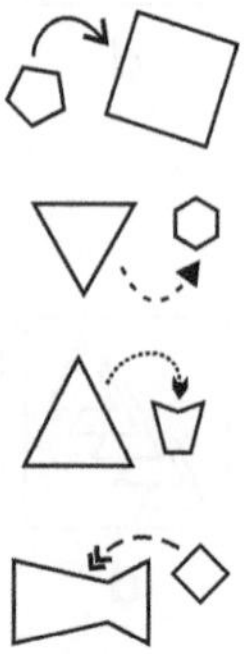

Shape	Code
	FYU
	FZV
	HYV
	GZU

GYU	FZV	HYU	FZU	HYV
a	b	c	d	e

For each question below there are two figures that are like each other in some way. Find which of the five figures on the right is most like the two figures on the left.

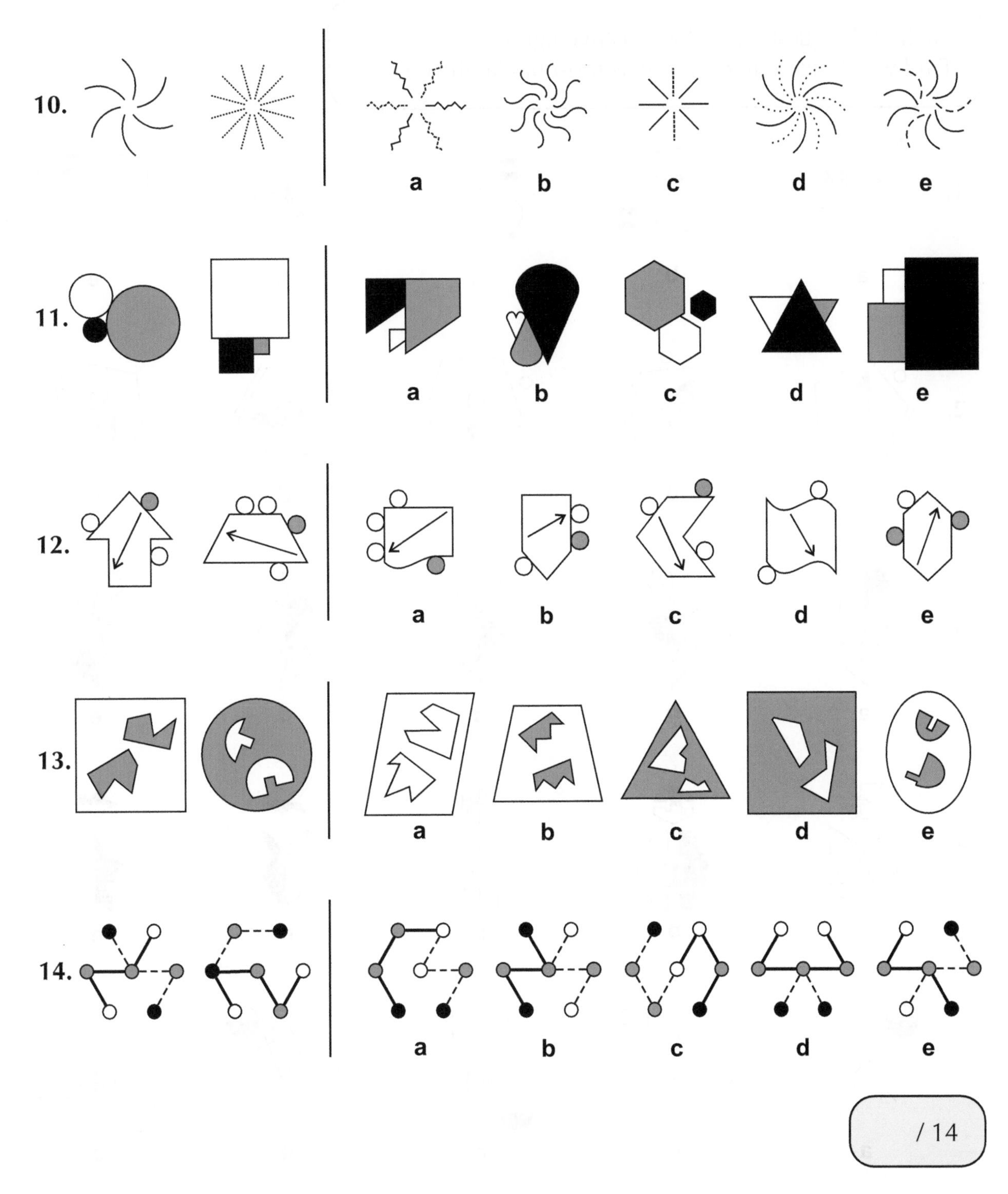

/ 14

Test 30

You have **10 minutes** to do this test. Circle the letter underneath each correct answer.

Each of the questions below has five figures.
Find which figure in each row is most unlike the others.

1.

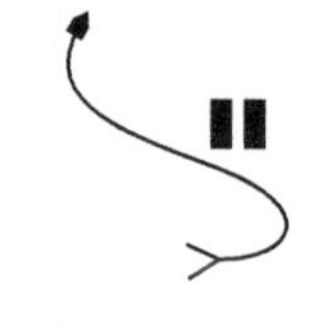 a

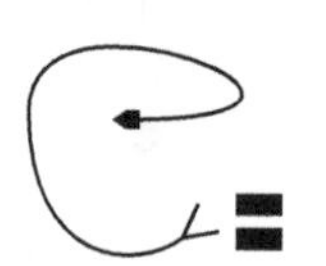 b

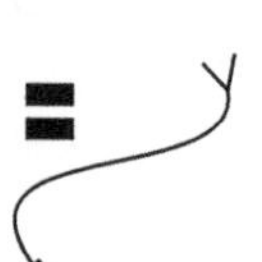 c

 d

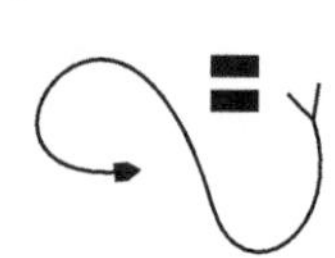 e

2.

 a

 b

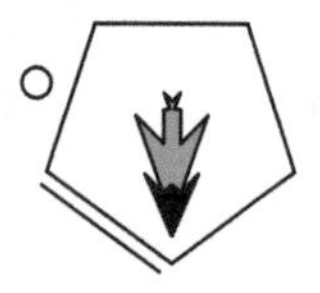 c

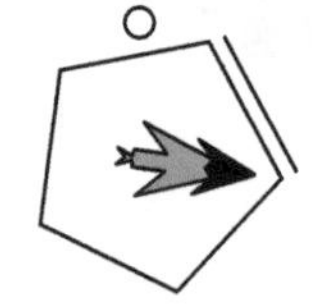 d

 e

3.

 a

 b

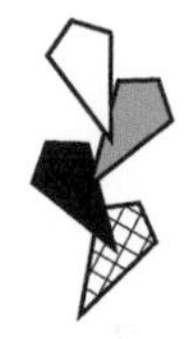 c

 d

 e

4.

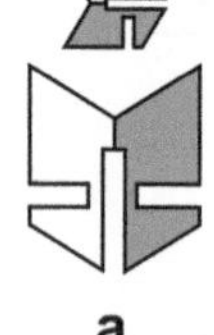 a

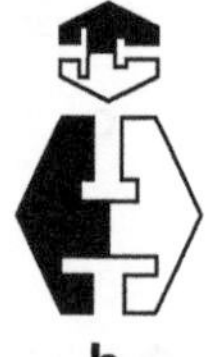 b

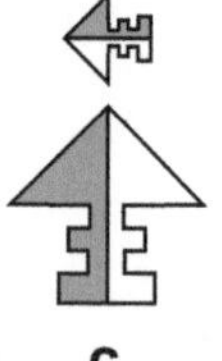 c

 d

 e

5.

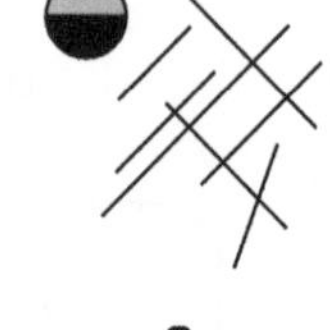 a

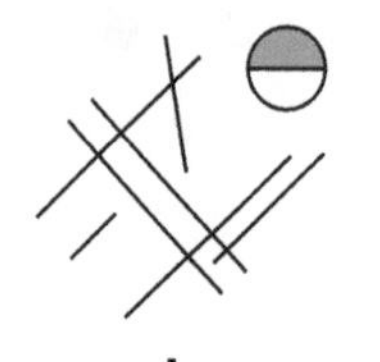 b

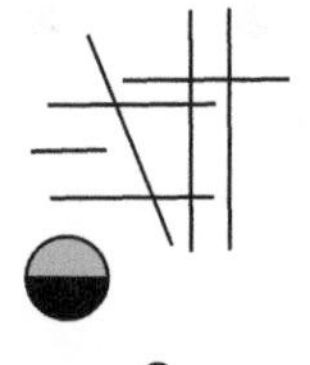 c

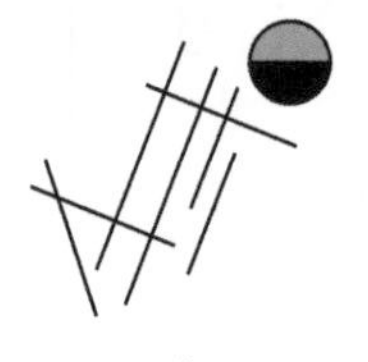 d

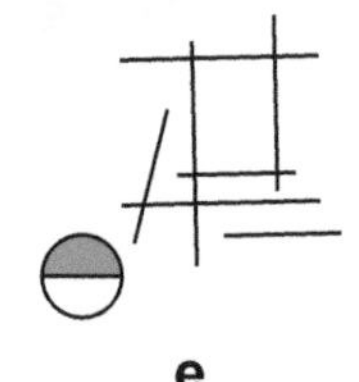 e

Each question has two shapes on the left with an arrow between them.
The first shape is changed in some way to become the second. There is then a third shape followed by an arrow and a choice of five shapes. Choose the shape on the right that relates to the third shape like the second does to the first.

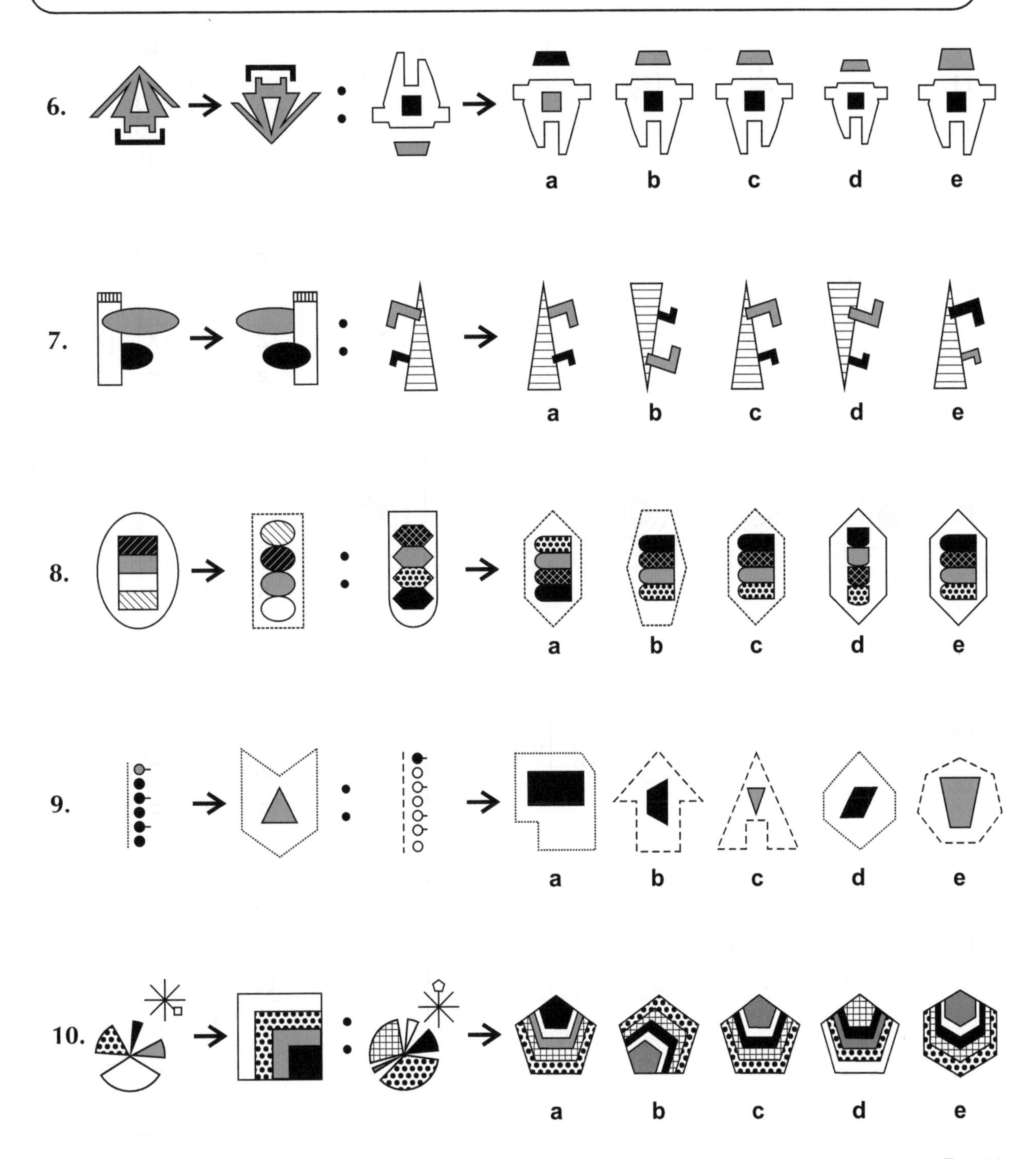

In the boxes on the left are shapes with code letters. The top letters have a different meaning to the bottom ones. Work out how the letters go with the shapes and then find the code for the new shape from the five codes on the right.

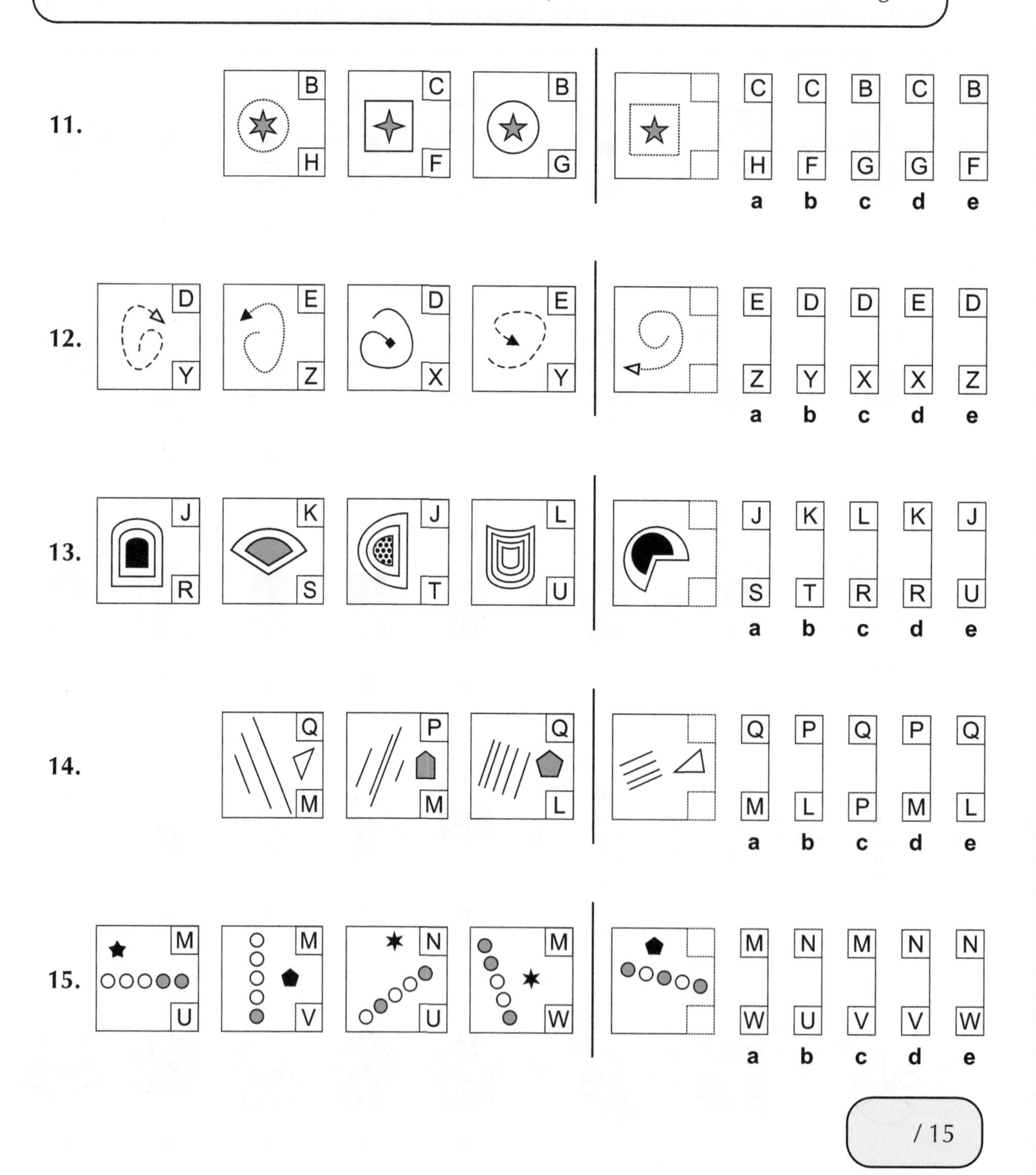

/ 15

Puzzles 10

It's puzzle time! This puzzle is great for helping you get to grips with **codes**.

Curious Codes

Use the codes given on the right to shade the grid squares on the left, in order to reveal Dr. Robotio's new secret creation. The top two rows have been done for you.

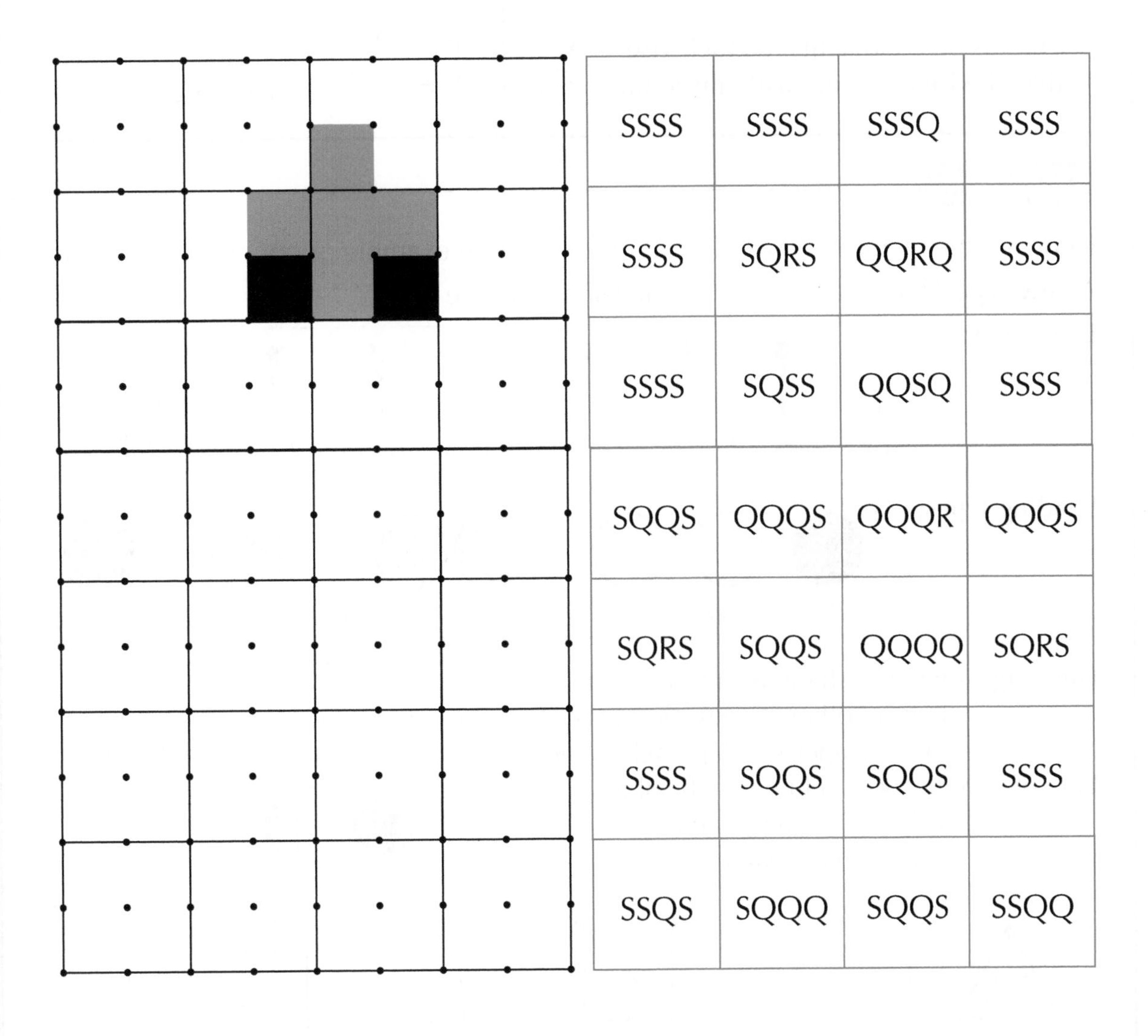

SSSS	SSSS	SSSQ	SSSS
SSSS	SQRS	QQRQ	SSSS
SSSS	SQSS	QQSQ	SSSS
SQQS	QQQS	QQQR	QQQS
SQRS	SQQS	QQQQ	SQRS
SSSS	SQQS	SQQS	SSSS
SSQS	SQQQ	SQQS	SSQQ

Glossary

Rotation and Reflection

Rotation is when a shape is turned clockwise or anticlockwise from its starting point.

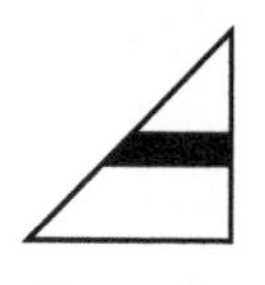
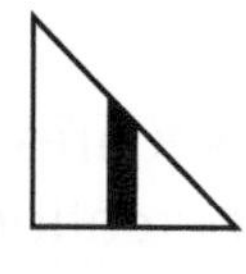

Example shape | 45 degree rotation | 90 degree rotation | 180 degree rotation

The hands on a clock move **clockwise**:
Anticlockwise is the **opposite direction**:

Reflection is when something is mirrored over a line (this line might be invisible).

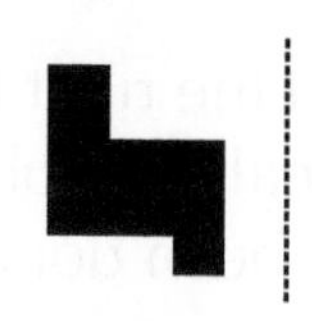
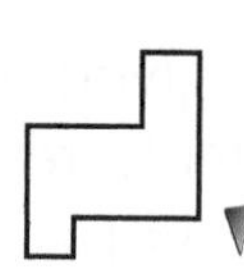

The black shape is reflected across to make the white shape.

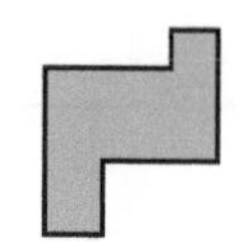

The black shape is reflected down to make the grey shape.

Other Terms

Figure — the picture as a whole that makes up one example or option in a question.

Arrow-style Line — a line with a small shape at one end.

Line Types:

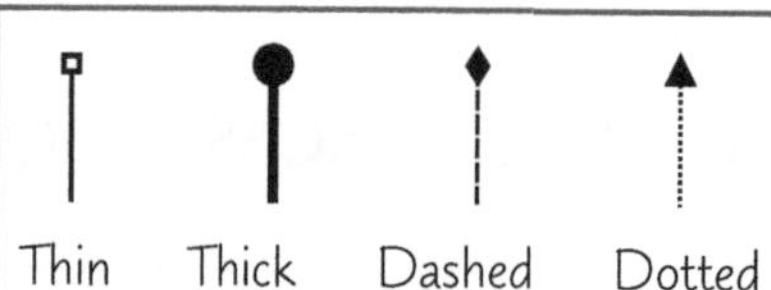

Thin | Thick | Dashed | Dotted | Curved | Jagged | Wavy

Arrow-style lines of different line types.

Shading Types:

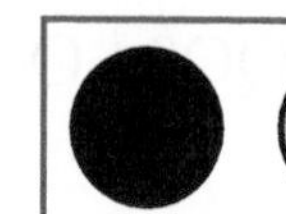
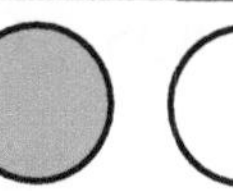
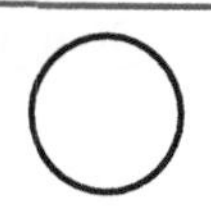
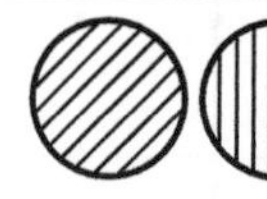

Black | Grey | White | Two types of hatching | Cross-hatched | Spotted

Layering — when a shape is in front of or behind other shapes, or if two or more shapes overlap each other.

Line of Symmetry — a line which splits a shape into halves that are reflections of each other.

Layering — the circle is in front of the square. The right-hand shape is a cut-out shape made from the overlap of the two shapes.

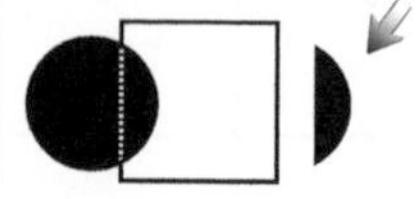

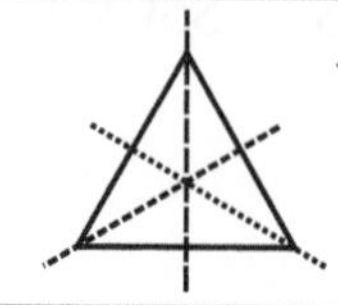

This triangle has three lines of symmetry.

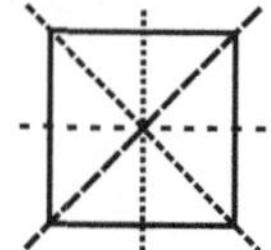

A square has four lines of symmetry.

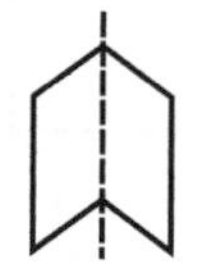

This shape has one line of symmetry.

Answers

Test 1 — pages 6-8

1. D
Working from top to bottom, the large shape and the line rotate 45 degrees clockwise. The small shape stays the same.

2. A
Working from left to right, the whole figure moves one place clockwise round the corners of the grid square. The circle moves one corner anticlockwise round the grey shape.

3. B
Working from right to left, the bottom shape moves to the top. The order of shading stays the same from top to bottom, except for the star that takes the shading of the shape it was in.

4. C
Working from left to right, the white part of the figure disappears and the grey part of the figure is reflected across to become the new white part of the figure. A new grey figure appears inside it. Each line type (solid, dashed, dotted) appears once as the outline of the white part of the figure in each row and column.

5. D
All figures must have a quarter-circle inside a larger shape. The larger shape must have a dashed outline.

6. D
All figures must have an arrow, a star and two straight lines. At least one of the straight lines must cross over the arrow.

7. E
Ignoring shading, all figures must have a horizontal line of symmetry.

8. E
In all figures, there must be a white copy of the small shape at the end of the line. It must be in the section of the large shape which has the same shading as the shape at the end of the line.

9. C
All figures must have two shapes which can fit together (without being reflected) to form a square. The shapes must overlap, and the one at the front must be hatched.

10. A
The figure reflects across and the shape that was at the back moves to the front.

11. B
The shading of the long shape changes to match the shading of the circles. The circles are replaced by a shape with the same number of sides as there were circles. The shading of this new shape matches the original shading of the long shape.

12. E
The top half of the right-hand shape disappears and the bottom half takes the shading of the left-hand shape. The left half of the left-hand shape disappears and the right half takes the shading of the right-hand shape. The two shapes join together.

13. B
The zig-zag line loops round to join to another corner of the larger shape. The number of sections in the line stays the same. The line changes to have the same line type as the outline of the small shape. The small shape moves inside the larger shape.

14. C
The large shape and the small shapes inside it rotate 180 degrees. The shapes on the outside of the large shape then move one place clockwise around the edge of the large shape.

Test 2 — pages 9-11

1. D
All figures must have a grey star. There must be two white circles on opposite points of the star.

2. A
All figures must have three arrows that all point in the same direction. One arrow must have a different arrowhead from the other two. This arrow must also have a circle overlapping it.

3. B
All figures must have three shapes which are identical apart from shading. One shape must be in the middle and touch both the other shapes. The other two shapes must touch only the middle shape.

4. A
In all figures there must be two white rectangles, two grey rectangles and two black rectangles. Rectangles of the same colour must have the same orientation (either horizontal or vertical).

5. B
In all figures, the three shapes on the line must be identical apart from shading. Moving clockwise (or anticlockwise) along the line, the line must enter each shape on the same side and exit each shape on the same side.

6. B (EM)
D = hatching goes diagonally up to the right,
E = hatching goes diagonally up to the left.
L = star has four points. M = star has five points.

7. C (AG)
A = shapes are the same, B = shapes are different.
G = right-hand shape is grey, H = left-hand shape is grey.

8. D (PY)
P = cross is a plus (+) sign, Q = cross is a multiplication (×) sign.
X = cross is split into three sections, Y = cross is split into four sections, Z = cross is split into five sections.

9. A (LSU)
J = four lines, K = five lines, L = six lines.
R = circles on corners, S = circles on lines.
U = three circles, V = four circles.

10. C
All figures must contain four squares.

11. D
All figures must be made up of triangles.

12. E
In all figures, the rectangles must all be different heights.

13. A
In all figures, the shape that is inside another shape must be repeated on the other side of the line.

14. E
In all figures, the arrow must point in a clockwise direction.

Test 3 — pages 12-14

1. D (MT)
M = large shape is a circle, N = large shape is a diamond.
T = small shape is a diamond, U = small shape is a circle.

2. B (DG)
C = moon is split by a horizontal line,
D = moon is split by a vertical line.
F and G = different rotations of the moon.

3. C (JX)
J = small square is outside the large shape,
K = small square is inside the large shape.
X = small square touches the left-hand side of the large shape,
Y = small square touches the top side of the large shape,
Z = small square touches the right-hand side of the large shape.

4. B (LR)
L = two parallel lines, M = three parallel lines,
N = four parallel lines.
R = five lines, S = six lines.

5. B (EW)
D = shape in the box matches the shapes at the front of the figure.
E = shape in the box matches the shapes at the back of the figure.
V = four circles, W = three circles.

6. D
All figures must have two shapes which are downwards reflections of each other.

7. A
All figures must be identical apart from rotation.

8. C
In all figures, the spiral must go anticlockwise from the centre outwards. The spiral must be joined to a corner of the small shape.

9. B
All figures must have an equal number of dashed lines going in two directions across the shape. The two directions must be perpendicular to each other.

10. D
In all figures, the circle must be on the right-hand end of the line. The line must curve around the other shape. The arrow must point away from the shape.

11. E
Working from left to right, the shaded corner of the shape moves one corner clockwise. Any grey shading becomes white and any white shading becomes grey.

12. B
Working from left to right, the figure gets larger and moves diagonally across the grid square. The black line alternates between being connected to the top of the white shape and the bottom of the white shape.

13. E
Working clockwise around the grid, each grid square is rotated 90 degrees clockwise to form the next grid square.

14. A
Working from top to bottom, the star moves to a new position in the grid square and a black circle appears where it used to be. Any existing black circles turn white.

Puzzles 1 — page 15

Cherry Picking

B. Jack's card has three differences to the centre card: the cherries have been reflected, the cherries aren't touching and the stalks are at the front of the figure. Card B only has two differences: the cherries have been reflected and the cherries aren't the same size. (Card A has three differences: the cherries aren't touching, the stalks are straight lines and the stalks are at the front. Card C also has three differences: the cherries have been reflected, the stalks are straight lines and the stalks are at the front.)

Spinning Circles

1 — B and E
2 — A and C
3 — D and F

Test 4 — pages 16-18

1. A
The small shape moves down, and the shapes swap shadings.

2. B
The black shape is reflected across the centre of the figure and moves behind the other shape.

3. D
The outline of the large shape becomes dashed. The small black shape rotates 90 degrees anticlockwise. The small white shape rotates 90 degrees clockwise.

4. A
The number of points on the star in the first figure becomes the number of circles in the second figure. The number of raindrops in the first figure becomes the number of sides on the large shape in the second figure.

5. B
The figure is reflected downwards. The shadings swap over.

6. E (AKP)
A = heart in the left shape, B = heart in the right shape.
J = larger shapes are white, K = larger shapes are grey.
P = larger shapes are triangles, Q = larger shapes are circles.

7. B (DY)
D = arrowheads are triangles, E = arrowheads are squares,
F = arrowheads are circles.
W = no arrows point right, X = one arrow points right,
Y = two arrows point right, Z = three arrows point right.

8. A (MQ)
L = no raindrops are grey, M = one raindrop is grey,
N = two raindrops are grey.
Q = star has solid outline, R = star has dashed outline.

9. C (BHT)
A = white triangle points left, B = white triangle points right.
F = spotted triangle is on the left, G = spotted triangle is in the middle, H = spotted triangle is on the right.
S = white and grey triangles point in the same direction,
T = white and grey triangles point in opposite directions.

10. E
In all figures, a smaller, black version of the white shape must be touching the edge of the white shape.

11. D
In all figures, there must be four arrows coming out of the large shape. The arrowheads must be the same shape as the large shape.

12. C
In all figures, a quarter of the large shape must be cut out. The hatching on the cut-out quarter must be rotated 90 degrees compared to the hatching on the large shape. Any small shapes must match the whole large shape.

13. B
In all figures, there must be several of the same shape stacked on top of each other. The number of shapes must be the same as the number of sides of that shape. There must be three lines overlapping the outlines of some of the larger shapes.

14. E
In all figures, there must be a six-sided shape, with a smaller grey shape on top of it on the right-hand side.

Test 5 — pages 19-21

1. E
In all other figures, the arrow points towards the white circle.

2. D
In all other figures, the large shape has the same number of sides as the star has points.

3. D
In all other figures, the black shape is a copy of the other shape cut in half vertically. (In D, the shape has been cut horizontally.)

4. B
In all other figures, the circle is shaded black.

5. C
In all other figures, the shape with the greatest number of sides is shaded grey.

6. D (EY)
D = solid outline on rectangle, E = dashed outline on rectangle.
X = star in centre, Y = raindrop in centre.

7. C (BK)
A = the smaller shape and larger shape match,
B = the smaller shape and larger shape are different shapes.
J = the arrow points to the left, K = the arrow points to the right,
L = the arrow points both ways.

8. B (GP)
F = there are three small circles, G = there are two small circles,
H = there is one small circle.
P = half the large shape is shaded grey, Q = a quarter of the large shape is shaded grey.

9. D (YB)
X = there are two grey triangles, Y = there are two grey squares.
A = two grey shapes are outside the white shape, B = one grey shape is outside the white shape, C = all grey shapes are outside the white shape.

10. E (TN)
R = the top shape is grey, S = the top shape is white,
T = the top shape is black.
M = the triangle is above the circle,
N = the triangle is below the circle.

11. E
In each series square, the flag is reflected across and alternates between black and grey. The circle moves anticlockwise around the corners of the square and alternates between white and black.

12. C
In each series square, the number of stars increases by one.
The stars alternate between pointing up and pointing down.
The line alternates between dashed and solid.

13. B
In each series square, the hourglass shape rotates 90 degrees clockwise and the white dot moves down by one place. When it reaches the bottom, it starts again at the top.

14. A
In each series square, the arrow rotates 90 degrees clockwise. The colour of the arrowhead changes in the sequence: white, grey, black. An extra line is added to the end of the arrow, alternating which side of the arrow it is added to. The heart alternates between being in the top left and the bottom right of the series square.

15. D
In each series square, the shape in the centre gets larger and alternates between a circle and a cross. In the squares along the top, the grey shading moves one square to the right, and the dot moves one square to the left. In the squares along the bottom, the two black squares move one place to the right. When they reach the right-hand edge, they start again at the left.

Test 6 — pages 22-24

1. B
The large shape gets smaller and its shading is inverted from black on white to white on black. The small shape gets larger and moves from the top left to the bottom right of the figure.

2. E
The grey shape rotates 90 degrees anticlockwise and moves behind the white shape. The black shape moves to the bottom of the figure.

3. A
The number of lines coming off the arrow becomes the number of sides on the large shape. The number of points on the star becomes the number of dots above the large shape.

4. D

All shapes move to the centre of the figure. The white shape rotates 180 degrees. The grey shape rotates 45 degrees anticlockwise. The black shape moves to the back and the grey shape moves to the front.

5. B

The number of circles in the first figure becomes the number of lines in the second. The colour of the rectangle in the first figure becomes the background colour of the second figure and the colour of the triangle becomes the colour of the lines.

6. B

All figures must have seven sides.

7. D

In all figures, the triangle must be at the front.

8. B

In all figures, all of the small shapes must have straight sides. Each small shape must be joined to the larger figure by a corner.

9. C

In all figures, the arrows must point to white shapes.

10. A

In all figures, the number of dots must be equal to the number of sides on the hatched shape.

11. A

Working from left to right, the figure in the second grid square is made by rotating the figure in the third grid square 90 degrees clockwise and adding it to the figure in the first grid square.

12. C

In each row and column, there is a vertical line, a horizontal line and a diagonal line. In each row and column, there is a grey shape, a black shape and a white shape. In each row and column, there is a square, a heart and a circle. Black shapes are always in the top left. Grey and white shapes are always in the bottom left.

13. E

Working from top to bottom, the figure is reflected across. Solid lines become dashed and dashed lines become solid.

14. A

Working from left to right, the white shape in the first grid square rotates 90 degrees anticlockwise, the grey shape moves behind it and the black shape moves to the top to give the figure in the second grid square. The black shape then moves to the centre of the white shape and the whole figure is reflected downwards to give the figure in the third grid square.

Puzzles 2 — page 25

Rotating Hexagons

E. Tile E rotates 30 degrees anticlockwise to fit into the centre of the pattern.

Locked Up!

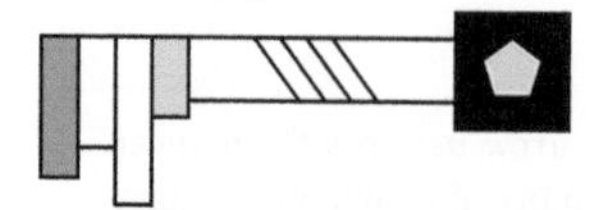

The number of stacked squares around the outside of the lock is equal to the number of diagonal lines on the key. Starting from the top and going clockwise around the lock, the rectangles in the centre of the lock match the ones on the end of the key, moving inwards. The shape of the top half of the keyhole matches the large shape at the end of the key. The four small shapes in the corners of the lock match the small shape on the key. Their shading matches the shading of the large shape on the key. The shading of the outermost square on the lock matches the shading of the small shape on the key.

Test 7 — pages 26-28

1. A

In each series square, the shape rotates 45 degrees anticlockwise and its shading alternates between black and white.

2. D

In each series square, the black triangle is reflected downwards, the heart rotates 90 degrees clockwise and the circle rotates 45 degrees clockwise.

3. E

In each series square, the number of horizontal lines changes in the sequence: one, two, three, two, one, and they alternate between the top of the vertical line and the bottom. The raindrop moves clockwise around the corners of the series square and alternates between black and white.

4. A

In each series square, the number of diagonal lines increases by two, and the lines alternate between being added in the bottom right and top left corners of the series square. The shape in the centre changes in the pattern: half circle, three-quarter circle, full circle, three-quarter circle, half circle and its colour changes in the pattern: black, white, grey, white, black.

5. C

In each series square, shapes that were black become grey, shapes that were grey become white and shapes that were white become black.

6. D (YB)

X = the shape on the right is a star,
Y = the shape on the right is a cross.
A = the shape on the left is a circle, B = the shape on the left is a square, C = the shape on the left is a triangle.

7. A (EN)

E = white shading, F = grey shading, G = black shading.
M = the figure has four lines of symmetry,
N = the figure has two lines of symmetry.

8. D (EPW)

D = diamond is at the front, E = heart is at the front.
P = large heart, Q = small heart.
V = diamond has a line across it, W = diamond has no line.

9. E (CLS)

A = arrow points down, B = arrow points up, C = arrow points left.
J = two dots are shaded grey, K = one dot is shaded grey,
L = three dots are shaded grey.
R = the arrow line is solid, S = the arrow line is dashed.

10. D

All other figures contain a (white) hexagon.

11. E
In all other figures, the black triangle points to the right and the grey triangle points to the left.

12. C
All other figures are made up of three pairs of shapes, where one shape in each pair is rotated 90 degrees to the first. (In C, the pentagon is not rotated.)

13. A
All other figures contain one more dot than the number of lines.

14. D
In all other figures, the arrow with the circular arrowhead is to the right of the arrow with the double arrowhead.

Test 8 — pages 29-31

1. B
Working from left to right, the shape is reflected across and split in half horizontally.

2. C
Working from left to right, the first grid square contains a whole shape, the second grid square contains three quarters of that shape, and the third grid square contains a half of that shape. Each type of shading (white, grey and black) appears only once in each row and column.

3. E
Working from right to left, the number of sides on the shape halves, extra hatching is added perpendicular to the existing hatching and the black bar moves one place clockwise around the sides of the grid square.

4. C
Working from left to right, the figure in the first grid square is reflected downwards and added to the figure in the second grid square to make the figure in the third grid square.

5. D
All figures must have two shapes that overlap each other.
The area where they overlap must be shaded black.

6. A
In all figures, there must be three of the same shape overlapping each other. The shapes must have different shadings and the grey shape must be at the back and the hatched shape at the front.

7. B
In all figures, the black shape must have the same number of sides as the number of grey and white shapes on the line.

8. C
In all figures, the large shape must have at least one black stripe through it and two smaller shapes to the right of all the stripes.

9. E
All figures must have one arrow with a black arrowhead which is pointing in the opposite direction to all the other arrows.
Each grey rectangle must overlap exactly two arrows.

10. C (UQ)
U = stripe is horizontal, V = stripe is vertical.
Q = small shape is a square, R = small shape is a pentagon,
S = small shape is a hexagon.

11. B (FW)
E = large shape has six sides, F = large shape has seven sides,
G = large shape has eight sides.
V = circle has vertical hatching, W = circle has horizontal hatching,
X = circle has cross hatching.

12. B (CL)
C = spiral goes clockwise (working from the centre outwards),
D = spiral goes anticlockwise (working from the centre outwards).
K = two small shapes are black, L = one small shape is black,
M = no small shapes are black.

13. A (TZ)
T = all shapes have the same orientation, U = one shape has a different orientation, V = all shapes have different orientations.
X = black shape at the front, Y = grey shape at the front,
Z = white shape at the front.

14. E (BN)
A = arrow points at the largest shape, B = arrow points at the medium-sized shape, C = arrow points at the smallest shape.
L = largest shape is hatched, M = largest shape is grey,
N = largest shape is spotted.

Test 9 — pages 32-34

1. D
In all other figures, the order of shading from largest shape to smallest shape is: white, black, white.

2. B
All other figures are identical apart from their rotation.
(B is a reflection of the shape.)

3. C
In all other figures, all of the right angles are at a different rotation.

4. E
In all other figures, the number of stars inside the shape is equal to the number of lines that cut through the shape.

5. D
In all other figures, the total number of sides is even.

6. C (BG)
B = square touches the edge of the grey shape,
C = square is in the centre of the grey shape.
F = grey shape has four sides, G = grey shape has three sides.

7. A (NT)
M = vertical lines, N = horizontal lines.
T = number of lines is one more than the number of circles,
U = number of lines is the same as the number of circles.

8. E (KS)
J = arrow points to white shape, K = arrow points to black shape.
S = square is black, T = square is white , U = square is grey.

9. A (HQX)
G = curled lines curl in different directions (clockwise and anticlockwise), H = lines curl in the same direction.
P = line through the centre of the rectangle is dotted,
Q = line through the centre of the rectangle is solid.
W = curled lines start from opposite sides of the rectangle,
X = curled lines start from adjacent sides of the rectangle.

10. B
In each series square, the figure is reflected across and the black rectangle moves closer to the centre of the spiral.

11. E
In each series square, the shape on the left-hand side moves to the right-hand side and goes to the back of the figure. The shadings move one shape to the right.

12. A
In each series square, the whole figure rotates 90 degrees anticlockwise and an extra line is added.

13. C
In each series square, one shape becomes larger than the others in the order: star, square, oval. The arrow moves up to point to the next shape. When it reaches the top shape, it starts again at the bottom shape. The star gains one extra point.

14. E
In each series square, the diagonal line moves one rectangle anticlockwise. Its direction alternates between going up from right to left, to going up from left to right. One grey circle disappears at a time, from bottom to top. When they have all disappeared once, they all reappear again.

Puzzles 3 — page 35

Strange Stars

Constellation C3 is the odd one out. Constellations A2, A3, B2 and C1 all have 3 stars. Constellations A1, B1, B3 and C2 all have a vertical line of symmetry.

Queen Bee

D. All the other bees have a pale blue wing in front of a darker blue wing.

Test 10 — pages 36-38

1. D (BY)
A = arrow points up, B = arrow points down.
X = hatching is horizontal and vertical,
Y = hatching is diagonal.

2. A (CP)
C = circles are in different columns of the grid,
D = circles are in the same column of the grid.
P = one circle is white and the other is black,
Q = both circles are black.

3. E (HT)
F = three dots, G = two dots, H = one dot.
R = large shape is a circle, S = large shape is a square,
T = large shape is a hexagon.

4. D (ZE)
X = triangle points down, Y = triangle points to the left,
Z = triangle points to the right.
E = circle is in front of the rectangle,
F = circle is behind the rectangle.

5. C (KR)
J = diagonal lines are on the left-hand sides of the shapes,
K = diagonal lines are on the right-hand sides of the shapes.
Q = black cross, R = grey cross, S = white cross.

6. B
All figures must have exactly four lines of symmetry.

7. D
In all figures, there must be circles over half of the corners of the large shape.

8. C
In all figures, the black shape must be a smaller, upside-down copy of the white shape.

9. A
In all figures, the dotted line must be perpendicular to the grey rectangle.

10. B
All figures must be made up of a combination of stars, circles, arrows and triangles. There must be ten shapes in total and two of them must be circles.

11. E
The number of sides on the larger shape decreases by two. The smaller shape is reflected downwards and gets smaller.

12. C
The shape at the top of the figure is reflected downwards and moves in front of the other shape. The two shapes swap shadings.

13. A
The shape at the back of the figure moves to the top of the figure. The shape in the middle of the figure moves to the bottom of the figure. The shape at the front of the figure rotates 90 degrees anticlockwise.

14. D
The number of diamonds becomes the number of sides on the grey shape. The number of grey squares becomes the number of lines at the bottom of the grey shape. The number of white squares becomes the number of white dots in the middle of the grey shape.

15. B
The shadings each move two columns to the right. The shape in the third column is reflected downwards and moves to the bottom of the column that matches its shading. The shape in the fourth column is reflected downwards and moves to the top of the column that matches its shading.

Test 11 — pages 39-41

1. B
In each series square, the whole figure moves one place to the right and the white shape moves one place down the rectangle.

2. D
In each series square, the figure rotates 45 degrees anticlockwise. An extra, solid line is added through the large shape. The line that was added in the previous series square becomes dotted.

3. D
In each series square, the star is reflected downwards and moves one corner anticlockwise. The circle moves diagonally across the series square from the top left to the bottom right. When it reaches the bottom right, it starts again at the top left. The circle alternates between being small and large and changes shading in the order: white, black, grey.

4. A

In each series square, the square and the heart alternate between the top left and bottom left of the figure. The bottom of the heart always points towards the centre of the series square. The rectangle takes on the shading of the square from the previous series square. The heart takes on the shading of the rectangle from the previous series square.

5. E

In each series square, the shape with the fewest sides disappears and is replaced by a shape with one more side than the shape with the most sides. The hatching moves one shape clockwise.

6. B

In all other figures, the rectangle is to the left of the circle.

7. D

All other figures have a side that curves outwards.

8. C

In all other figures, the shape at the front of the figure is on the left-hand side.

9. B

All other figures have a grey square.

10. C

All other figures are identical apart from rotation. (C is a reflection.)

11. B

Working from top to bottom, the line is reflected across and the grey shape is reflected downwards.

12. B

Working from top to bottom, the star moves one place to the right and one place upwards. When it reaches the top, it starts again from the bottom. When it reaches the right, it starts again from the left.

13. A

Working from right to left, the whole figure is rotated 90 degrees anticlockwise. Any black shading becomes white, any white shading becomes grey, and any grey shading becomes black.

14. E

Working from top to bottom, the first grid square is made by reflecting the third grid square downwards. Any small shapes disappear, and the areas of the grid square they were in take their shading. The remaining areas of the grid square take the shading of the second grid square. A larger copy of one of the small shapes appears in the centre. It has a line through it in the same orientation as the line in the second grid square.

Test 12 — pages 42-44

1. C

In all figures, the large shape must be split into three equal parts. Each of these parts must have one smaller shape on it.

2. A

In all figures, there must be three different shapes with the same number of sides. There must be two lines that connect one of these shapes to the other two.

3. E

In all figures, the shapes must all be the same and have the same shading. Working along the line, the shapes must alternate between being on each side of the line.

4. B

In all figures, working clockwise, the shadings of the shapes must go in the order: diagonal hatching, spots, white, cross hatching. There must be a circle at the top.

5. C

All figures must have three triangles. Two shapes must be grey.

6. C (YF)

X = the top circle is white, Y = the middle circle is white,
Z = the bottom circle is white.
E = the large shape is an oval, F = the large shape is a rectangle.

7. B (QU)

P = the circle is split into two, Q = the circle is split into four.
T = one small grey shape, U = two small grey shapes,
V = three small grey shapes.

8. D (GW)

F = the shapes have four sides, G = the shapes have five sides,
H = the shapes have six sides.
V = the top and bottom shapes are grey, W = the top and bottom shapes are white, X = the top and bottom shapes are black.

9. B (LR)

L = arrowheads are pentagons, M = arrowheads are triangles,
N = arrowheads are squares.
R = one rectangle is behind the arrows, S = two rectangles are behind the arrows, T = three rectangles are behind the arrows.

10. D (JB)

J = the star is in front of the triangle, K = the star is to the right of the triangle, L = the star is to the left of the triangle.
A = three black raindrops, B = two black raindrops,
C = one black raindrop.

11. B

Working from left to right, the small shape rotates 180 degrees, and the small and large shapes swap shadings.

12. A

Working from left to right (or from top to bottom), the number of sides on the shape increases by one. Each type of hatching only appears once in each row and column.

13. C

Working from right to left, the black shape moves behind the grey shape. The white and grey shapes rotate 180 degrees.

14. D

In each row, the figures in the second and third grid squares are added together then rotated 90 degrees anticlockwise to make the figure in the first grid square.

Puzzles 4 — page 45

Hidden Path

5, 1, 2, 6, 10, 11, 12, 8.

Misleading Mirrors

C. The figure has been reflected across.

Test 13 — pages 46-48

1. D

The whole figure is reflected downwards. The grey shape moves behind the white shape.

2. B

The grey shape gets taller. The hatching changes from going diagonally down to the left to going diagonally down to the right.

3. B

The shape made by the overlap of the two original shapes becomes the whole figure. The shape rotates 90 degrees clockwise. The dashed lines become solid lines and the solid lines become dashed lines.

4. E

A copy of the figure is rotated 180 degrees and joined to the original figure along its straight vertical edge. The whole figure becomes black.

5. A

The figure is rotated 45 degrees anticlockwise. The two arrows at the bottom of the figure swap positions. The two arrows at the top of the figure change direction.

6. B (BX)

A = arrow points diagonally upwards,
B = arrow points diagonally downwards.
X = two different shapes, Y = two identical shapes.

7. D (TG)

S = vertical line of symmetry, T = horizontal line of symmetry.
E = two dots, F = three dots, G = four dots.

8. C (NSY)

M = circle is black, N = circle is grey.
S = circle overlaps top edge of rectangle,
T = circle overlaps left edge of rectangle.
Y = circle in front of rectangle, Z = circle behind rectangle.

9. E (PCJ)

P = top arrow has arrowhead made of two lines,
Q = top arrow has triangle arrowhead.
B = white shape on bottom left corner of square,
C = white shape on top left corner of square.
J = one-quarter of square shaded grey, K = one half of square shaded grey, L = three-quarters of square shaded grey.

10. D

In all figures, the shape must be split into three sections. The order of the shading from left to right must be: grey, black, white.

11. C

In all figures, there must be two smaller, white copies of the grey shape in front of the grey shape. There must be a straight line crossing the grey shape. The two smaller shapes must be on opposite sides of the line.

12. B

In all figures, there must be dashed lines along every line of symmetry of the white shape. The number of crosses outside the shape must be equal to the number of lines of symmetry.

13. A

In all figures, the arrow must point to the shape with diagonal hatching. The black shape must be at the back of the figure.

14. E

In all figures, there must be two white shapes joined by a straight line. The sum of the number of sides of the two shapes must be nine. The shape with more sides must have a black dot inside it.

Test 14 — pages 49-51

1. A

In each series square, the two white ovals rotate 30 degrees around the circle. The black oval changes its position on the circle in the order: bottom, middle, top.

2. D

In each series square, the figure rotates 90 degrees anticlockwise. The shape that is shaded black changes in the order:
circle, triangle rectangle.

3. B

In each series square, the small shape from the previous series square becomes the large shape and a new small shape appears. The shading of the small shape alternates between grey and white.

4. B

In each series square, the shading moves inwards by one ring. The shading of the outer ring always matches the shading of the centre circle.

5. E

In each series square, the triangle moves one grid square in the direction that the arrow was pointing in the previous series square. A circle appears in the grid square that the triangle has moved from.

6. C (XH)

X = four-sided shape, Y = five-sided shape.
F = one dot, G = two dots, H = three dots.

7. D (FN)

E = hatched circle is at the back, F = hatched circle is in the middle.
M = hatching is vertical, N = hatching is horizontal.

8. B (AR)

A = arrow points right, B = arrow points up, C = arrow points down.
Q and R = different reflections of the shape.

9. C (QF)

P = heart and star are on different sides of the line,
Q = heart and star are the same side of the line.
D = two grey shapes, E = one grey shape, F = three grey shapes.

10. E (UK)

S = semicircle is on the left-hand side of the rectangle,
T = semicircle is on the right-hand side of the rectangle,
U = semicircle is in the middle of the rectangle.
J = circles are on the same side of the rectangle as the line,
K = circles are on the opposite side of the rectangle to the line.

11. C

In all other figures, there are only two types of shading.

12. E

In all other figures, the black shape overlaps the large white shape.

13. C
All other figures have just one line of symmetry.

14. A
In all other figures, the longer arrow points to the cloud shape.

15. E
In all other figures, the layout of the shapes is the same except for rotation.

Test 15 — pages 52-54

1. E
In all figures, there must be a white square on a corner of the large shape. The white square must have a black cross inside it and be the same orientation in each figure.

2. C
All figures must have a series of small, black shapes positioned on one line. The small shapes must be the same shape as the large shape at the end of the line. The number of small shapes must match the number of sides on the shape inside the large shape.

3. A
In all figures, the grey shape and the white shape must be touching and one of them must be the same shape as the black shape.

4. C
In all figures, there must be the same number of lines going in each direction. For each direction, the lines must alternate between two different styles.

5. C
All figures must have a black circle and a grey star. The dotted line must be a 90 degree clockwise rotation of the portion of the outline of the large shape between the black circle and the grey star, moving clockwise.

6. D (WZ)
U = black circles on top row, V = grey circles on top row,
W = white circles on top row.
Y = circles don't overlap, Z = circles overlap.

7. A (FNS)
E = left-hand shape is grey, F = right-hand shape is grey.
M = solid line, N = dashed line.
R = right-hand shape is a reflection of left-hand shape,
S = right-hand shape is a 180 degree rotation of left-hand shape.

8. D (DGQ)
C = shaded corner of large shape is an obtuse angle,
D = shaded corner of large shape is a right-angle.
G = large shape doesn't point towards line,
H = large shape points towards line.
P = shaded corner of large shape is black,
Q = shaded corner of large shape is white.

9. B (JT)
J = bottom shape is white, K = bottom shape is black,
L = bottom shape is grey.
S = shape made by the overlap of the other two shapes is the same shape as the other two shapes,
T = shape made by the overlap of the other two shapes is a different shape to the other two shapes.

10. D
The hatching is reflected across and swaps shading with the shape it is in.

11. E
The shadings move one shape inwards and the smallest shape becomes larger.

12. B
The figure rotates 45 degrees clockwise and a white copy of the largest shape appears in its original position.

13. B
The left-hand stripe inside the large shape disappears and the other stripes widen to fill the space. The whole figure is then reflected across and a rectangle appears at the bottom of the figure. The rectangle has the same shading as the stripe that disappeared.

14. A
Lines with shapes that match the central shape rotate 90 degrees anticlockwise around the centre of the figure. Lines with shapes that don't match the central shape stay where they are and the shape changes to match the central shape (but it keeps its shading).

Puzzles 5 — page 55

Teacup Conundrum

D. On all the other teacups, the dashed line crosses the thick line.

Permitted Path

The figure rotates 90 degrees anticlockwise each time.
The quarter-circle alternates between grey and blue.
The number of lines changes in the order: one, two, three.

Test 16 — pages 56-58

1. B
In all other figures, the hatching goes diagonally down to the left.

2. B
In all other figures, the star inside the black circle has the same number of points as the number of sides on the grey shape.

3. C
In all other figures, the white shape overlaps the black shape.

4. D
In all other figures, the dashed line ends with a white circle.

5. D
In all other figures, the dotted line and the solid diagonal line(s) are on adjacent sides of the shape.

6. A

Working from left to right, the figure is rotated 90 degrees clockwise.

7. C

Working from left to right, the number of equal parts the circle is split into increases by one in each grid square. In the first row, there is a pentagon in each section of the circle, in the second row, there is a circle in each section of the circle, and in the third row, there is a triangle in each section of the circle.

8. C

Working from left to right, the hatching inside the large shape rotates 90 degrees and the small circle moves one corner clockwise around the grid square. In each row and column, there is one black circle, one grey circle and one white circle. Each type of shape (diamond, pentagon, hexagon) appears once in each row and column.

9. B

In each row, the third grid square is made up of the first grid square rotated 90 degrees anticlockwise and the second grid square rotated 90 degrees clockwise.

10. E

All figures must contain three identical shapes of different sizes and shadings layered on top of each other. The largest shape must be grey, the second-largest shape must be white with a dashed outline and the smallest shape must be black.

11. C

All figures must have a four-sided shape with a curved arrow pointing clockwise.

12. A

All figures must contain at least one white star, one black star and one grey star. The total number of stars must be equal to the number of sides on the large shape.

13. C

All figures must be made up of identical shapes. Half of the shapes must be shaded grey and the other half must be shaded white. There must be two black dots on top of adjacent shapes.

14. A

In all figures, there must be a large shape joined by straight lines to two smaller copies of the shape – one of which has been reflected downwards. The reflected copy must be shaded white and attached to the larger shape by a dashed line.

Test 17 — pages 59-61

1. A (AV)

A = square has a solid outline, B = square has a dashed outline, C = square has a dotted outline.
U = line to the black circle points up,
V = line to the black circle points down.

2. D (FM)

F = left-hand rectangle is raised, G = middle rectangle is raised, H = right-hand rectangle is raised.
L = left-hand rectangle is grey, M = left-hand rectangle is black, N = left-hand rectangle is white.

3. C (KZ)

J = one star is on a large shape, K = no stars are on large shapes.
X = shape at the front points right, Y = shape at the front points down, Z = shape at the front points up.

4. B (DS)

D = two shaded sections of the circle are next to each other, E = no shaded sections of the circle are next to each other.
Q = small shape is in the bottom right section of the circle,
R = small shape is in the top right section of the circle,
S = small shape is in the middle right section of the circle.

5. D (BM)

A = more shapes on the left, B = equal number of shapes on each side, C = more shapes on the right.
K = shapes on the left are triangles, L = shapes on the left are circles, M = shapes on the left are pentagons.

6. E

In all figures, there must be a small shape with a solid outline inside a large shape with a dashed outline. The small shape must be a 90 degree anticlockwise rotation of the large shape.

7. E

In all figures, from top to bottom, the shapes must go in the order: circle, square, triangle, circle, square, triangle.

8. C

In all figures, there must be one more shape on one side of the line than on the other. On the side with fewer shapes, each shape must have a dot in it, and there must be no dots on the other side.

9. B

In all figures, there must be a small black shape overlapping each of the larger shape's straight sides.

10. D

In all figures, the large shape must be the same shape as the area where the two small shapes overlap, reflected down. The arrows must point in the same direction and have different arrowheads.

11. C

In each series square, the small square moves one corner clockwise, and its shading alternates between black and white. The central shape alternates between a circle and an oval.

12. E

In each series square, one more grey shape is added and the figure is reflected down. The left-most black bar is removed, until there are none, and then the pattern reverses (the right-most bar is added back in).

13. A

In each series square, a new straight line is drawn from the end of the previous line. The connected circles move one side clockwise around the series square, and their shading follows the pattern: both white, one black one white, both black, one black one white, both white.

14. B

In each series square, the black dot and grey raindrop move along one square. When they reach the end, they start again at the other end. The whole figure is rotated 90 degrees clockwise.

15. C

In each series square, each shape on the left is rotated 180 degrees and the shadings in these shapes move up one place, beginning at the bottom again when they reach the top. The star has the same number of points as the number of sides of the black shape.

Test 18 — pages 62-64

1. B

In all figures, a quarter of the shape must be shaded white.

2. A

In all figures, the two lines must be parallel and there must be a line of symmetry between them.

3. C

In all figures, the two lines must be identical apart from rotation. The shape made by the overlap of the lines must have four sides.

4. E

All figures must contain one grey shape and two shapes with a dashed outline. Working clockwise, the order of shapes must be: arrow, triangle, square, star, hexagon.

5. E

In all figures, half the shape must be shaded white. The arrow must start at a grey segment and end at a black segment.

6. E (YAN)

X = both shapes have a solid outline, Y = one shape has a dashed outline, Z = both shapes have a dashed outline.
A = large square, B = small square.
M = one shape is grey, N = both shapes are white.

7. C (EP)

D = the two inner shapes are different,
E = the two inner shapes are the same.
P = the line joins the middles of the circles, Q = the line joins the tops of the circles, R = the line joins the bottoms of the circles.

8. B (GJ)

G = the dot is inside one of the shapes,
H = the dot is outside the shapes.
J = the arrow is above the shapes,
K = the arrow is below the shapes.

9. D (TCW)

S = outer shape points downwards, T = outer shape points right,
U = outer shape points upwards.
B and C = the direction of the stripes.
W = outer shape is white, X = outer shape is grey,
Y = outer shape is black.

10. A

The figure rotates 180 degrees.

11. D

The two shapes on the right swap shadings and the inner shape moves to the top of the outer shape. The shape to the left becomes smaller and moves inside the outer shape.

12. C

The figure reflects upwards and the outline of the small shape becomes solid. A copy of the original large shape appears below the reflection. The copy has the same outline type as the original small shape.

13. E

The shapes move one square anticlockwise and the shadings move one square clockwise.

14. D

The figure is reflected across and the spotted shape moves to the front. The inner white shape rotates 90 degrees. The white, grey and black shapes then reflect downwards and the black and grey shapes swap shading.

Puzzles 6 — page 65

Related Robots

A — 1, B — 3, C — 4, D — 2, E — 5

The number of black bars on the battery is equal to the number of antennas on the robot. The grey shape on the right of the battery is the same as the shapes on the ends of the robot's antennas. The number of hearts on the battery is equal to the number of large shapes used to make the robot.

Cracked Code

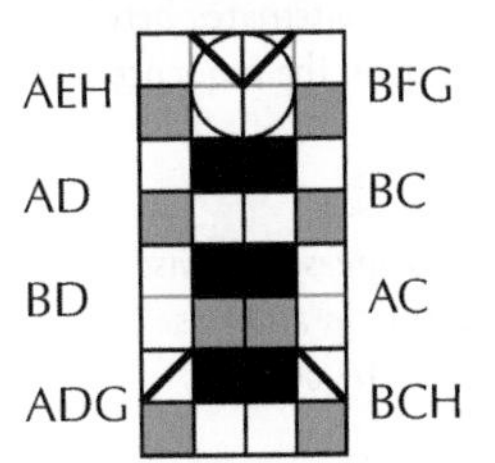

Test 19 — pages 66-68

1. B (BF)

A = the white shape is a smaller copy of the grey shape,
B = the white shape is different to the grey shape.
E = the grey shape has four sides,
F = the grey shape has five sides.

2. E (PX)

P = the hatching goes diagonally down to the left,
Q = the hatching goes diagonally down to the right.
W = the hatched shape is a square,
X = the hatched shape is a triangle.

3. E (KT)

K = two dots, L = three dots, M = four dots.
S = dots have different shadings, T = dots have the same shading.

4. A (ZC)

X = the medium-sized circle has a solid outline,
Y = the medium-sized circle has a dashed outline,
Z = the medium-sized circle has a dotted outline.
A = the smallest circle has a dashed outline,
B = the smallest circle has a solid outline,
C = the smallest circle has a dotted outline.

5. C (UH)

U = total number of shapes is odd,
V = total number of shapes is even.
F = shape in the bottom left corner is a white circle,
G = shape in the bottom left corner is a grey square,
H = shape in the bottom left corner is a black triangle.

6. B
In all figures, there must be a black shape in front of a hatched shape. The hatching must go diagonally down to the left.

7. D
In all figures, the small shape made by the overlap of the arrow and the large shape must be a triangle.

8. E
In all figures, there must be three shapes.
The shape with the most sides must have spotted shading.

9. D
In all figures, a single, straight line must cross the edge of the grey shape four times. There must be one white dot inside the shape.

10. E
In all figures, the white arrow must change direction twice.
The two small shapes must combine to give a whole circle.
The arrow must point to the larger of the two shapes.

11. A
In each series square, the position of the shapes alternates between top/bottom and left/right. The shapes change in the sequence: black circles, white diamonds, grey crosses.

12. A
In each series square, the arrow rotates 90 degrees clockwise.
The position of the dots alternates between the tip and base of the arrow and the number of dots increases by one.

13. D
In each series square, the small white circle moves anticlockwise one third of the way round the inside of the circle. The grey circle alternates between being at the front of the figure and the back.

14. B
In each series square, the figure reflects across. The hatching moves down by one square each time. When it reaches the bottom of the figure, it moves to the top square and starts again.

15. E
In each series square, the small white shape from the previous series square becomes the large grey shape and a new white shape appears in the grey shape. The number of lines behind the grey shape changes in the order: one, two, three.

Test 20 — pages 69-71

1. E
The whole figure rotates 90 degrees clockwise and the two shapes swap shadings.

2. D
The large shape gains a side. The small shapes on the corners of the large shape are replaced with small copies of the original large shape. The new small shapes have the same shading as the original small shapes.

3. B
The small arrow changes to point in the opposite direction and then the whole figure is rotated 90 degrees anticlockwise.
The arrows swap line types.

4. A
The small black shapes move two corners clockwise around the large white shape. The small white shape is reflected downwards. Copies of the large white shape appear so that there are the same number of these large shapes as there were lines.
The lines then disappear.

5. C
Black squares become white, and the squares to the right of them become hatched. The hatching is in the opposite direction to the hatching in the first figure. Hatched squares become white, and the squares to the left of them become grey.

6. E
In all other figures, the large shape is identical apart from rotation.

7. A
All other figures have the same number of wavy lines as zig-zag lines.

8. B
In all other figures, the arrow is pointing in a clockwise direction around the shape.

9. B
All other figures contain three black shapes.

10. C
In all other figures, going clockwise around the pentagon, the shading of the circles is in the order: black, white, grey, black, grey.

11. B
Working from left to right, the left-hand shape gets larger and the right-hand shape gets smaller. The right-hand shape reflects downwards.

12. C
Working from top to bottom, the arrow rotates 45 degrees clockwise and the small shape moves one place anticlockwise around the corners of the grid square.

13. E
Working from left to right, two more circles become white, moving anticlockwise around the circles. One more line is added between the circles, moving clockwise from the original line. The original line becomes dotted.

14. D
Working from left to right, the star gains one more point, and alternates between being in front of and behind the right-hand shape. For the right-hand shape, each type of shape (circle, square, pentagon) and shading (white, grey, black) appears only once in each row and column.

Test 21 — pages 72-74

1. B
In all figures, the two shapes must be horizontal reflections of each other, and an arrow must point towards where the shapes overlap.

2. E
All the figures must be identical apart from rotation.

3. C
In all figures, the tallest line must have a black triangle pointing left. The grey rectangle must be on top of the first two lines.

4. A
All figures must have five shapes.
All triangles must have a dotted outline.

5. B
In all figures, the number of lines crossing the sides of the large shape must be equal to the number of raindrop shapes.

6. D (SJ)
R = bottom two shapes are rectangles,
S = bottom two shapes are trapeziums.
J = arrow points left, K = arrow points up, L = arrow points right.

7. B (FU)
E = line is made of seven segments,
F = line is made of nine segments.
T = black dots at the top of the figure, U = black dots in the middle of the figure, V = black dots at the bottom of the figure.

8. E (CY)
A = outer shape is white, B = outer shape is black,
C = outer shape is grey.
X = three shapes, Y = four shapes, Z = five shapes.

9. A (GLU)
G = grey shape is behind the lines,
H = grey shape is in front of the lines.
L = one arrow points right, M = two arrows point right,
N = three arrows point right.
S = top arrow is solid, T = top arrow is dashed,
U = top arrow is dotted.

10. B
In each series square, the square rotates 45 degrees and moves down. The circle moves right and alternates between grey and black.

11. C
In each series square, one more circle becomes dotted, working from right to left along the bottom row and then right to left along the middle row. A new horizontal line is added to the long vertical line.

12. A
In each series square, the shapes are reflected across the diagonal line. The triangle gets bigger, and the shading of the triangle changes in the sequence: grey, black, white.

13. E
In each series square, the figure rotates 90 degrees anticlockwise. A new arrow is added, two corners clockwise from the previous arrow. The arrowhead of the new arrow alternates between black and white.

14. B
In each series square, the black shading moves one small shape to the right. The large shape at the back of the figure disappears, and a new large shape appears at the front, which is a downward reflection of the small shapes from the top of the previous series square. From front to back, the shadings of the large shapes must be in the order: hatched, grey, white.

Puzzles 7 — page 75

Pumpkin Patterns

Sequence: 9, 5, 3, 4, 8
In each pumpkin, the number of grey shapes increases by one.
The pumpkin stalk is reflected across, and the black semicircles are reflected down.

Haunted House

House number 2 is haunted.
In all the other figures, the large white shape has seven sides.

Test 22 — pages 76-78

1. B
In all figures, the grey star must be inside the large shape.
The grey star must be next to the corner where the two dashed lines meet.

2. D
In all figures, there must be a white circle directly above a grey diamond.

3. E
All figures must be made up of one continuous line. The line must not cross itself. The ends of the line must not join up.

4. E
In all figures, there must be two overlapping white shapes inside a larger grey shape. The grey shape must be a larger, 90 degree anticlockwise rotation of the shape made by the overlap of the two white shapes.

5. A
In all figures, following the line from the square, it must turn right, then left, then left again to reach the circle.

6. E
In all other figures, exactly half of the figure is shaded white.

7. C
In all other figures, the shape at the end of the arrow matches the large white shape.

8. A
In all other figures, the raindrop points towards a dot.

9. D
In all other figures, the dot is inside the square at the back of the figure.

10. B
In all other figures, there are the same number of solid and dashed lines.

11. D
Working from left to right, the shape in the second grid square is reflected down and takes on the shading of the shape in the first grid square to give the shape in the third grid square.

12. C
Working from right to left, the square is rotated 90 degrees anticlockwise. The grey shape becomes white and its left half disappears.

13. B
Working from left to right, the two small squares in the corners of the grid square swap positions. The two overlapping shapes disappear and are replaced by a number of small shapes. The small shapes are the same shape as the shape with the dotted outline. The number of small shapes is equal to the number of sides on the shape with the solid outline.

14. C
Working from left to right, the number of sides on the shapes increases by one. The grey shape changes position in the order: front, middle, back. In each row and column, there's one figure that has two shapes with a dotted outline, one figure that has one shape with a dotted outline and one figure that has no shapes with a dotted outline.

Test 23 — pages 79-81

1. D (LE)
K = black square, L = grey square.
E = heart is inside square, F = heart is outside square,
G = heart overlaps edge of square.

2. B (XS)
X = middle arrow is dashed, Y = outer arrow is dashed.
R = all arrows are pointing in the same direction,
S = arrows are pointing in two different directions.

3. E (NR)
M = grey shapes are 180 degree rotations of each other,
N = grey shapes are reflections of each other.
Q = arrowhead is black, R = arrowhead is white.

4. E (FC)
F = top section of shape is grey, G = top section of shape is white.
B = top section of shape is the largest section,
C = top section of shape is the smallest section.

5. C (UB)
S = shape at the top of the figure has four sides,
T = shape at the top of the figure has five sides,
U = shape at the top of the figure has six sides.
B = shape at the front is white, C = shape at the front is black.

6. C
All figures must have an arrow that is pointing at a black circle. Working in an anticlockwise direction from the point of the arrow, the arrow must have a grey circle on the fourth corner.

7. B
All figures must have equal numbers of each type of arrow. Two of the arrows must cross.

8. C
In all figures, three-sided shapes must be black, four-sided shapes must be grey, and five-sided shapes must be white. The figure must contain four shapes.

9. D
In all figures, there must be more small triangles on the left-hand side of the line than on the right-hand side.

10. A
In all figures, the number of squares on the bottom row must be equal to the number of squares shaded grey.

11. D
The figure rotates 90 degrees anticlockwise and the arrow becomes dashed.

12. C
The spiral is reflected across, and the circle moves further around the spiral, towards its centre. The circle changes its shading to grey.

13. E
A large shape appears that is the same shape as the overlapping parts of the two original shapes. The two original shapes get smaller and overlap the edges of the new shape.

14. D
The two smaller shapes join together and are reflected downwards to become the large shape. The large shape is reflected downwards and splits into two halves to become the two small shapes. The shapes swap shadings, and the hatching reflects across.

15. A
The number of black circles on the right-hand side of the figure gives the number of sides on the outer grey shape. Counting down from the top, the grey circle that the arrow is pointing at gives the number of sides on the inner black shape.

Test 24 — pages 82-84

1. A
In all other figures, the grey shape has a vertical line of symmetry.

2. D
In all other figures, the oval is at the front.

3. E
In all other figures, the arrow points in the same direction as the black raindrop.

4. D
In all other figures, the number of lines making up the outer shape is one more than the number of dots.

5. D
In all other figures, the black shape and the hatched shape can be rotated 90 degrees clockwise and joined together to make the grey shape.

6. B (BM)
B = arrow is pointing towards the square,
C = arrow is pointing away from the square.
K = one quarter of the square is grey,
L = half of the square is grey,
M = three-quarters of the square is grey.

7. D (FR)
E = number of stars equals the number of sides of the white shape,
F = number of stars is half the number of sides of the white shape.
R = white stars, S = black stars, T = grey stars.

8. C (YVG)
Y = shapes are the same size, Z = shapes are different sizes.
V = shapes overlap, W = shapes don't overlap.
G = grey shape is a 90 degree clockwise rotation of the white shape,
H = grey shape is a 180 degree rotation of the white shape.

9. B (BLQ)
A = circle is black, B = circle is hatched.
L = two arcs, M = one arc.
Q = arrow is pointing in a clockwise direction,
R = arrow is pointing in an anticlockwise direction.

10. C
In each series square, the arrow points to the next corner moving in a clockwise direction. The star decreases in size, before increasing again.

11. A
In each series square, the heart moves towards the bottom of the figure. The black shading moves one shape backwards. When it reaches the shape at the back, it starts again at the front.

12. E
In each series square, the arrow rotates 90 degrees anticlockwise. The square rotates 45 degrees. The square and the star swap shadings in each series square, and alternate being at the back of the figure.

13. E
In each series square, the black arrow moves anticlockwise to the next corner and reflects downwards. The number of sides of the grey shape decreases by one. The raindrop rotates 45 degrees, pointing towards the right-hand side of the series square in the sequence: bottom corner, side, top corner, side, bottom corner. The shading of the raindrop changes in the sequence: spots, hatched, cross-hatched.

14. B
In each series square, the black dot moves around the shape one corner at a time in an anticlockwise direction, and alternates between being in front of and behind the white shape. The figure is reflected down. The number of grey rectangles decreases by one.

Puzzles 8 — page 85

Abra-card-abra

C B A E D

Perplexing Post

A — the rule is that the dark blue letter must always be behind the grey letter.

Test 25 — pages 86-88

1. C
Working from left to right, the figure is rotated 90 degrees clockwise. Any grey shapes become white, and any white shapes become grey.

2. B
Working from left to right, the shape disappears and lines appear where all of the shape's lines of symmetry were.

3. A
Working from left to right, an extra line is added, starting from the circle. The new line alternates between being dashed and solid. All existing lines also alternate between dashed and solid. The circle moves to the end of the new line and alternates between white and grey.

4. C
Working from left to right, the shapes rearrange and the circle moves behind a different shape. In the second and third grid squares, an arrow points to the shape that was in front of the circle in the previous grid square.

5. D (BM)
A = right-angled triangle, B = isosceles triangle.
L = grey circle, M = black circle, N = white circle.

6. E (CR)
C = shape has curved sides, D = shape has straight sides.
Q = line goes diagonally down to the left,
R = line goes diagonally down to the right.

7. B (GX)
G = front rectangle has more black shading than white,
H = front rectangle has more white shading than black.
X = rectangles are split into two sections, Y = rectangles are split into three sections, Z = rectangles are split into four sections.

8. B (LT)
J = shape at the end of the straight line is a 90 degree clockwise rotation of the shape at the end of the spiral,
K = shape at the end of the straight line is a 180 degree rotation of the shape at the end of the spiral,
L = shape at the end of the straight line has the same rotation as the shape at the end of the spiral.
S = straight line goes through centre of spiral,
T = straight line doesn't go through centre of spiral.

9. C (GW)
F = there are the same number of lines with each rotation,
G = there are different numbers of lines with each rotation.
V = grey circles are on lines with the same rotation,
W = grey circles are on lines with different rotations.

10. A
In all figures, there must be a dotted line from the centre of the star to each point.

11. A
All figures must be made up of four arrows. The direction of the arrows must alternate. Arrows pointing in the same direction must have different arrowheads.

12. E
All figures must contain a heart, a hexagon and a diamond. The shape at the top of the figure must be at the back and the shape at the bottom of the figure must be at the front. Working from top to bottom, the direction of the hatching must alternate.

13. D
In all figures, there must be a large four-sided shape and a small four-sided shape. The small shape must be a horizontal reflection of the large shape. The small shape must be on a left-hand corner of the large shape.

14. C
In all figures, all shapes with the same shading must be joined by lines. White shapes must be joined by dashed lines, black shapes must be joined by dotted lines and grey shapes must be joined by solid lines.

Test 26 — pages 89-91

1. B
The figure reflects across. A grey rectangle appears at the back.

2. C
The line that the arrow is pointing to disappears. The direction of the arrow is reversed.

3. A
The black shape in the middle of the figure gets smaller and becomes grey. Working from the outermost shape inwards, the outline of the second shape becomes dashed.

4. E
The whole figure reflects downwards. The circle on the right becomes a square. The circle in the middle and the circle on the left swap shadings.

5. C
The whole figure disappears except for any parts of the shape at the back that are visible around the other shapes. These are rotated 90 degrees anticlockwise and take the shading of the shape at the front in the original figure.

6. E (FNY)
E = shapes have different shading,
F = shapes have the same shading.
M = small and large shapes are the same shape,
N = small and large shapes are different shapes.
X = arrowhead is a triangle, Y = arrowhead is two lines

7. A (BW)
A = three lines inside rectangle, B = four lines inside rectangle.
V = triangle is in a section of the rectangle that touches the star,
W = triangle is in a section of the rectangle that doesn't touch the star.

8. E (GP)
G = smaller shape shaded grey, H = larger shape shaded grey.
P = arrowhead made up of one shape, Q = arrowhead made up of two shapes, R = arrowhead made up of three shapes.

9. C (SLC)
S = two dashed lines connected, T = two separate dashed lines.
J = equilateral triangle, K = scalene triangle, L = isosceles triangle.
C = hatched shape is a square, D = hatched shape is a circle.

10. B
In all figures, there must be a square at the front.

11. E
In all figures, there must be a curved arrow starting in a shape with a dotted outline and finishing in a shape with a solid outline.

12. D
In all figures, there must be five small shapes inside a rectangle with a dotted outline. The small shapes with an even number of sides must be shaded black. The small shapes with an odd number of sides must be shaded white.

13. E
In all figures, if the grey shapes disappeared, the figure must have exactly one line of symmetry. There must be an arrow pointing in the direction of that line of symmetry.

14. A
In all figures, the shape that touches the sides of the fewest other shapes must be shaded black.

Test 27 — pages 92-94

1. E
In each series square, another grey triangle is added.
A black dot is added to the bottom corner of the triangle that was added in the previous series square, alternating between the right and left corners.

2. A
In each series square, the spiral rotates 90 degrees anticlockwise, and the outermost line is removed. The shading of the heart alternates between white and black.

3. D
In each series square, the arrows on the small squares show the directions the small squares will move in the next series square.

4. C
In each series square, the semicircle moves one side anticlockwise around the large shape and the raindrop moves one side clockwise. The hatching rotates 90 degrees. The shading of the raindrop and the semicircle each change in the order: black, grey, white.

5. B
In each series square, the figure is reflected across, and the white triangles alternate between being in front of and behind the oval. One triangle is removed, starting from the bottom and working around the oval.

6. D (EM)
E = horizontal hatching, F = cross hatching, G = vertical hatching.
L = two circles, M = three circles.

7. A (JQ)
J = three shapes, K = four shapes.
P = smallest shape is grey, Q = smallest shape is black,
R = smallest shape is white.

8. E (UC)
T = small shapes are triangles, U = small shapes are squares,
V = small shapes are pentagons.
A = small shapes are outside the large shape,
B = small shapes overlap the sides of the large shape,
C = small shapes are inside the large shape.

9. D (DT)
D = three lines, E = four lines, F = five lines.
R = dashed lines are behind the rectangle, S = solid lines are behind the rectangle, T = dotted lines are behind the rectangle.

10. A (LX)
L = large shape has one line of symmetry, M = large shape has three lines of symmetry, N = large shape has two lines of symmetry.
X = arrow points right, Y = arrow points down, Z = arrow points up.

11. C
In all figures, the white shape must be a reflection across the dotted line of the grey shape. The white shape must be at the top.

12. B
In all figures, the largest shape must have six sides. There must be a small grey circle between two small black circles.

13. E
In all figures, all shapes must be identical apart from shading and rotation. The number of shapes must be one more than the number of sides on each shape.

14. D
In all figures, the arrow must have a white arrowhead and be pointing towards the shape with curved sides.

15. B
In all figures, the shape must be split into seven parts, three of which are larger and the same size, and four of which are smaller and the same size. There must be a different number of black dots in each of the larger sections.

Puzzles 9 — page 95

Puzzling Pairs

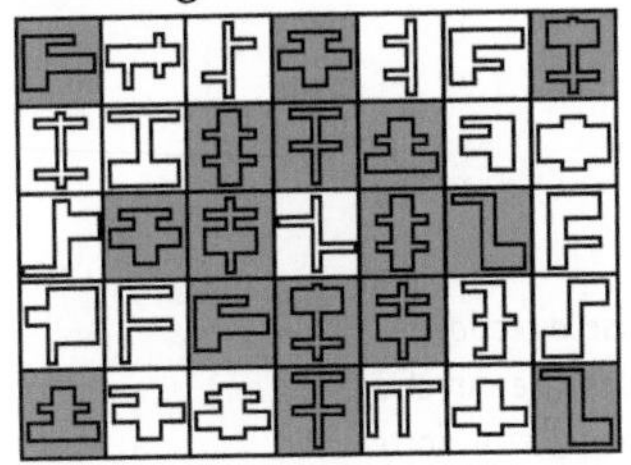

Decode the Bug

ASX.
A = bee is not symmetrical, B = bee is symmetrical.
R = bee has hatched eyes, S = bee has grey eyes.
X = bee has four black stripes, Y = bee has five black stripes.

Test 28 — pages 96-98

1. D
The completed grid is symmetrical both horizontally and vertically.

2. B
Working from left to right, the figure is reflected across. The star and the shape at the back swap shadings. The star gets smaller.

3. A
Working from left to right, the shading of the outer and inner shapes in the first grid square combine with the shading of the middle shape in the second grid square to give the shading in the third grid square. Working from top to bottom, the arrow moves to the next corner in a clockwise direction, rotating 90 degrees clockwise each time.

4. D
Working from left to right, the shapes created by the crossing of the lines in the first grid square rotate 180 degrees around the centre of the grid square to give the figure in the second grid square. These shapes then decrease in size and line up vertically to give the figure in the third grid square. The shading in the second and third grid squares match.

5. B
All figures must have a white triangle inside a four-sided black shape.

6. E
All figures must have two identical overlapping shapes.
The shape formed by the overlap must have four sides.

7. D
All figures must be identical apart from rotation.

8. A
In all figures, there must be a black square directly between the arrow with a circle arrowhead and the arrow with a triangle arrowhead. All arrows must be pointing in the same direction.

9. A
In each figure, there must be an odd number of shapes.
Exactly two of the shapes must be shaded black.

10. C
In all other figures, each row contains four types of shading.

11. E
In all other figures, the star is positioned on the side of the grey shape that's nearest to the arrow with the solid black arrowhead.

12. E
In all other figures, the number of lines equals the number of sides on the shape with the dashed outline.

13. B
In all other figures, there is only one line of symmetry across the whole figure.

14. C
In all other figures, the number of crosses is one more than the number of curved sides on the grey shape.

Test 29 — pages 99-101

1. E
In each series square, another grey rectangle appears above the others. The border alternates between black and white.

2. C
In each series square, the arrow begins at the place where the arrow was pointing to in the previous series square.

3. B
In each series square, the number of lines of symmetry that the shape has decreases by one. The shape changes position within the series square in the order: top, middle, bottom.

4. E
In each series square, the triangle in the top left corner rotates 90 degrees clockwise. The shape in the top right corner rotates 120 degrees anticlockwise. The black circle gets larger.

5. A
In each series square, the hatching in the shape at the bottom rotates 45 degrees anticlockwise. The number of shapes is equal to the number of sides on each shape in the previous series square.

6. A (ES)
D = line crosses itself once, E = line crosses itself twice.
S = circles are different colours, T = circles are the same colour.

7. E (YPK)
X = circle on the left, Y = circle on the right.
P = circle in front of square, Q = circle behind square.
J = vertical hatching, K = horizontal hatching.

8. C (CM)
B = circle above the line, C = circle below the line.
L = square to left of triangle, M = square to right of triangle.

9. C (HYU)
F = total number of sides is nine, G = total number of sides is ten,
H = total number of sides is eight.
Y = arrow curves clockwise, Z = arrow curves anticlockwise.
U = arrow points to large shape, V = arrow points to small shape.

10. B
All figures must only contain one type of line.

11. E
In all figures, there must be three of the same type of shape, and each shape must touch both of the other shapes.

12. C
In all figures, there must be one grey circle touching the outside of a larger shape. The arrow must not point towards any circles.

13. C
In all figures, the two smaller shapes must have different shading to the larger shape. When rotated and attached together, the two smaller shapes must be the same shape as the larger shape.

14. D
In all figures, there must be a path between the white dots made up of thick lines. There must be a path between the black dots made up of dashed lines.

Test 30 — pages 102-104

1. D
In all other figures, the tail of the arrow splits in two, leading away from the arrowhead.

2. E
In all other figures, the black end of the black and grey shape points towards a corner of the pentagon.

3. D
In all other figures, the second flag from the top is shaded grey.

4. B
In all other figures, the top shape is a smaller, 90 degrees anticlockwise rotation of the bottom shape (with the shading reversed).

5. C
In all other figures, the shape formed by the crossing of lines is a rectangle.

6. B
The whole figure rotates 180 degrees.

7. A
The whole figure reflects across. The grey shape moves to the back. The black shape moves to the front.

8. C
The larger shape and the smaller shapes swap and rotate 90 degrees. The outline of the larger shape changes from solid to dashed. The shadings in the four smaller shapes move down one place (the shading at the bottom goes to the top).

9. B
The number of dots in the first figure gives the number of sides of the outer shape. The number of dots with lines, and the shading of the top dot, gives the number of sides and shading of the inner shape. The line type of the line on the left in the first figure gives the line type of the outer shape.

10. C
The shape attached to the star at the top of the first figure gives the shape of the second figure. The position of this shape relative to the centre of the star gives the alignment of the smaller shapes within the second figure. Each circle segment represents the shading of a shape in the second figure. The size of the segments gives the order and layering of the shapes in the second figure, going from largest at the back to smallest at the front.

11. D (CG)
B = a circle, C = a square.
F = a four-pointed star,
G = a five-pointed star,
H = a six-pointed star.

12. E (DZ)
D = arrow pointing in a clockwise direction,
E = arrow pointing in an anticlockwise direction.
X = a solid line, Y = a dashed line, Z = a dotted line

13. D (KR)
J = three shapes, K = two shapes, L = four shapes.
R = front shape is black, S = front shape is grey,
T = front shape is spotted, U = front shape is white.

14. B (PL)
P = the number of lines does not equal the number of sides of the shape,
Q = the number of lines equals the number of sides of the shape.
L = the lines are the same length,
M = the lines are different lengths.

15. E (NW)
M = the white dots are next to each other,
N = the white dots are split into two groups by a grey dot.
U = there are two grey dots,
V = there is one grey dot,
W = there are three grey dots.

Puzzles 10 — page 105

Curious Codes

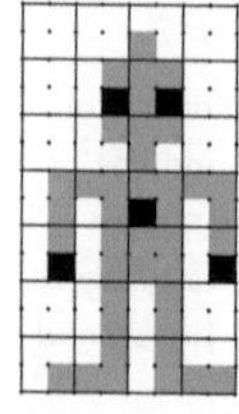

Each grid square must be split into four smaller squares.
The four-letter code for each grid square represents the smaller squares in the order: top left, top right, bottom right, bottom left.
Q = grey square, R = black square, S = white square.

N6XP2E1